1993

A Very Good
Place to Start

A Very Good Place to Start

Approaches to Teaching Writing and Literature in Secondary School

Edited by

Craig Thorn

Phillips Academy
Andover, Massachusetts

Boynton/Cook Publishers
HEINEMANN
Portsmouth, New Hampshire

Boynton/Cook Publishers, Inc.
A Subsidiary of
Heinemann Educational Books, Inc.
361 Hanover Street, Portsmouth, NH 03801
Offices and agents throughout the world

We would like to thank the following for permission to reprint previously published material:
Pages 156–158: "Last View of Four," by Adlai S. Hardin (III), was previously published in *The Christian Science Monitor*, April 25, 1986, and is reprinted with permission of the author.

We would like to thank the students and parents who have given their permission to include material in this book. Every effort has been made to contact copyright holders for permission to reprint borrowed material where necessary, but if any oversights have occurred, we would be happy to rectify them in future printings of this work.

Library of Congress Cataloging-in-Publication Data

A Very good place to start: approaches to teaching writing and
  literature in secondary school/edited by Craig Thorn.
      p.   cm.
   ISBN 0–86709–283–1
   1. English language—Composition and exercises—Study and teaching
(Secondary) 2. Literature—Study and teaching (Secondary)
I. Thorn, Craig.
LB1631.V47 1991
808'.042'0712—dc20

91–11035
CIP

Cover designed by Jenny Jensen Greenleaf.
Printed in the United States of America.
91 92 93 94 95   9 8 7 6 5 4 3 2 1

To my high-school English teacher,
Frank Sullivan, who handed me
Macbeth one day and said, "Take a
look at this."

Contents

Preface

At Phillips Academy we've found that there are as many ways to teach writing and literature successfully as there are teachers concerned with teaching it. Here you'll find theories, exercises, course designs, and case studies with but one thing in common: they focus on teaching writing and literature. You'll find essays that summarize useful exercises, apply complex linguistic/rhetorical theory to classroom teaching, propose syllabi for courses emphasizing writing, and describe ways to use classroom techniques. None of these essays are meant to be the final word on anything. They're presented only as what thirteen English teachers do in one department. In fact, we began this project with the express purpose of helping ourselves help ourselves. We each wanted to know what the others were thinking about teaching composition. So we decided to write about whatever interested us and share it with one another. As we shared our work, it occurred to us that one of the strengths of any teaching department is its diversity. Furthermore, the autonomy we enjoy in the classroom has enhanced and encouraged that diversity. At a time when administrators and pedagogues seem poised to impose more and more restrictions on the classroom, we thought that our efforts represented the advantages of leaving teaching to the teachers and their students.

We believe that the classroom is ultimately the source of all good teaching and learning. Students succeed when they're challenged. We believe the same goes for teachers. The classroom is where these challenges should take place. We hope the essays in this book challenge your thinking about teaching composition, not threaten it. We hope they raise more questions than they answer. They're an argument for autonomy in the classroom. In the broadest sense, they're presented as questions. They're an invitation to use your classroom as an opportunity to experiment and learn with your students. In the final analysis, they're a celebration of teachers as students and students as teachers.

The essays are grouped into three general categories: introductory writing courses, introductory literature courses, and advanced writing and literature courses. Naturally, the essays vary in point of view as well as content and approach. Nevertheless, they speak with one clear voice. Successful writing is an empowering experience. These teachers are willing to go to great lengths to give students that experience.

In Section 1, Peter Gilbert explores ways to encourage conviction in student writing; Tom McGraw demonstrates that formal research papers on the classics make great works less, not more, intimidating to young readers; Ed Germain discusses writing assignments that invite students to use writing as a tool to influence and understand events in their immediate environment; Paul Kalkstein employs a grading style that encourages a dialogue between students and their drafts; and I show how lengthy writing projects developed in the classroom enable students and teachers to understand writing as they write.

In Section 2, Lynne Kelly argues that training students to write as readers and read as writers has profound educational implications for both student and teacher; Kevin O'Connor applies James Kinneavy's and James Britton's theories of discourse to possible writing assignments in an introductory literature course; Carole Braverman teaches students how to read poetry by teaching them how to write it; Thylias Moss dramatically demonstrates the validity of the variety of voices teachers might encounter from students of different cultural backgrounds; and I argue that New Criticism and prose models are best used as means toward the ends of good writing, not as ends in themselves.

In Section 3, Ada Fan outlines the advantages of using film to teach narrative techniques; John Gould offers an exercise that enables students to show rather than tell how they feel in an essay; Seth Bardo studies how students write in response to politically and socially challenging literature; Sheila McGrory Klyza explores how students can learn about literature and their own writing by studying how written works might be performed; and I offer examples of courses that link classic and contemporary works as well as literary and contemporary experience.

All these efforts taken together make one important point, the real point of this anthology. Any group of teachers can produce a useful, ongoing colloquy about composition. The first step is simple: recognize what goes on between you and your students as the best place to start.

C. T.

Acknowledgments

I would like to acknowledge the Abbot Academy Association, Kelly Wise, and Skip Eccles for their generous support of this project. I would also like to thank the other members of our English Department for creating a wonderful atmosphere in which we can all learn as teachers, from each other and from our students. I would particularly like to thank Lou Bernieri, who made this book possible.

Introductory Writing Courses

1

Read 'Em and Weep
Encouraging a Love of Language

Peter A. Gilbert

One might think that writers' greatest love would be the subjects they write about — people's lives, people themselves. But innumerable interviews and memoirs suggest that even more than life, writers love language — wrestling with it, working it, molding it, polishing it. Those tasks are a writer's great challenge and source of great joy. Many writers confess that they couldn't possibly stop writing because they love playing with language. One of our goals as English teachers should be to promote an equally strong love of and sensitivity to language.

As English teachers we strive to teach students to read with care and sensitivity, and to write with clarity, grace, and power. We encourage students to become increasingly articulate — in oral as well as written form. Central to all these educational goals is an awareness and an appreciation of language — the ways it is used; its beauty, euphony, and rhythm; the relationship of style to content. Perhaps we can do more to encourage students to love language itself and not just the tale the author tells with it.

As teachers of writing, we seldom insist that the challenge of using words effectively is a joy separate from the joy of the tale told, even though our students know that *telling* a joke well brings a delight different from the humor of the joke. Through rewriting they may discover the pleasure of finding and using just the right word, even as a baseball player feels the joy of hitting the ball cleanly and sending it right where he intended. Too rarely do we as literature teachers ask our students to focus not only on the picture the words of the story so magically conjure within the mind but also on the stunningly compelling combination of words on the page and to consider how the words give rise to that powerful mental image. Some might call it reading as a writer. I'd also call it loving language used well.

With so little attention to language and how writers use it, it is no wonder how unpopular poetry is in the United States, for poetry is the consummate art form of the wordsmith. We wonder why so few students love to read for pleasure, or if they do read, why so many turn only to best-selling page-turners, in which language is the transparent vehicle for conveying plot. With little sense of language, they are only doing what we have asked them to do—reading for plot and perhaps "meaning," but not for the sake of appreciating the writing.

Clearly there are innumerable ways to encourage students to notice and appreciate language well used. One, of course, is to examine a compelling passage from literature. But we are English teachers and that's literature, and students consider literary examples suspect and unconnected to the world outside the classroom. Carrying more weight is a comparison between an article from the well-edited *Rolling Stone*, for example, and an article from, say, any one of several popular hunting or celebrity magazines. One might also take the first two pages from a best-selling thriller and compare them with the beginning of a contemporary book with richer language. Because their syntax and diction are typically simple and unsurprising, page-turners can be read more quickly than books that are stylistically more sophisticated.

To pique students' interest in language itself, I have also compared two writers' versions of a familiar children's story, such as *Goldilocks and the Three Bears* or *The Brementown Musicians*. Students quickly see that it is often not plot that matters, but style. They come to see that a writer has many choices to make concerning diction (word choice) and character or scene development—whether, for example, to make it scary, funny, or satirical. The plot of each version may be the same, but the stories are radically different.

An entire class might be asked to write a paragraph-long spatial description of the same scene or room, each student describing the scene in such a way as to convey a dominant mood or impression. The assignment encourages students to write coherent paragraphs and to describe with concrete particularity, and reading their paragraphs in class emphasizes the variety of possible impressions the scene might give and the importance of diction in conveying the desired effect.

The most effective way I know to encourage interest in language well used—what one calls *rhetoric*—is to expose students to language that is powerful, compelling, and *not* literary, and then ask them to write and read aloud in class some rhetorically powerful prose. Perhaps the best source is great political rhetoric. Teaching famous political speeches has several advantages: their historical context inevitably involves an interesting story that most students should but often do not know. Moreover, the subject of such speeches is important, interesting, and moving.

Play for your class a recording of excerpts from Winston Churchill's most famous speeches, John Kennedy's inaugural address, and Martin Luther King, Jr.'s "I have a dream" speech, to name a few fine examples of stirring prose. Examine their transcripts, available in any library. Ask your students what it is about the way the ideas are expressed that makes them so compelling and memorable. Ask students to identify parallel constructions, word repetitions, uses of contrast, word pairing for rhetorical effect, series, alliteration, metaphors and similes, and periodic sentences.

Let's begin with a careful look at the "Gettysburg Address" (Abraham Lincoln, November 19, 1863, in Boutwell 1965, 217−18): it is only two paragraphs — ten sentences. I provide the students with a copy of the speech in which I have shuffled the order of the sentences. For homework I ask them to reorder each paragraph without looking at the original and to be prepared to justify their decisions. The students discover a veritable daisy chain of connections between sentences, transitions binding the speech together and making it easy to follow. The annotated copy shown in Figure 1−1 suggests many of the links between sentences and ideas, and identifies some of the speech's rhetorical devices. Class discussion should elicit most of these connections.

In addition to the links between sentences (many of them the demonstrative pronouns *that* and *this*), your students might note the contrasts contained in the speech (birth/death, then/now, who and how one can dedicate a battlefield). One might notice Lincoln's insistence on focusing on the concrete — the sense of particularized place (*here*) and his involving the audience in the ceremony (*we* and *us*). I ask students, What one word is the speech's keystone? (*Dedicate*: Our country is *dedicated* to the proposition of equality; we came to *dedicate* a battlefield. But we *cannot dedicate* the battlefield because those who fought here consecrated it by their actions. And so we must *dedicate ourselves* to winning the war so that those who died "shall not have died in vain" and that the country "shall not perish.")

The student historian in your class might observe, in response to a question, that the speech's very form suggests Lincoln's commitment to the survival of the Union: the first and last sentences deal with it. Lincoln asserts not once but twice that the Union soldiers who died at Gettysburg died to save the Union: they "gave their lives that that

Figure 1-1
Annotated "Gettysburg Address"

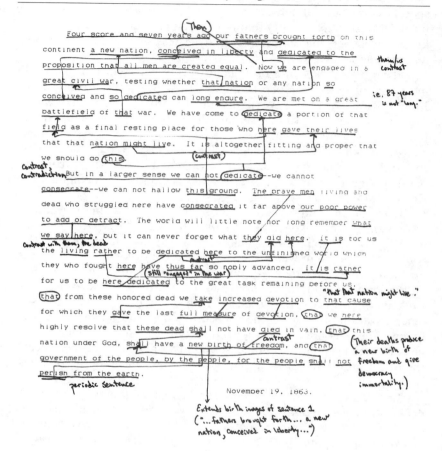

nation might live." The nation's survival was "that cause for which they gave the last full measure of devotion." The historical biographer might assert that the speech also suggests the author's humility: the entire speech is based on the notion that he, the president of the United States, is less able to dedicate a cemetery than those soldiers who fought there. Moreover, Lincoln was being sincere when he said that his speech would not be memorable. And yet he was mistaken when he said, "The world will little note nor long remember what we say here, but it can never forget what they did here." While a few students may recall hearing of Pickett's charge and Cemetery Ridge and while some students may understand that Gettysburg was the turning point of the Civil War, most Americans know Gettysburg as the site of Lincoln's speech. The pen can be more memorable as well as mightier than the sword.

It is no coincidence, then, that Martin Luther King, Jr., begins his "I have a dream" speech (August 27, 1963) with an allusion to the "Gettysburg Address":

> Five score years ago, a great American, in whose symbolic shadow we stand today, signed the Emancipation Proclamation. This momentous decree came as a great beacon of light of hope to millions of Negro slaves who had been seared in the flames of withering injustice. It came as a joyous daybreak to end the long night of their captivity.
>
> But one hundred years later, the Negro is still not free. One hundred years later, the life of the Negro is still sadly crippled by the manacles of segregation and the chains of discrimination. (In Linkugel 1972, 289–93)

His paragraph structure here, like Lincoln's, is one of contrast. His imagery vivifies such abstract notions as injustice and makes compelling the suffering of slavery. He knows intuitively that pairing words and images adds power — that "the manacles of segregation and the chains of discrimination" is rhetorically more powerful than "the chains of segregation and discrimination," for example. "Manacles of segregation and the chains of discrimination" are, of course, metaphors King uses to emphasize that segregation and discrimination are a kind of continuing slavery of black Americans, notwithstanding the century-old Emancipation Proclamation.

Reverend King knew the power of presenting coordinate ideas in parallel form, for the rhetorical technique appears frequently in the Bible, and in no place more effectively than the Beatitudes (Matthew 5:3–12):

> Blessed are the poor in spirit: for theirs is the kingdom of heaven.
> Blessed are they that mourn: for they shall be comforted.
> Blessed are the meek: for they shall inherit the earth.
> Blessed are they which do hunger and thirst after righteousness: for they shall be filled.

The "I have a dream" refrain repeats in his speech six times, while "Let freedom ring" (lyrics he quotes from the song "America") repeats no fewer than ten times in a crescendo that builds to his dramatic and rhetorically elegant conclusion:

> Let freedom ring from every hill and molehill of Mississippi, from every mountainside, let freedom ring.
> And when this happens, and when we allow freedom to ring, when we let it ring from every village and hamlet, from every state

and city, we will be able to speed up that day when all of God's children — black men and white men, Jews and Gentiles, Catholics and Protestants — will be able to join hands and sing in the words of the old Negro spiritual, "Free at last, free at last; thank God Almighty, we are free at last." (Linkugel, 293)

I wonder whether anyone can listen to a recording of King delivering this speech and remain unmoved. I should emphasize perhaps that while class discussion might call attention to King's use of rhetorical devices, they are important not in themselves but in how they help convey important and inspiring ideas with clarity and power. It is not great ideas alone that move people's hearts and minds, but great ideas eloquently expressed.

Take, for example, Jimmy Carter's inaugural address. After students have read Lincoln's "Gettysburg Address" and his second inaugural address (Boutwell 1965, 78−79), Kennedy's inaugural address (Boutwell 1965, 4−8), Elizabeth Cady Stanton's speech at the first Woman's Rights Convention (1848) (Boutwell 1965, 141−43), and King's "I have a dream" speech, they will be able to critique Carter's speech, recognizing its significant strengths and weaknesses.

President Carter begins with a generous acknowledgment to Gerald Ford, who was president immediately after the Watergate scandal, Richard Nixon's resignation, and America's military involvement in Vietnam. The rhetorical continuity and thematic unity of the sentences that follow, however, lack the clarity of other speeches the students have read:

For myself and our nation, I want to thank my predecessor for all he has done to heal our land. In this outward and physical ceremony we attest once again to the inner and spiritual strength of our nation.

As my high school teacher, Miss Julia Coleman, used to say, "We must adjust to changing times and still hold to unchanging principles."

Here before me is the Bible used in the inauguration of our first President in 1789, and I have just taken my own oath of office on the Bible my mother gave me just a few years ago, opened to a timeless admonition from the ancient prophet Micah:

"He hath showed thee, O man, what is good; and what doth the Lord require of thee, but to do justly, and to love mercy, and to walk humbly with thy God." [Micah 6:8]

This inauguration ceremony marks a new beginning, a new dedication within our government, and a new spirit among us all. A president may sense and proclaim that new spirit, but only a people can provide it.

Two centuries ago our nation's birth was a milestone in the long quest for freedom, but the bold and brilliant dream which excited the founders of our nation still awaits its consummation. I have no new dream to set forth today, but rather urge a fresh faith in the old dream. (*New York Times*, January 21, 1977, B1)

What happened to Micah's message? And Miss Julia Coleman's? President Carter has touched on a number of important, meritorious ideas, but they have yet to be dealt with or related one to the next. They are in fact related, but the connections between them are too abstract to be appreciated at the first hearing, and neither the diction nor the syntax makes the connections more accessible. And certainly, if these sentences were shuffled, it would be impossible to put them back in order. No teacher could have asked for a better lesson in rhetoric, coherence, transitions between sentences, and thesis development.

Yes, Carter's rhetoric utilizes repetition, parallelism, and contrast, but the results are not wholly successful:

> We have learned that "more" is not necessarily "better," that even our great nation has its recognized limits and that we can neither answer all questions nor solve all problems. We cannot afford to do everything, nor can we afford to lack boldness as we meet the future. So together, in a spirit of individual sacrifice for the common good, we must simply do our best. (*New York Times*, January 21, 1977, B1)

President Kennedy also asked for personal sacrifice for our country at the conclusion of his inaugural address, and he, like President Carter, recognized that not all our attempts would meet with success. But President Kennedy put it this way:

> And so, my fellow Americans: Ask not what your country can do for you — ask what you can do for your country. ...
> With a good conscience our only sure reward, with history the final judge of our deeds, let us go forth to lead the land we love, asking His blessing and His help, but knowing that here on earth God's work must truly be our own. (Boutwell 1965, 8)

Also worth examining, for example, is Senator Edward M. Kennedy's (1968) eulogy for his brother Robert F. Kennedy (see "Tribute to His Brother in Cathedral," *The New York Times*, June 9, 1968, 56). This speech also uses rhetoric well to move its audience. Those who hear a recording or watch a videotape of Ted Kennedy speaking about Bobby, the second brother he had lost to an assassin's gun, will not forget his voice's cracking toward the end of the speech when he recalls how Bobby had seen the Vietnam War and "tried to stop it." The speech concludes:

> My brother need not be idealized or enlarged in death beyond what he was in life. He should be remembered simply as a good and decent man who saw wrong and tried to right it, saw suffering and tried to heal it, saw war and tried to stop it.

> Those of us who loved him and who take him to his rest today pray that what he was to us, and what he wished for others, will some day come to pass for all the world.
>
> As he said many times, in many parts of this nation, to those he touched and who sought to touch him: "Some men see things as they are and say why. I dream things that never were and say, why not."

Does one have to be able to remember the pain of 1968 to be deeply moved by those words? My students tell me no.

Also worth studying is the brilliant speech given before a joint session of Congress by Czechoslovakia's president, Vaclav Havel. The former dissident playwright spoke about the democratic ideal, human responsibility, and America's potential role in the post—Cold War world. (For a verbatim transcript see *Time*, March 5, 1990, 14—15.)

Any collection of famous speeches will provide a number of texts worth reading in class, including perhaps William Faulkner's Nobel Prize acceptance speech (Boutwell 1965, 10—11) and speeches by Winston Churchill. Here are excerpts from three Churchillian masterpieces:

> What General Weygand called the Battle of France is over. I expect that the Battle of Britain is about to begin. Upon this battle depends the survival of Christian civilization. Upon it depends our own British life, and the long continuity of our institutions and our Empire. The whole fury and might of the enemy must very soon be turned on us. Hitler knows that he will have to break us in this Island or lose the war. If we can stand up to him, all Europe may be free and the life of the world may move forward into broad, sunlit uplands. But if we fail, then the whole world, including the United States, including all that we have known and cared for, will sink into the abyss of a new Dark Age made more sinister, and perhaps more protracted, by the lights of perverted science. Let us therefore brace ourselves to our duties, and so bear ourselves that, if the British Empire and its Commonwealth last for a thousand years, men will still say, "This was their finest hour." (Churchill, "Their Finest Hour," in Cannadine 1989, 177—78)

> In this crisis I hope I may be pardoned if I do not address the House at any length today. I hope that any of my friends and colleagues, or former colleagues, who are affected by the political reconstruction, will make all allowance for any lack of ceremony with which it has been necessary to act. I would say to the House, as I have said to those who have joined the Government: "I have nothing to offer but blood, toil, tears and sweat."
>
> We have before us an ordeal of the most grievous kind. We have before us many, many long months of struggle and of suffering. You ask, what is our policy? I will say: It is to wage war, by sea, land and air, with all our might and with all the strength that God can give us:

to wage war against a monstrous tyranny, never surpassed in the dark lamentable catalogue of human crime. That is our policy. You ask, what is our aim? I can answer in one word: Victory—victory at all costs, victory in spite of all terror, victory, however long and hard the road may be; for without victory, there is no survival. Let that be realized; no survival for the British Empire; no survival for all that the British Empire has stood for: no survival for the urge and impulse of the ages, that mankind will move forward towards its goal. But I take up my task with buoyancy and hope. I feel sure that our cause will not be suffered to fail among men. At this time I feel entitled to claim the aid of all, and I say, Come, then, let us go forward together with our united strength. (Churchill, "Blood, Toil, Tears and Sweat," in Cannadine 1989, 149)

The other day, President Roosevelt gave his opponent in the late Presidential Election a letter of introduction to me, and in it he wrote out a verse, in his own handwriting, from Longfellow, which he said, "applies to you people as it does to us." Here is the verse:

> ... *Sail on, O Ship of State!*
> *Sail on, O Union, strong and great!*
> *Humanity with all its fears,*
> *With all the hopes of future years,*
> *Is hanging breathless on thy fate!*

What is the answer that I shall give, in your name, to this great man, the thrice-chosen head of a nation of 130 millions? Here is the answer which I will give to President Roosevelt: Put your confidence in us. Give us your faith and your blessing, and, under Providence, all will be well.

We shall not fail or falter; we shall not weaken or tire. Neither the sudden shock of battle, nor the long-drawn trials of vigilance and exertion will wear us down. Give us the tools, and we will finish the job. (Churchill, "Give Us the Tools," in Cannadine 1989, 212–13)

After they have looked at several famous speeches and discussed some rhetorical devices, I ask students to write a speech, advertisement, or letter that moves its audience. I invite them to break my heart, make me cry, make me mad, move me to action, make me dedicate my life to some important purpose or give up my life for a worthy cause. They might write a presidential speech, a eulogy for a friend, a private, heartfelt letter, a solicitation for a charity, a call to arms, a plea for peace. Whatever they choose, I encourage them to write not only *about* something moving but *in a moving way*, to experiment with the rhetorical techniques that, when used well, can make important ideas and sentiments unforgettable.

Two brief caveats: I do warn students to beware of sentimentality and overwritten prose. Sentimentality appeals cheaply to surface emotions and lacks heartfelt sincerity; television commercials and politics are teeming with examples. Overwriting produces sickeningly sweet prose, à la travel brochures and wine labels. But I do not overemphasize these dangers — I want the students to take risks — and most of them can tell when enough is enough.

The exercise helps the students understand, among other things, that it is not only *what* one says, but *how* one says it; indeed it becomes clear that the distinction between the thing said and the way it is said is a false dichotomy. Supreme Court Justice Oliver Wendell Holmes once observed that *every* idea is an incitement — a call to action. The writer's or speaker's challenge is to make the language carry the power of the idea. Even the most compelling idea can be lost if it is not made incarnate in compelling words.

Focusing on rhetoric — language well used — reminds students that effective use of language is important not only in what they may consider a rarefied classroom world of poetics and intellect but also in the everyday world of action. If students do come to love words, they will be more likely to continue to read, to challenge themselves to use language well, and to derive joy from words well used. Students may become more discriminating citizens if they can understand not only how great language works but also how manipulative language works. Such understanding should help them distinguish the saccharine from the tender, the sentimental from the heartfelt, the thoughtless from the thoughtful, the demagogue from the leader, even — dare I say it — falsehood from truth.

Works Cited

Boutwell, William D., Wesley P. Callender, Jr., and Robert E. Gerber, eds. 1965. *Great Speeches*. New York: Scholastic.

Cannadine, David, ed. 1989. *Blood, Toil, Tears and Sweat: The Speeches of Winston Churchill*. Boston: Houghton Mifflin.

Carter, James. January 21, 1977. Inaugural Address. *The New York Times*, January 21, B1.

Churchill, Winston. May 13, 1940. "Blood, Toil, Tears and Sweat." In *The Speeches of Winston Churchill*, 148–49. See Cannadine 1989.

——. June 18, 1940. "Their Finest Hour." In *The Speeches of Winston Churchill*, 166–78. See Cannadine 1989.

——. February 9, 1941. "Give Us the Tools." In *The Speeches of Winston Churchill*, 202–13. See Cannadine 1989.

Faulkner, William. December 10, 1950. Nobel Prize Acceptance Speech. In *Great Speeches*, 10–11. See Boutwell 1965.

Havel, Vaclav. 1990. Address Before a Joint Meeting of Congress on February 21. "The Revolution Has Just Begun." *Time*, March 5, 14–15.

King, Martin Luther, Jr. August 27, 1963. "I Have a Dream." In *Contemporary American Speeches*, 289–93. See Linkugel 1972.

Kennedy, Edward M. 1968. "Tribute to His Brother in Cathedral." *The New York Times*, June 9, 56.

Kennedy, John F. January 20, 1961. Inaugural Address. In *Great Speeches*, 4–8. See Boutwell 1965.

Lincoln, Abraham. November 19, 1863. "Gettysburg Address." In *Great Speeches*, 217–18. See Boutwell 1965.

——. March 4, 1865. Second Inaugural Address. In *Great Speeches*, 78–79. See Boutwell 1965.

Linkugel, W. A., R. R. Allen, and Richard L. Johannesen, eds. *Contemporary American Speeches*. 3d ed. Belmont, Calif.: Wadsworth.

2

Meeting the Author
The English Research Paper

Tom McGraw

How can a class of fledgling writers fire their enthusiasm for using a library? How can teachers introduce the research paper without feeling like they're sending their students over the top at Verdun? Surely the students know their academic futures hold many hours of plowing through dusty stacks, gleaning quotes, annotating bibliographical sources, and presenting papers that reflect their curiosity and resourcefulness in tracking down ideas. But too often, composition courses demand essays disembodied from day-to-day classwork. The introductory writing course focuses on argument/persuasion through the practice of rhetorical strategies that are the staples of expository prose: comparison/contrast; analogy; classification/division; example; definition. Students hone these skills daily on narrow assignments whose scope promotes the merge of style and oomph. They zoom in on what they want to say, then plug in these rhetorical devices to achieve greater clarity. But to argue some of the monolithic controversies that suggest themselves to students as fertile ground for argument requires them to reduce unwieldy and deep questions to facile abridgments. How many papers can one read about gun control? abortion? capital punishment? How many "current affairs" topics can be reduced to the narrow scope a moderate-length (eight- to fifteen-page) research paper demands? Even students who write fine papers know their topics would be better suited for history or social studies courses.

To orient the research paper toward the writing course's ultimate goal (to teach students to apply newly acquired fundamentals of expository writing to the study of literature), the teacher must show young writers how fiction, its criticism, and authors' biographies offer manageable and vivid material for a research paper of sharp focus. If the composition course were tailored to move the class from writing expository prose to writing expository prose about fiction, the teacher could use a library-oriented unit to excite each student about a particular author and the critical heritage of the author's work.

Here's a way to go about it. Assign a three-part paper in which each student is asked to choose a favorite writer. The first part is a biographical sketch, the second an overview of the critical reception of the author's work, and the third a close examination of a particular work using the information in the first two parts. If the class uses anthologies for its fiction and poetry, for four weeks assign a half-dozen short stories to be read each week, and about a dozen poems. In literary journals, students respond to the week's reading, explaining how and why a particular story or poem has hit them. After a few weeks of such entries, they are asked to review what they've read and reread their literary journals. Teachers then call for a short essay on students' choice of a writer to investigate, which particular work(s), and why. A typical sampler: O. Henry, William Carlos Williams, Edgar Allan Poe, George Orwell, Willa Cather, John Updike, Sylvia Plath, Guy de Maupassant, James Joyce, and William Butler Yeats. The writer ought to be prominent enough that ample biographical and critical information is available from a wide variety of resources.

Part One

By using various compendiums (*American and British Writers Series, Magill's Critical Survey of Fiction*, and biographies), students garner information about the life and times of their writer of choice. Allow at least three class meetings for supervised reading and note taking. The first part of the paper, the biographical "thumbnail sketch," ought to run between three and five pages. Because students often become swallowed up by plumbing the biographies, the challenge is to jettison anything that will not pertain to the specific work they have chosen for the third and final part of the paper. For example, a student might be smitten by Mark Twain's silver-mining career in Nevada, but if his work is *Huckleberry Finn*, he'd get closer to the bone focusing on Twain's piloting days by skimming *Life on the Mississippi*.

Such investigation can yield insights into a writer's later work. In this student's paper about William Carlos Williams, she connects family dynamics with the writer's subsequent poetic vision:

> Williams' father . . . spent much of his time away from home. William George Williams slowly blended into a shadowy figure in his son's life. Although he taught William Carlos the writings of Shakespeare and became the force behind Williams' formal education, he left his

wife to fill the vacuum his stern silence created. It was at this early age that Williams developed his reliance on a motherly figure that carried on into his marriage. An unpassable silence grew between father and son. Perhaps it was the unmistakable line separating duty and emotion.

Later, the student returns to this idea when she describes Williams's early writings:

On the twelfth of December, 1912, Williams and "Floss" were married, simply, in Rutherford. They ... developed a strong, complicated love for each other. She remained a constant influence in his life, supporting him in his [medical] practice and writing. It was for her that he wrote the poem "Asphodel, That Greeny Flower," which Randall Jarrell claims to be one of the few perfect love poems in the English language.

Other students would mention equally compelling facts: Orwell's virtual imprisonment at a British boarding school; O. Henry's jail term for embezzlement; Poe's dissolution; Willa Cather's ambiguous sexual identity. Part of the value of this biographical element of the paper is to give a period flavor to the literature, deepening the student's imaginative grasp of the work and its cultural/historical setting. Who could read about the murder of Boggs in *Huckleberry Finn* without revulsion, knowing Twain actually witnessed a brutal murder on a dusty street in Hannibal, Missouri, when he was eight? Is not the world of *1984* the same world of sensory deprivation and repression Orwell lived in at St. Edward's School when he was nine, as testified to in his essay "Such, Such Were the Joys"? Students begin to understand how important it is to keep their own antennae extended to help them understand their own motivations, what fires their own imaginations, what historical and social forces give them their own special visions.

Part Two

In the middle section of the paper, the students are asked to summarize the characteristics of the writer's work. They are introduced to resource works such as *The Explicator,* Magill's critical surveys of fiction and poetry, and *Contemporary Literary Criticism/20th Century Literary Criticism.* Here they learn the vocabulary of criticism and a context into which their specific work can be placed. At first, the students are inclined to parrot the language of these sometimes lofty entries. Take care to make them translate what they uncover into their own vernacular (or a serviceable one). One function of this overview of each author's work is the demystification of what they will be fed in future literature classes. They are empowered to know that they, too, could come up with the same "insights" as their teachers. Such deep, dark mysteries about the "hidden meaning" are not the purview of the teacher alone. This tends to check frustration and anger at the library doors. Here the students begin to appropriate and denominate the off-putting language of academia. Here, also, the students are encouraged to disagree with the "canonical message" as set down by academic authorities. Few students have been able to set out an author's style as concisely and clearly as this student does:

> Willa Cather's novels and stories can be divided into three groups. The first speaks of the lives of foreign-born farmers and their descendents. The second group consists of short stories and novelettes, influenced by Henry James and Edith Wharton, dealing with artists and sophisticated Easterners. The third group merges almost into legend, being influenced by Willa's conversion to Roman Catholicism in 1922. ... Her stories are not stories of plot, but rather chronicles of death and significance. In these stories, her characters are deeply affected and motivated by their surroundings; thus, her best short stories are set against the land. Her stories are filled with an emotional vitality stemming from the people who populate her books, human beings devoted to living. Her works are human truths that appeal to the five senses. She was able to relate the beauty of the land, the simplicity of pioneer life and the bitter and hard existence with lyricism and simple realism.

The students enjoy playing a little parlor psychology; having devoured the information about these literary lives gives them the license. Often, their diagnoses are pointed. This, from the same paper about Willa Cather:

> Her writing was a search for her erased self. In searching, she recovered ancestors, reviving them from forgotten places, making them speak, integrating her identity with her past-life. The dangers of Willa's sexual desire also evidence themselves in her writing. In her writings, sexual desire often results in the loss of identity. Passion is often intertwined with death, for it is the ultimate state of self-dissolution. She frequently used male characters and narrators to confront an erotically compelling woman, placing a barrier between herself and the maternal presence she was always seeking in her lesbian relationships. Her need to conceal her lesbian love led her to the slavish imitation of male writers in order to cloak her own feelings.

The middle part of the paper ought to connect with the first part, overlapping where biography supplies a motive for writing. The following is from a paper about Orwell:

> I believe Orwell's main motive was to write with "political purpose," as he always wrote to uncover what he perceived to be injustice. Orwell had always hated the unfairness of the British Caste System,

and . . . based his short stories, essays and journalism on the oppression the class system brought upon his people.

Part Three

The final section of the paper is the student's chance to plug in all that's gone before to a single, specific work. This explication is proof that the student has understood the forces that converged on the writer to shape his or her work, and shows how those forces are reflected in one short story, novel, or poem. Poems lend themselves to a more pointed investigation than novels. If by this time in the school year (spring) the class has discussed rhythm, phrasing, rhetorical devices, and other elements of fiction, the student may use such a vocabulary to illuminate the work of choice. This example taken from a paper about Sylvia Plath's poem "Daddy" combines technical explication with psychological implication:

> The rhyme scheme of the poem is that of a nursery rhyme — sing-song — setting up a great irony with the poem's subject matter. Some think the emotional anguish of the poem might have caused her to use the rhyming pattern in order to maintain control in at least one way throughout the entire poem. The father/husband figure, often represented as a Nazi, is one that haunts a number of her other poems, like "Lady Lazarus" and "Little Fugue." In "Daddy," the speaker expresses conflicting feelings for her father. In the second stanza, he is described as "marble-heavy, a bag full of God,/Ghastly statue with one grey toe/Big as a Frisco seal." He commands the respect of an everlasting, impressive statue; the "one grey toe" refers to Otto Plath's amputated foot. She is afraid of him, yet feels adoration for him ("I have always been scared of you/ . . . Every woman adores a Fascist"). The vampire comparison of blood-drinking, or emotional, perhaps physical pain, links the speaker's father and husband, by far the two men Sylvia loved most, and the two most alternately horrible and wonderful men in her life. The major conflict is that of the psyche of the speaker with its final knowledge, from which she can escape only into death, and that love expresses itself only in terms of violence and brutality.

This project combines library skills, close reading, gleaning of biography and criticism, and a sense of having taken on a writer and investigated him or her in depth. It requires close personal monitoring during the stages of independent research and reading, careful checking on note taking, and immutable standards on presentation, format, and time frame. A fifteen-page paper completed over four weeks is about average. The choice of writer ought to have been preceded by a broad exposure to fiction; the final section of the paper hangs in part on the class's exposure to the language of literary investigation. But apart from all that, it comes to this: when students read something that really turns their heads, what better way to pursue this interest than the English research paper?

3

Our Problems With Water
Writing to Make a Difference
Ed Germain

We were partway through the fall term, a tenth-grade composition class talking about punctuation and looking at this passage from James Joyce's *Ulysses*:

> Did it flow?
> Yes. From Roundwood reservoir in country Wicklow of a cubic capacity of 2,400 million percolating through a subterranean aqueduct of filtre mains of single and double pipeage constructed at an initial plant cost of £5 per linear yard by way of the Dargle, Rathdown, Glen of the Downs and Callowhill to the 26 acre reservoir at Stillorgan, a distance of 22 statute miles, and thence, through a system of relieving tanks, by a gradient of 250 feet to the city boundary at Eustace bridge ... (1946, 654)

That is the long-winded, catalogue version. You could compress it, as poet Donald Hall does:

> A column of water
> miles long
> moves, suddenly, to the faucet ... (1969, 84)

I sat at one end of the oval table, drinking water. The kids were noisy, enjoying Joyce's and Hall's different kinds of exaggeration. Then we were sitting looking at the half-full glass of water on the table.

"So where does it come from, David?" I asked.
"Water?"
"Yeah."
"Uh [pause] from some reservoir somewhere?"
"Where?" Silence followed by silence.

"Where *does* it come from?" Jadie asked me.
"Want to find out?"

Behind the seeming improvisation in this class is a lot of planning that students needn't see. What they should notice is the lesson that following your curiosity can make you knowledgeable and articulate.

For the next class I told the students to meet me in "Siberia"—our farthest athletic field—and to bring a notebook and pencil. Sitting on the grass in the soccer field on crimson, orange, and yellow leaves, we started talking about school: what was good and bad about it. Some of the kids had much to say. Others answered them. I kept the atmosphere easy, contemplative. Jadie toyed with grass stems.

"Do you remember going to school for the first time?" I asked them. They reminisced. Kindergarten, first grade: fear, bewilderment, hope. "I was so little then," someone said. About fifteen minutes had passed.

"Try this," I said. "Make yourself that little person you were. Go back to your feelings of expectation. And add this: you have just begun wondering where the water comes from." Groans from some kids, puzzlement from others.

"So here's the situation: you're going to school for the very first time. You have in your mind, back in some corner, this question: 'Where does the water come from?' It's not a burning issue, just a question. But the time has come to go to school, and it's your first day. OK?"

A couple of questions and then silence.

"Are you all in your child's mind, now?"

They were alert. Jadie was sitting quite straight with her legs crossed and Jim was kneeling, sitting back on his heels. We were still and quiet—we'd been getting to this for half an hour.

"OK, you can take your notebooks because you can write, even though you are little. Your school is right across the street; you'll see the road there, just to the left of that shed. Go to school, and keep the question in the corner of your mind just in case."

Of course they were confused, and surprised. I had to explain that there really was an elementary school there, and that they were free to walk into it, to go anywhere they wanted, to enter and leave classes in session. "Go be a child again," I said. "Leave by noon, and write me what it was like—for tomorrow's class, anything you want, any way you want. If you don't see anything about the water, that's fine."

"Do we have to use only words a kid would know?"

"You can use any words you want. Observe what you feel and see. Then make those things clear on paper."

And so off they went — rather randomly as little kids might: three girls together, but one a little apart; a boy throwing a stone into the woods. They disappeared up the leaf-littered road. No one paid any attention to the shed, with its water valves and gauges inside, visible through the window.

Anything is worth observing: an old tree; bricks in your building; bells in a church steeple (take your class up); the cemetery; the sidewalks; dumps (one school used to have a class that met in the city dump).

Bancroft Elementary School, a public experiment, looks like a child's sand castle turned stone. The essays made much of its fantasy architecture. Several mentioned getting a drink at a fountain, but otherwise water remained mysterious. We spent the class period reading papers to each other, appreciating what was human and vital, overlooking what sounded as if it was written for English class. Some of the students were beginning to get that point.

Toward the end of the class, kids raised the water question. "Where was it?" they asked. "What were we supposed to learn about water?"

"Well, what you've written here is interesting enough," I said. "Let me take your papers and see if I can make some useful comments, and we'll talk tomorrow about how some of you went about creating a child's view of Bancroft school. But let me ask you, where did you write your notes, if you made any?"

Some hadn't made any notes, other had jotted notes while moving around the school. But Kathleen had written hers outside.

"And where were you when you were writing the notes?"

"I sat outside on that hill."

"What hill?"

"The hill down the road, before you get to the school." When I professed puzzlement, she continued: "You pass the green shed, then the hill starts on the left."

"Oh," I said, "that's not a hill, that's a five million gallon underground water reservoir." That ended class for Tuesday.

Is there a more rewarding lesson for a student to learn than to discover how to pursue what interests her?

Potentially, anyone can become interested in anything. The high school teacher's basic problem becomes one of tricking or goading or inspiring a student to become interested. With particularly able students, it may just be a matter of setting out material and getting out of the way, but with others it often demands a kind of "sleight of mind" on the teacher's part. For example, if you can show a student that she's sitting right on top of an answer *and she doesn't even know it*, you've got a good start towards getting her curiosity aroused. Perhaps you then can get her to open her mind and pursue that interest. One wonderful teacher at this school brings a flower into class and asks the kids to describe it, day after day, all term long. Their essays get better and better as the rose wilts; because they are learning to see, students look for the flower even after it has fallen to dust. By the term's end, "flower" means vastly more to them than when they began. For some it has become a symbol or a metaphor. Others have begun to observe their own observing. One student may by now be a botanist. Everyone sees that there are worlds of other words in a simple "flower."

At least one of my students had sat on five million gallons of water and not known it. And in spite of my hint, not one of them had asked a teacher or any of the children in the elementary school about water (I had; that's how I knew the reservoir was there).

The next day they arrived in class noisy and feeling a little tricked. We talked about their descriptions, letting water go for a while. (After all, if they were going to describe the water-treatment plant, they had to have some practice in describing, first.)

Nothing can be uninteresting from all points of view.

The primary focus of the class discussion was *point of view*. The school essays had differed markedly depending on whether the writer had imagined himself a little kid with a little kid's vocabulary, or as a teenager who was speaking his own language, whether she was writing as a participant or as an observer. When the class began arguing which was the best point of view, I told them to meet me the next day in the cemetery.

Point of view has always seemed to me analogous to a physical position: an ironic point of view is from outside looking satirically in; a sympathetic point of view is inside; and so on. The exercise describing Bancroft School had been aimed at getting the students to use a child's concrete imagery. Now I had a chance to show them how physical and material their point of view could be.

The next day was rainy, but I had some plastic stuffed in my pocket. We stood not far from where Harriet Beecher Stowe is buried, looking at the only modern marker in the cemetery, the grave of scholar, poet, and Andover teacher Dudley Fitts. The grave marker is aluminum, perhaps three inches thick and maybe three feet long. Exactly in the middle is a pole that holds the thing up. "Here's the assignment," I told them. "Just describe this grave marker."

"It's weird," they said. "It looks like a metal slab, on a pole about a foot high." "It's got a bunch of rods going through it that stick out on both sides." "Some stick out two inches, others stick out five inches."

"We could measure them!" somebody volunteered. It was raining fairly hard. Some kids wanted to get indoors. There was a name and two dates on the marker, not much more. "Let's go, OK?" "We can write descriptions inside" — they all said that. But we didn't go. We kept standing in the water, looking at the grave marker.

Why did the dowels penetrate the slab? Why were they different lengths? Why was a classics scholar's grave made of aluminum, a metal neither the Greeks nor Romans knew?

Then out of nowhere Cintra said, "The rods are like flowers." We all paid attention to her idea.

But no, that wasn't quite right; everybody said so. The rods were stiff and straight. "Well, flowers penetrate two worlds," she said, like Persephone.

"But these don't *look* like flowers," Jon said. And then a tall, agile girl whose dark hair I remember, but whose name I cannot, said, "Well, if not flowers, then like music."

That sounded so nonrational that nobody had an answer. We were getting used to silences in this class, so we just stood there in the white noise of the rain, mostly puzzled. It was Caroline who started to lie down. "Ohhh, ick, what are you doing!" Jadie blurted.

"I wanted to be like he is," Caroline said — startled by Jadie's warning as though she were suddenly waking up. I handed her the plastic from my pocket. "Here, put this down first."

She did. And when she was looking at the marker from the point of view of Dudley Fitts, she understood some of the answers. In turn, each of us assumed his point of view, saw what we could write about, the line from a poem etched into the thin bottom edge of the aluminum:

AND NOW THE QUICK SUN ROUNDING THE GABLE PICKS OUT A CHAIR
   A VASE OF FLOWERS WHICH HAD STOOD TILL THEN IN SHADOW.

As class ended, we recalled that it was raining and we were wet.

The day afterwards was clear, and the glass of water appeared on the table again.

"How much does it cost?" I asked.

"It's free," they answered.

Well, no, it isn't really free; the school probably pays something for it, and we pay for it indirectly through tuition, and so on, but who cares, really, nobody thinks about it . . .

"How much do you think the school's water costs?"

"For how long," David asked, "a semester?"

"Yeah."

"About seven or eight thousand dollars."

"No, no, that's too high," Caroline said.

"Too high?" Cintra butted in; "It's *way* too *low*."

"No, I think the school pays twenty thousand for a semester of water," said the girl with the long brown hair. Voices were rising as kids searched for a handle to this question.

"You have to know how much water the school uses," Jadie said.

"How do we find that out?" I asked quickly.

"Look it up," several voices said.

"Yeah, OK. Go ahead," I said. Sudden silence.

"Where?" This was from bright, withdrawn Ted. More silence — but an anticipatory one.

"The administration building," Jadie said.

"OK," I said, "let's go."

It took less than five minutes for my class of fifteen kids to crowd into the treasurer's office. I had called the day before, so the water records were ready for us. But the secretary waited until the class explained to her what they wanted before she said, "Those records aren't tallied. We have the receipts from the town water bills for each month, but you'll have to add them up."

Individual work, while essential, can be overstressed; group collaboration, pooling of ideas, sharing of hunches, even confusions, can engage students and stimulate creativity.

There were hundreds of receipts. Each water meter in the entire school was represented by one receipt for each month — we have sixty dormitories alone, not to mention the other buildings. We broke into teams, but in the half hour remaining hadn't come close to finishing. Cintra asked if the town offices might not have the compiled figures, so we could bypass this adding up. Everyone thought that was a hopeful idea, so she and Ted decided to go there (about eight blocks) after sports. I encouraged a small group of students, however, to return that afternoon and complete the figuring here. That way we could be sure we had the right amount in class the next day. I'm still not sure why I insisted on this. But sometimes to pursue what interests you, you follow hunches.

The result was that the academy paid about $65,000 for water for one academic year. Strangely, however, the town's bill and the school's record of payments didn't match. There was a discrepancy of about $4,500.

Now we had plenty to do. First Cintra and Ted decided we ought to get a complete breakdown from the town and check month by month to see where the discrepancy lay. When the class agreed to do this, I knew that, at last, they had gotten interested. But some members of the class were more interested in the thousands of gallons we used.

How much is all that water, when you put it into a swimming pool or into glasses or showers? That group decided to write one-page descriptions of a year's water usage. And David reminded everyone that while this statistical stuff was fairly "bizarre," we still didn't know where the water came from. So I just told him to find out.

Every community is a learning place. You don't need special assets or endowment. When one class read Hard Times, *it discovered that Charles Dickens had visited Lowell, Massachusetts, to observe a modern, well-run mill. So everyone took the bus to Lowell, about fifteen miles away. The mills hadn't yet been renovated, and the present historical district was just an idea. Nevertheless, the kids "ran into" an ex-marine who remembered the mills from his grandmother's stories—she had worked there. They got a key and with his help brought that abandoned mill back to life one October afternoon.* Hard Times *was tangible after that.*

The next day David reported back: "Water comes from the water treatment plant."

"'From Roundwood reservoir in county Wicklow of a cubic capacity of 2,400 million gallons, percolating through a subterranean aqueduct ...'" chanted Nick.

Where was the plant? One of the girls knew, since she lived in town. No student had ever gone there, though, so I set up a tour for the following Saturday morning. There was some resistance to this, but not too much. Everyone showed up. My wife drove a car, I drove a school van. When we arrived, the water quality engineer met us.

What did the kids see? There were fifteen different points of view in the papers they wrote. These essays grew longer—not because I assigned a length, but because the problem of describing was bigger. Two kids got bogged down, lost focus, and called me at home. Caroline had gotten really interested in the fact that all the pipes in the water plant are painted in shiny enamel primary colors. She'd asked the engineer and discovered that they'd been painted by an artist from New Hampshire, who had arrived each day on her bicycle. This was as unpredictable as a public school that looked like a castle, and she had wanted to pursue it but didn't know how. Instead, because the paper was due, she started talking about "flocculation tanks" and "caustic soda"; she had lost interest and gotten stuck. She asked me what to do.

The best solution would have been to help her get in touch first with the bicycling artist, then with those who authorized painting those cheerful, streaming colors. But I didn't have the time, so we worked on the practical problem: how to find a point of view that made flocculation tanks interesting to her and to her readers, and how to shape the description so that it didn't turn into dead encyclopedia prose (partial answer: include the story of the colored pipes). I reminded her of the Joyce excerpt; encyclopedism doesn't need to be dull.

While these descriptions were being written, Cintra and Ted came back with the discovery that the school appeared to have overpaid its town water bill. The whole class poured over the data and agreed. Then they wrote, as a class, a letter to the treasurer documenting it.

The descriptions of our water consumption came in next. These brought up the question: what part of the school uses the most water? When I asked if they thought boys used more or less water than girls, the class came unglued. Whew, what a controversial issue! But after standing up and raising my hands and shouting "Enough!" I was able to say, "OK, let's find out."

We rearranged the water receipts and discovered that certain girls' dorms used twice as much water as comparable boys' dorms. Strangely, the girls' dorm that used the most water had the same name as the school where the underground reservoir was located, Bancroft. Nobody thought that signified anything even when I called it the mystery of the universe at work, but one of the girls who lived in Bancroft organized a study to figure out why her dorm was using all that water. And another group of kids set out to investigate disproportionate water usage by a distant boys' dorm.

The answers came back: Bancroft "has lots of jocks and we all shower all the time and nobody turns off the showers all the way." And for the other: "The boys in the small dorm do not use the water that the meter shows is being used!" As an in-class exercise, we wrote a note to the girls in Bancroft asking them if they really wanted to be known as water hogs. Then we all went out to look at the dorm that used more water than it used.

We finally concluded that there must be a leak in the water line somewhere. Three students wrote to the Office of the Physical Plant explaining why we thought so. (The leak was subsequently found — oh, and the school eventually did receive its refund from the town for overpayment.)

By this time we had spent about five weeks discovering that in a wet year pumps suck water from Haggett's Pond (otherwise, from the Merrimack River), propel it through the treatment plant and eventually out into several huge reservoirs, one of which, miles away and underground, is ours. We had described a fairy-tale school, a mysterious modern tombstone, that invisible reservoir, a gargantuan water tower on Holt Hill, and what it felt like for a bunch of kids to walk into the treasurer's office and ask to see water records. We had written fairly big papers that explained where water came from. Many of those papers dwelt on the fact (which we had discovered) that Andover's water treatment plant was world-famous when it was built, that visitors from as far away as Japan had signed its guest book, that it integrated modern high technology with a policy of adding as few chemicals as possible to water. One paper that focused on the burying of the town water mains used material discovered in the town library and historical society to reveal that much of this work had been performed by Chinese laborers at substandard wages.

The less successful papers tended toward being catalogues of mechanical processes. The most successful grew from concrete imagery and a clear point of view. These papers had theses that interested other kids. We recognized them when they were read in class. We did not read the least successful ones in class.

For the longer papers, I had received three drafts from each student. Usually I didn't specify that what was handed in was a draft; I just treated it like one. That caused another version to be written, which I treated as draft two. When a paper had progressed as far as it should go, I asked the student for a final version, compiled from the best parts of all the drafts. Several of those were rewritten, too, after comments. One girl wrote essentially failing versions right up to the end, then must have worked straight through a weekend because she totally revised all of them for a final essay that reflected nearly all of the suggestions I had made for weeks.

The structure of an assignment should appear to derive from its content. When a teacher tells students that they must write on one topic, have at least three sources, a full page of footnotes, and a bibliography, groans will be audible. Curiosity can die right there.

On the last day of the term, when students read their essays in class, two of the papers got spontaneous applause. Then when we had finished, David said, "You remember at the treatment plant when we drank that water?"

Out of his knapsack, David brought a jar of water. "This is some of that water. I went back and got it."

Then he pulled out another jar of water and set it on the table, too. "This is water I got out of the tap in our dorm this morning."

It was duller, slightly brownish in tint; there was some sediment on the bottom of the bottle.

"What happens to the water in between the treatment plant and my dorm? And why does it taste so bad when it gets here, when it tasted great at the plant?" He brought out a paper cup. "Here, you can taste it."

Nobody wanted to drink. Nobody knew the answer to David's question.

And at that precise moment, the term was over!

When one class can continue a project another class began, the "I am alone here trying to survive" feeling breaks down. It helps kids bond to a group of successful kids who have learned and passed the lessons along to them.

So, a year later, I told my winter composition class what their predecessors had done. I brought out two bottles of water (newly refilled). They could see the difference. And, gingerly, they tasted the difference.

"So, do you all want to discover the answer to the question that class ended with?"

"Why don't you just tell us," said a crew-cut kid in a jacket with The Dead Live on it. I had just picked up this class, and was still learning their names, but I recognized the question's mild sarcasm.

"Because I don't know the answer," I told him honestly.

So, with just a hint of that nervous energy I look for, we started asking how we could discover what we wanted to know. That energy is a kind of hungriness; in the best writers I've taught it can flower into short stories and poems and sinewy essays.

We spent two days speculating on what could cause the difference in taste. We made lists and divided them into sublists. At one point the blackboard contained the somewhat illogical but useful outline shown in Figure 3–1.

That night we all took water samples from our dorms, and the next day our specimens were neatly lined up on the table. They didn't look the same, and we couldn't tell whether or not they tasted the same — some people said yes, some no: much hilarity during our "water tasting." (Jen: "Tastes like Blatz." Zach: "What's Blatz?")

All thought we needed some standard measurement. We walked down to the English Department lounge and called the school's chief engineer, who said simply that the school got its water from the town (out of Haggett's Pond, we already knew that) and didn't check it or treat it.

I decided these kids, too, ought to see how the town treated the water, so I organized another tour of the water treatment plant. This time their assignment was to focus on how the water was treated: what went into it, what came out of it. It was to be a short, clear paper. The facts.

That tour, which was as fascinating to them as it had been for their predecessors, left the kids puzzled. They saw the lab where water was

Figure 3—1

Possible Causes of Bad-Tasting Water

```
Given: 1) treatment plant's output tastes OK and looks clear
       2) Dorm A's water doesn't and isn't
       3) Dorm A gets its water from the Treatment Plant

Then:                                                       If    If
      Is Dorm A the only dorm with yucky water?   Yes?  No?
          --  check other dorms' water?
          --  check ALL dorms?!


      Then focus on Dorm A:
          --Something must be getting into pipes?
          --Other possibilities?
          --Resource people:
              1.   Head of Physical Plant
              2.   School engineer for water (if any)
              3.   Interview kids in dorm
              4.   Ask town water treatment engineer
          --Is water bad throughout dorm?
          --Is it really bad?  i.e. what does "bad" mean?
          --Some way to scientifically verify yuckyness?


      Then focus on whole school!
          --Some one cause?
              --are all buildings the same?
              --need some way to scientifically verify the yuck
              --how to tell?
          --Many causes?
              --then the degree of yuck must vary from
                    building/bldg (in all probability)
          --Q: Should we first verify the degree and
                    extent of yuckyness?
```

tested and saw the water test OK. It looked clear. They put their cups under the stream. It tasted pretty good. They heard the town's water quality engineer tell them that the water mains were old, that over the years minerals and deposits had built up, and that these undoubtedly accounted for the bad taste. Those dorms where water tasted the worst probably had the oldest input pipes. What more was there to ask? The kids were beginning to feel we had spent a week doing very little.

But I wasn't willing to let this opportunity go by. If they could find out something interesting about the water, then I could pass *that* on to the next year's class. Maybe I could eventually get to the waste treatment plant on the other side of the city, and from there to environmental pollution. I could see this chain of student investigations bearing fruit for several years—if it didn't disintegrate now. If we were at a dead end, we'd have to go back to the library and I'd have to fight the "standard-research-paper blues" (five papers on drugs, five on abortion, one on rock music, maybe an interesting one in there somewhere).

I called a friend in New Hampshire, owner of a water-analysis company called WaterTest, which tests water from all over the United States. Yes, he would be willing to test a few samples of water for us, for free. Yes, the kids could come through WaterTest's lab and watch the tests in action. WaterTest would provide test kits and a printout of results.

When the test kits arrived overnight, and the kids stopped by my house to pick them up, curiosity was flowing. We organized carefully. Each student was responsible for proper testing of water in one dormitory. The test was to be done before anyone used the water in the morning — about 5 A.M. The student was to write (in a journal — something we invented at this point) a short account of what it was like doing the test, what the dorm sounded like at dawn, what it felt like — anything, just a paragraph. It wasn't much of an assignment, but it would keep us going.

The kids brought all the test kits in, and we scheduled a field trip for Wednesday. When we rode in a cold bus up to New Hampshire, most of the kids slept in their seats.

Gene Rosov personally gave us a tour. He told us about water quality on a national and regional scale, showed us graphs and a copy of a report WaterTest had made for a Congressional subcommittee. Kids took notes; after a few minutes, everyone had questions. Whatever was happening, we were in business again: that nervous, curious energy had come back to the group.

"What's the biggest problem, aside from supply, with the water in the U.S.?" Kim asked.

"Lead pollution," Gene Rosov answered. "About a third of the houses in the U.S. have it. It comes from the lead solder used in copper plumbing and from old lead water mains."

"My house has copper plumbing," reported Leonard.

"Don't drink the water!" yelped Sam.

I asked each student to write a personal essay about the experience at WaterTest. I wanted to cut against the tendency to write very "scientific," tensionless prose. I told them to write for another class member, to tell what the experience had been like for them. No generalizations (e.g., "It was neat!"), but pictures and conversations and thoughts they had had. We read some of these in class waiting for the results from WaterTest. We didn't have to wait long.

Gene called me at 11 P.M. "I think you've got trouble," he said. Next day his report shocked the kids silent. What we had found had little to do with the way the water tasted. Half of their dorms had dangerous lead readings. Levels sometimes exceeded ten times the maximum tolerated by proposed EPA recommendations.

The kids wanted to know immediately all the implications of high lead content. An early reaction was "We've got to warn everybody!"

But more conversation showed them that they didn't understand enough even to explain the situation clearly. We talked about what kind of confusion, even panic, might be caused by wild assertions based on lack of understanding. We left class early and went to the library. I let each student follow whatever leads he or she wished, however inefficiently. The assignment was to come up with a list of sources we ought to check before going further. We knew what we were interested in, but we needed to discover where to learn more about how that lead might be affecting our lives.

By the end of the next class each student had a research project in mind. None were the same; all explored various sources and aspects of the lead question. We decided to work independently for a week, then meet together to share what we had learned. Logistically, this meant that we met in the library during the next four class days. Students would check in with me, then work on their own. I circulated, working with different students each day. Every student did go to the library; some went beyond it. A week later class was filled with excerpts from the *Congressional Record*, *The New York Times*, two dozen books on water quality and environmental pollution, notes from conversations with the school's engineer and the town's water quality engineer. Animated class discussion pieced together the likely scenario: lead came mostly from old solder joints; although, in at least one instance (my own dorm, which has no soldered connections), it might come from an old lead intake pipe.

Clear questions formed: (1) If the lead levels were this high before anyone had used the water, would they continue that high while water was frequently used during the day? We postulated that probably these high readings came from the steady buildup overnight of leached lead and that the day's normal water use would see much lower levels. But how could we find out? (2) What was the clearest and most nonthreatening way to alert students and faculty throughout the school? We all felt we must do this, and with dispatch! But because the issue was complicated, and because the extent of the threat still remained somewhat unclear, we agreed that our alert should be done in some detail and with special care not to panic anyone unnecessarily. After all, no one had died from the leaded water at school—so far as we knew!

After debate, we agreed that another couple of weeks shouldn't make a drastic difference in what must be a decades-old problem. We decided to finish our research papers, then to write a class article for the school paper, *The Phillipian*. And that's what we did for the final weeks of class.

As you may guess, however, there was considerable other activity going on while the class worked. Immediately after receiving the computer analysis from WaterTest, I went to our headmaster. "There's lead in the drinking water," I told him. I won't print his immediate response.

Neither of us knew enough at that point to speculate what this meant for the school, but we agreed that the school would have to take some action. The headmaster said he would make the issue the charge of a particular administrator, and that he wanted to be kept informed of what we found.

We both understood, too, that the students knew they had discovered something important. They believed it their duty to report it to their community, and they needed to learn enough about it so they could report responsibly. The report would come out — and it would be in the school paper. I volunteered that I would do my best to keep the report informed, calm, unsensational. "Even though they are excited, slightly alarmed tenth graders, I want the work to be theirs. That's what the class is all about," I said.

The headmaster nodded with a look of a man bracing for an experience he knew might be good for us all, but that might not be pleasant. "Thanks," he said, with only a trace of irony. I left his office proud of my school.

When the student essays were in, we had one week to write the newspaper article. In the meantime, the newspaper had gotten wind of our project and had assigned an inexperienced student reporter to the case. It didn't take long to convince him that our class would do a much better job.

So we started out with everyone sketching the kind of article they thought we should write. These were awful! I realized I'd not shown them anything about newspaper writing. In haste we talked about putting the most important facts first, and so on. By the week's end, we had a new draft from everyone and had elected an editorial committee of three students to meld these drafts into a final report. I gave advice frequently, but let the students do the writing. We met after class, in the evening, the night before the article was due. We cut and pasted, scribbled transitions in the margins. I typed the final version because the kids ran out of time, editing as I went along. The kids checked it in the morning, making two more changes and approving the story; we all knew we needed more time, but the deadline was at hand. The committee took it to the paper. We all waited for the paper to come out.

The first sign of trouble was a curt note to me from a middle-level administrator. I answered the summons to appear.

At that meeting, I was told that the article was irresponsible, inaccurate, uninformed, and that I was abusing my privilege as a teacher. Then a member of *The Phillipian* staff arrived, paper in hand. I saw the printed article for the first time, published mostly as we had written it, with only a few strange changes in the text but with headlines and illustrations that we never envisioned. The news staff had done just what the tenth-grade class had struggled to avoid—sensationalized the issue. I pointed out the distinction between the captions and illustrations on the one hand and the text on the other, said my class and I would stand behind the text, and left. I wondered if the issue was really going to blow up further. I felt like Dr. Stockman in Ibsen's *An Enemy of the People.*

The next day I received a note of apology from the administrator. In that day's class we talked about the press's responsibility not to sensationalize with headlines or cartoons. But the news was out; the student felt proud of their work. We spent the last few minutes of the term discussing what we had learned from one student's essay: the U.S. government had been aware of the danger of lead solder for decades, but had made no national effort to ban it; Russia, however, had banned high-lead solder in the 1950s. You can bet that made us think!

Shortly thereafter, WaterTest offered, for a reasonable fee, to test the water throughout the school. But the town of Andover's water quality engineer volunteered to do it without charge as a test case. His tests subsequently confirmed ours, as well as our hypothesis that the lead levels were most dangerous at the first draw of water in the morning. Our class warning to the school is now institutionalized; many faucets have RUN WATER FOR 90 SECONDS signs. Remodeling work at school now routinely includes replacing high-lead solder wherever practical.

After its own study, the town modified the alkalinity of the town's water to retard lead-leaching in everyone's home. Working independently, Massachusetts has made high-lead solder illegal in input water pipes.

All in all, our project made us all think. And, truly, every student had excelled. They had gotten involved, done their work, and made a difference.

Afterthoughts

Recently, Nanao Sakaki told me of a teacher in Japan who asked her students to bring an adult with them when they came to school on Saturday morning, and to meet by the river instead of in the schoolroom. Moreover, no one should eat anything before class. The adult should bring a sharp knife.

When they arrived, they saw brightly burning charcoal braziers lined up along the side of the river. Next to them in a pen were chickens.

"Each of you kill a chicken," the teacher said, "then we will cook it for your lunch."

Think of the essay assignments that could come out of an experience like that! Of course, better let the principal in on it first before you order the chickens! (That teacher used the resulting stunned silence to talk about where food comes from, and then she told the kids—to their relief—that they didn't have to kill the birds. From behind the bridge marched butchers who had volunteered their time, who dispatched the chickens. Then the teacher presented one bird to each student and parent to gut and pluck. It was one o'clock when the meal was ready. "It smelled great," Nanao said, "and there was lots to talk about over lunch.")

Another idea is the question of where our water *goes*. That will lead to the local sewage treatment plant, into the controversies about waste management, and who knows where from there. It might help your school or town start recycling more of its by-products. Perhaps some kids might start asking why we don't utilize compost. Maybe one of them would think about majoring in waste management in college.

A third idea: most schools are made out of bricks; we build whole towns of the little clay things. What would happen if we got kids to ask what is a brick? Perhaps each student could make a brick; is there a potter at school who could help? Is there a local bricklayer who might give a demonstration? Could kids help build a building for a day? How could they become curious about different kinds of bricks? What are all the uses of the different kinds of bricks, anyway? From what points of view would a high school student find a brick fascinating? Could kids in a writing class build something useful out of bricks, writing about it for kids that follow?

Not all ideas work, of course. One idea I tried that didn't work as well as I'd hoped began with my question to a class, "Why does the light light when you turn the switch?" At first it was fun. We wrote what we thought the answer was; then we went to the physics lab. We stood in a circle hooked up to a static electricity generator, daring each other to let go—and we wrote about that. We built a small AC motor, and walked to the school's power plant where the engineer did his best to explain to the tenth graders how his diesel turbines generate electricity and steam. But the technicalities proved too much for some of our kids, so we switched that topic off.

Or how about people? A senior-level class in prose writing got talking about interviews. One day, with no forewarning, the students found a stranger in their classroom to be interviewed. They found he was a musician, recently divorced, painfully shy, not well educated, but honest and extraordinarily open. They asked some emotional questions; he answered them. Not one of them had ever met anyone like this man. They transcribed their interviews with him, then incorporated these into extensive written profiles. No two were alike. We rewrote these essays several times, sharing information, comparing impressions. Long after class ended some of the students would ask about the gentleman. After spending fifty minutes with him, they had begun to care about his life.

I have learned to believe in assignments like these. Getting kids to ask a few childlike questions can excite their interest. Then if you can think a little quicker than they do, and can invisibly orchestrate events in advance when necessary, you can show kids how to empower themselves, how to learn and write down what they have become curious about. Cooperation helps everyone. Writing a "We-search!" paper can be just as good as writing a research paper, sometimes better.

Sometimes getting out of class and moving around the school or community helps everyone wake up.

Works Cited

Hall, Donald. 1969. "Light Passage." In *The Alligator Bride: Poems New and Selected*. New York: Harper & Row.

Joyce, James. 1946. *Ulysses*. New York: Random House, Modern Library.

4

Marking Papers
Let the Student Do the Work
Paul Kalkstein

As a faculty admissions reader, I note with special interest the English paper that is a part of each applicant's portfolio. The admissions office requires that this paper come marked by the applicant's English teacher. The papers are various; they include poems, expository pieces, critical analysis, and even (alas) grammar exercises from a workbook. The variety of teacher responses to the papers is as wide as the range of papers. Sometimes I see a full page of appended comments, sometimes merely a grade at the end, sometimes interlinear commentary.

Many reasons exist for the diversity in marking styles. The bare A− on one paper may bespeak a pupil load of 130 and the requirement of an essay each week. The interlinear suggestions may proceed from a need or desire to guide a student through the writing process. One of my own colleagues, when asked why she wrote such lengthy remarks at the end of her students' papers, said that she did so because of a sense of guilt that attacked her when she wrote less than her students.

Over the years I have asked secondary school teachers from all sorts of schools around the country why they marked papers as they did. I discovered that very few of them had a cogent personal philosophy for marking papers. Some of them were driven by institutional guidelines; others marked as their own teachers had marked their papers. Almost no one worked backwards. That is, teachers did not generally pay attention to what happens when students have their work returned to them and then develop a marking scheme that would make maximum use of that potentially galvanic moment.

What actually happens when papers are returned? It is true that our best students pay attention to what we write on their papers. Some of them even read marginal comments before they flip to the end to

37

see the grade. But others go right for the bottom line, and if the grade is a bad one, they are turned off; that paper is history. How much time did we spend trying to help that writer by writing helpful, caring comments on the paper, and what was this time worth to the writer — or to us?

Even when a student carefully reads our comments, how sure are we that those comments have communicated what we wished them to? After all, we have been marking since 6:00 P.M. (that was thirty essays ago) and perhaps our word choice is not so sharp as it was when we started. Further, we know how difficult it is to find the right words to help a writer perceive issues of clarity and style. Sometimes what we say is not actually what we mean; and sometimes, even if we say precisely what we mean, our students miss our meaning by 180 degrees.

Marking papers can surely be onerous. How sad if marking papers were a waste of time as well! It mustn't be a waste of time: it's too important to our students. And it needn't be so onerous. The answer lies in an understanding of writing as process. Of course, everyone knows about writing as process. No strategy of teaching composition has ever received more lip service than this one. Unfortunately, teaching writing as process takes a lot of time and patience and is hard to build into a unit-oriented approach to English/language arts.

Without going into the theory of writing process, let me assert that crucial factors are the timing and nature of the response writers receive from the reader/editor between drafts. Ideally, the response should be swift; the problems of composition should be fresh to the writers when their papers come back. And the response should lead the writers to improve the work themselves rather than supply changes for the writers to plug in. A very limited form of editing may best suit most students' development as writers.

Writing is a struggle. Teachers who write and writers who teach know this, of course, and they also know that learning is the product of this struggle. Much of the struggle is solitary and internal, but it is more than a comfort to have help nearby. The questions for teachers of writing are: how can we ensure that our students will struggle with their writing, and how can we make that struggle as productive as possible?

Central to answering these questions is the marking process. I believe that *marking* is a more useful term than *grading* or *correcting*. Grading suggests that the teacher is reading the papers primarily to judge their quality, rather than to assist the writer's development. Correcting implies that the teacher is supplying the "right" version of something that the student has done wrong — hardly a way to build confidence and competence, or anything much at all. Marking simply means that the teacher is making some sort of written response to the writer's ideas and words, not necessarily judging, and certainly not replacing, those ideas and words.

What sorts of things should we mark? Misspellings, certainly; these are clear-cut and not appropriate for commentary (I circle them). Punctuation errors: fragments, run-ons, misused punctuation marks. Other usage errors. Redundant words, phrases, sentences. All of these sorts of problems are usually marked, or corrected, by composition teachers. But also suitable for underlinings are stylistic inconsistencies, tone lapses — and places where "you just can do it better." This approach signals that we are not just error hunting. We are most interested in provoking the writer to improve the paper. Such improvement is not limited to the correction of miscues but involves constant revision as the writer searches for the most felicitous way of saying what he or she means. In that search we provide some direction and lots of encouragement, but the search belongs to the writer, not to the teacher.

We shouldn't mark everything on each draft. Too much blue pencil is daunting; the editing task seems hardly worthwhile. We should remember, too, that a conversation will complement the marking. Orally, we will comment on the ideas in the paper, and on its composition as a whole. *Let the student do the work* is both good pedagogy and sound self-defense — as long as we as teachers don't wholly disappear. Markings on a paper should help a writer to see where to concentrate in the process of revision. On the other hand, they should not accomplish the revision for the writer. The struggle, to avail, must be real. Merely "copying over" someone else's ideas is not of service. Yet even when we recognize that writers must do their own writing, we find it hard to hold back the more knowledgeable hand with the marking pen.

How to fight the strong tendency — whether produced by guilt, work ethic, or love of precision — to write complete, lengthy comments on papers? Choice of weapon can help. Instead of a sharp pencil, pilot pen, or even a felt-tip, a crayon or fat highlighter can limit our activity.

To illustrate, here are two marked copies of three student paragraphs, written in haste in class, on courage in the face of an angry mother grizzly bear. The first set (Figure 4—1) is minimally marked with a crayon; the second (Figure 4—2) is corrected by a conscientious colleague. The top paragraph has some problems: dangling modifier, sentence fragment, awkward pronoun usage. Both sets of markings are directed to these problems. In the second set, however, the teacher not only has identified one of the errors but has corrected all of them and left nothing for the student to do. Even the redeeming feature of the paragraph, the synecdoche at the end, has been corrected. What does the student think? The first set of markings invites and demands revision but does not humble the writer or give the answer.

Figure 4-1

Courage while facing an angry grizzly bear
has to be strong. Because you know that you may very
well be killed right there. You must not panic,
because it will bring an immediate assault of ripping   *Good*
claws and shart teeth.

Courage while facing an angry mother grizzly
bear is not very common. Since a grizzly bear is so
much larger than all humans to be courageous is often
suicide. More commonly people will turn and run up a
tree which while perhaps being cowardly at least the
person may live to meet another angry mother grizzly
bear some other time. Courage in a case such as this
can be defined as stupidity.

While facing an angry mother grizzly bear,
one must have the courage to face such a dangerous
situation. If the bear begins to approach the
individual in any angry state, do not run away. Stand
straight and motionless, allowing the bear to sniff
and familiarize itself with your body. If it begins   //
to attack, kick it in the stomach.

Figure 4−2

When you face ~~Courage while facing~~ an angry grizzly bear

your courage must ~~has to~~ be strong, *because* ; Because you know that you may very *(fragment)*

well be killed ~~right there~~. You must not show panic,

because *obvious fear may cause* ~~it will bring~~ an immediate assault of *the bear's* ^ ripping

claws and sharp teeth.

Courage while facing an angry mother grizzly

rare bear is ~~not very common~~. Since a grizzly bear is so

(sp.) much larger *than* ~~then~~ *a* ~~all~~ human~~s~~, to be courageous ~~is often~~ *may be to commit*

suicide. More commonly people ~~will~~ climb ~~and run up~~ a *(redundant)*

(d-m) tree ~~which~~ *this action appears* ~~While perhaps being~~ cowardly, at least the

climber ~~person~~ may live to meet another angry mother grizzly

bear! ~~some other time.~~ ^ *Showing* Courage in a case such as this

can be defined as stupidity.

While facing an angry mother grizzly bear,

one must have ~~the~~ courage ~~to~~ ~~face~~ such ~~a~~ ~~dangerous~~ *(redundant)*

situation. If the bear begins to approach [the *you*

keep person consistent individual] ~~in any~~ angr~~y~~ *ily* ~~state~~, do not run away. Stand

straight and motionless; allowing the bear to sniff

and familiarize itself with your body. If it begins

to attack, kick it in the stomach.

The same differences in approach and emphasis characterize the middle and bottom paragraphs as marked by two teachers. In the middle selection, both markers hope to help the writer find precision and straighten out some twisty syntax; however, one marker does the work for the writer and leaves wreckage behind, whereas the other leads the writer to grope for improvements on his own. Similarly, concision is the aim for a revision of the bottom paragraph. Note that this writer has a good grasp of sentence structure and usage (except for inconsistent person) but can still profit from revision.

What happens when the papers come back? In the first case (Figure 4–1), the student must revise the paper, replacing all of the underlined words, phrases, and sentences. The returned paper is a draft in the writing process. But in the second case (Figure 4–2), the work is done. The teacher has already revised the paper, and there is no process.

It should be obvious that the minimal marker with the crayon is spending much less time marking the paragraphs than the other teacher. But in each case the initial reading and assessing of the paragraphs have been performed with the same care; each marker has tried to help with the same problems. That is important.

"Let the student do the work" means that the teacher can assign more papers and respond in a helpful way to more papers. It means that the students will write more—not just more first drafts but more revisions as well. It means that the papers may be returned to the writers in the next class meeting, not a week later. There will be more paper to keep track of, naturally, but this is the student's job. And, most significantly, with practice comes growth.

Longer papers also lend themselves to minimal marking. Again, the examples in Figures 4–3 and 4–4 show two different types of marking. The student paper was written as homework on the topic of mismanagement of time. Both teachers see similar strengths and weaknesses in the paper, but they approach marking it differently. In this example, the time saved by the teacher who works with a crayon is clear, and so is the need of the student who is presented with such a marked paper to struggle anew with issues of logic, structure, and phrasing. But how profitable will the struggle be, relatively unguided as it is?

If we do not write detailed comments on the paper, and we limit ourselves to underlining and perhaps a terse assessment at the end, how can we convey our feelings about the writer's work and our suggestions for the next draft? Such communication is necessary; the writer must have a sense that his or her words are being heard, ideas considered, and growth in composition nurtured. In fact, we have no choice but to communicate verbally.

Figure 4–3

To mismanage time at school is a habit which many students have since there are many tempting options rather than doing homework. For example, a relaxing and enjoyable activity to take part in during a free period is to play a Sport. Returning from a class, a student may want to let his tensions out. He may enjoy slaughtering a close friend in a tennis match in order to lose some of this tension. In addition, after staying up late at night, one may want to sleep through his free period. A free period is the ideal time for these particularly tired students to "catch up" on their slumber. Second, in the dormitory at night a student would rather socialize with other kids than complete his homework. For example, most students like to watch TV while discussing sports teams or academics. The loud noises came from the students who were watching "Jaws" in the dorm TV room. The discussion, as usual, was about how impossible grammar is to understand as well as the latest football scores around the NFL. Moreover, to play board games while listening to music is quite common amongst students. The radio was blaring the Grateful Dead and two students were sitting on a bed playing backgammon. In the back of the room a student was hustling a friend in poker. Mismanaging time at school is caused by a student's lack of discipline for there is plenty of time available for fun yet there is also a certain time for one to study or do homework.

NTB

Figure 4–4

[handwritten: Mismanaging]

~~To mismanage~~ time at school is a habit which many   *[handwritten: Good Topic Sentence]*

students have since there are many tempting options

[handwritten: don't waste words] rather than doing homework. For example, a relaxing

and enjoyable activity ~~to take part~~ in during a free

period is to play a Sport. Returning from a class, a   *[handwritten: ?]*

student may want to ~~let his tensions out~~. He may   *[handwritten: What does this mean?]*   *[handwritten: Combine sentences for emphasis]*

[handwritten: good verb] enjoy slaughtering a close friend in a tennis match in

order to lose some of this tension. In addition,

[handwritten: having stayed   the   before]
after ~~staying~~ up late ~~at night~~, ~~one~~ may want to sleep

through his free period. A free period is the ideal

[handwritten: take transitions] time for these ~~particularly~~ tired students to "catch   *[handwritten: this]*

up" on ~~their~~ slumber. Second, in the dormitory at   *[handwritten: his]*
[handwritten: redundant]
night a student would rather socialize ~~with other kids~~

than complete his homework. ~~For example~~, most

students like to watch TV while discussing sports

teams or academics. The loud noises came from the   *[handwritten: When?]*   *[handwritten: Change in tone here]*

students who were watching "Jaws" in the dorm TV room.

The discussion, as usual, was about how impossible
[handwritten: how the NFL teams]
grammar is to understand as well as the latest
[handwritten: were doing]
~~football scores around~~ the NFL. Moreover, ~~to play~~   *[handwritten: playing]*

board games while listening to music is quite common   *[handwritten: (weak)]*
[handwritten: time again]
amongst students. The radio ~~was blaring~~ the Grateful
[handwritten: while]
Dead and two students were sitting on a bed playing

backgammon. In the back of the room a student was   *[handwritten: false conclusion—]*

hustling a friend in poker. Mismanaging time at   *[handwritten: you've not]*

school is caused by a student's lack of discipline for   *[handwritten: proved this]*

there is plenty of time available for fun yet there is

also a certain time for one to study or do homework.

[handwritten: I like your eye for detail and the examples at the end. But this is very wordy, and you'll have to work on agreement and transitions.]

Verbal communication between teacher and student replaces much of the written commentary. The chances of misunderstanding are lessened because give-and-take is part of the process. Nothing beats personal contact with the writer, especially when it goes on daily or at least regularly in the context of a composition class. The need to communicate verbally with most students each day means that most class plans must be restructured to make time. But this process need not use the whole class period, by any means.

A strong writer needs few words about the returned paper but does need some: praise for what has gone well, suggestions for even more strength, or perhaps a hint of a different (not necessarily better) direction the paper might have taken in tone or idea. There is no need to linger.

At the other end of the scale, when we deal with clear usage miscues, it may be that models are appropriate. In any case, the issues are clear, and most of us are used to dealing with usage problems in ways that are efficient relative to the way we deal with ideas or with the logic of an argument.

In the middle we probably spend the most time. Here the writer has "almost got it"; here the matters are difficult ones of definition. With such writers we find it helpful to spend more time, to pin down the gains of the writer. However, perhaps we will spend less time with that writer on the next paper.

It is important to develop a strategy and a procedure for speaking in class to individual students about their work. Here are some suggestions:

When the papers go back, do not begin to speak to the students until they have begun to struggle with their papers, with the beginnings of their next draft. Let them face the underlinings solitarily first; then, as a discrete next step, let them look for help on real puzzles from a neighbor. Only when this process is well underway is it profitable for a teacher to begin giving feedback. To begin earlier is to short-circuit the process of creative editing.

Peer editing is a powerful tool in this process. Work with a peer is often helpful, and sometimes it may be more comfortable than working with the teacher. Peer editing can save time for the teacher and can help keep the verbal-response segment of the class period from being too long.

Principles for editing by peers should be similar to those applied by us as teachers. In other words, a student should not, in the first place, hold out an underlined phrase and ask a neighbor, "What's the matter here?" The writer should struggle alone at first and attempt a revision before seeking a response from either peer or teacher. In so far as possible, peer responses should be helpful and not negative—though they should be honest. Classroom time spent on discussion of the peer editing process will pay dividends later.

Once the editing is going strong, I scuttle from group to group, acting as mediator, respondent, goad, or cheerleader. It is easy in this process to assure that my comments will be positive in tone: there is no need to respond to everything, and there is always some good work going on somewhere.

When students are working by themselves on their own papers, I continue to circulate. This is the time for comments on their ideas. I try to focus also on the development of the whole paper: how does the opener set up the middle, the end? Do the parts cohere? Are transitions clear? Does the paper make a point?

Brief conversations with a class of fifteen can take fifteen minutes. Or I can stretch it to the full period. With more students in the class, we need to be more selective about who hears how much. It is a subjective matter; some students love and need a lot of response, while others need a few crisp words and an encouraging smile.

Students should keep a file of their own papers, arranged chronologically. It would be nice if they would respect their own writing enough to *want* to keep it, but we can help them by requiring them to retain all work. The file of papers is important for conferences, to show growth or continuing problem areas.

At the end of a marking period, the student should review the papers, assessing in writing his or her own strengths and areas of needed growth. Then teacher and student should look over the papers. At this time we may wish to announce the grade for the marking period, so that the basis for the grade is not misunderstood and there are no unpleasant surprises on the report card.

What if a student conveniently loses weak papers while retaining strong ones? The most clear, direct response is to award a 0 for missing papers; naturally, it is crucial to announce this policy ahead of time, and remind students of it along the way.

When I have had a manageable teaching load I have not kept a grade book for my composition classes. I have told this to students in the context of my grading policy and my requirement that students preserve all of their work. Then the accumulating file of each writer becomes the grade book. Having lost a grade book early in my career, I find this latter method preferable!

We talk often about the grades we assign to papers; that is, about the evaluation of the quality of our students' work, both on individual assignments and over the course of a grading period or a year. Some of us would like to give more grades, or higher grades, or lower grades, or no grades at all. To some extent, what we do about assigning grades is out of our hands, mandated by administration or department guidelines. Yet our students care about how we grade, and so should we, even though most of us do not believe that students should be principally grade driven.

I believe that it is not helpful to withhold judgment about a student's writing. While most teachers acknowledge the value of positive response to student work as against negative response, the fact is that some writers are better than others, and some papers by some writers are better than other papers by the same writers. We hope that in a writing course the quality of a student's writing will improve. It may hang on certain plateaus, but overall the direction should be up, perceivable by student as well as teacher.

It is grades that testify to progress, or to its lack. They may be a source of pride. Of course low grades, especially when they are consistent, are discouraging; they may bear with them a social stigma, at school or in the home, that hampers a writer's progress by undercutting his self-esteem. How can grades serve the function of assessing quality while not discouraging or limiting the writer? Further, can grades written on papers provide information beyond merely a judgment on relative quality?

Perhaps grades can indeed so serve. One approach to grading is to *transpose the grading system.*

At the bottom of the first version of the paper on mismanagement of time (Figure 4–3), the teacher has written "NTB." This is the grade. What does it mean? Eventually the recipient may figure out that it means "Not Too Bad." And what does that mean? It can mean just what it says. It can also mean C+, although the student wouldn't know that.

For some years I have used a grading system that includes such acronyms as PDG, NTB, CBW, NSH, and so forth. The highest grade is D (Dynamite), and the lowest, A (Awful), though students are never quite sure how these grades rank hierarchically. In addition, some grades may reinforce editing principles while withholding judgment: WOF reminds the writer to Wipe Out Fragments and does not assess the quality of this particular draft.

Such grades are silly, to be sure. However, students adjust quickly to them, puzzle them out when they are obscure, and, sometimes, take them to heart. At the end of the term they receive a standard grade. Through conferences they will already know what it is and why. Meanwhile, the acronyms have provided enough response to the quality of their work, as well as some guidance along the way. The pressure has diminished, too.

After a time, students come to understand the writing process and come to see themselves as writers always "on the way" from draft to draft. A final step may be to suggest that this is actually the way things work in the real world of writing: publication.

I encourage students to try to publish their work. Organs exist for this purpose in every school; but it is more exciting to go outside. A blurb about a student athlete may be published, or even a recipe. Once a student of mine published in a church magazine a long piece on the canonization of a saint—what an excitement that was! In some cases an editor may request additional information on a subject, and often the published article is much changed—by writer and editor—from the first draft. If even one student achieves publication, the class is excited.

Of course, there is usually a long wait between acceptance of a piece and its publication. More important are the joy and pride that most students feel when they hold the smooth "final" draft of a composition that they have taken, sweating, through a number of editings—the reward of the writing process for everyone.

5

Soaking Students in the Language of Writing

Craig Thorn

Major writing projects are an effective way to teach composition and reading at an introductory level. These projects, which I call models, usually take ten to fifteen class periods or two to three weeks. Though the final product is ordinarily a longer piece of writing, the student writes short pieces, works on relevant exercises, and covers rudimentary material as steps toward editing, revising, and completing the major work. Approaching introductory composition and reading this way has many advantages, the chief of which is that the student and teacher are "drenched" in the language of writing and reading.

I remember the way I learned Italian with Lorenzo Harvey. He used the Rassias method, a system of constant reinforcement and challenge that literally made the language a matter of instinct after a few weeks. Students would sit in a circle while the teacher wheeled around the room, snapping questions and phrases at them. You learned by doing, not solely by thinking. The material you absorbed expanded in concentric circles; you did not learn Italian in a linear fashion. So, on the second day of class you were speaking in sentences, even paragraphs. They may not have fully resembled Italian, but you were speaking nevertheless. You learned everything you needed to know at once, and you learned it over and over again in different ways in more complicated situations. Furthermore, the focus was on the dramatic possibilities of the language, what it could do for you in the physical world, not simply in the abstract world of intellectual growth. If Lorenzo was about to drop a chair on your head, you needed to remember how to say "For God's sake! Put down the chair!" So, breaking down the barriers between us and the language became Lorenzo Harvey's business. Learning became a means toward immediate ends, a method that developed in all directions through reinforcement and recognition, a matter of doing. You learned Italian as if you were quite suddenly in Italy.

Our own students view English as a second language, something foreign and not a little overwhelming. Using models breaks down many barriers between student and language because they can change the relationships students have with the material in the course, particularly the material they produce. The teacher's relationship to the students in the course changes as well; he or she becomes a colleague. Longer writing projects during which the class covers a variety of techniques and ideas engage students and teacher alike in the process of writing. With the emphasis on development rather than just on completion, the language of writing is no longer simply a matter of identifying discrete terms only the teacher knows, but a language of shared experience. Students and teachers demonstrate rhetorical models, audience and voice, grammar, style in varied and relevant contexts. Furthermore, students and teachers discover complex issues in writing as they naturally appear during the process of writing. Learning writing becomes a function of doing writing. Writing, not the teacher, becomes the center of attention.

Courses consisting of many short writing assignments run counter to writing as an ongoing process. Writing frequent short pieces makes for a less coherent course that deemphasizes writing to write in favor of writing to complete specific exercises. Courses like this separate the various aspects of writing. For instance, two weeks are devoted to grammar, three weeks to paragraphing and methods of development and organization, one week to audience and voice, and four weeks to argumentation in a multiparagraph essay. The relationships between the students and the course material, their own work, and the teacher's instructions break down into strictly formal codes that raise more questions than they answer. How is grammar related to paragraph development? How does the teacher judge a student's writing while counting the number of dependent clauses used because they were the chief goal of the writing exercise? Is style solely a matter of word choice? What patterns can the student discover in twenty distinct writing assignments over the course of a term or semester? Is there a definable goal behind all this writing besides the contractual grade the student will receive from the teacher?

Work models create a writing classroom in which the living text of student writing replaces the grammar textbook, and the writing workshop replaces the formal relationship between instructor and instructed. In this essay, I first address the advantages of the work-model approach for student and teacher and then give a brief description of one work model. Finally, I suggest that the work-model approach facilitates the planning and organization of writing courses. Suggesting new theories of writing or practices in the writing classroom is not the primary purpose of this essay. Rather, I hope to show that this type of model best applies the current thinking about process writing.

Ends and Means (Students and Their Work)

When students realize that their writing assignments are final and not final at the same time, they begin to see writing as an ongoing process that is valuable in itself. During a model on character sketches (the second of the fall term in my introductory composition class), I introduced four rhetorical modes of paragraph development as ways to look at people: cause/effect, classification/division, comparison/contrast, and example. We read four essays that applied these rhetorical approaches to the problem of character: "Cinematypes," by Susan Allen Toth (1985), "Uncle Myers," by Mary McCarthy (1984), "Stallone vs. Springsteen," by Jack Newfield (1987), and "No Name Woman," by Maxine Hong Kingston (1987). I had students choose one of these patterns of organization to write about their subjects (a partner in class). The process of imitating one of these writers, then, became a means towards a desired end — figuring out who this person was — and not just the exercise of a technique. It was part of a series of exercises designed to generate information about the subject. Consequently, students viewed the writing they produced with a healthy mix of enthusiasm and curiosity. Quite inadvertently, I had stumbled on a way to encourage in these young writers that balance of subjectivity and objectivity Peter Elbow (1981) says is needed in the writing and rewriting process. These students simultaneously viewed the paragraphs as finished products and as experimental ways to get at their subjects. They came to think of methods of paragraph development as great ways to discover information, not just organize it.

The work models instilled a pervasive understanding of writing as a process that is recursive as well as expressive. Because much of the writing students did during the term took the form of pre-writing, or preparatory writing, for a major writing project, they no longer thought of writing as the finished product. Rather, students began to see writing as a thinking process. This simple idea had profound implications for my introductory composition class. For instance, writing became for them a means of discovering as well as communicating meaning. The students saw editing as part of writing. They found writing about their writing very useful. They began to understand where good writing comes from by observing how their longer essays developed. Consequently, they could speak theoretically of writing itself precisely because they experienced theories of writing themselves. They developed a surprisingly sensitive understanding of the process of creation leading to painting, music, and literature. For them, writing was a way of knowing more about writing. Most importantly, performance was a matter of personal investment.

When assignments were intrinsically related to performance on a major project, I had little to do to generate student interest. In the second model of the winter term, I presented my students with two issues: Israel's occupation of the West Bank and lawyer/client confidentiality in capital punishment cases. The class broke up into groups of two, each person taking a position on one of the two issues. They were to present arguments, questions for rebuttal, and closing statements in a filmed debate. In this context, students were more than happy to learn everything there was to know about outlining, summarizing, and the logic of arguments — precisely what I hoped to teach. They knew that other classes would "elect" winners. They knew that succeeding in this project would help them in the next. The work models enabled me to arrange for larger audiences for the simple reason that I had plenty of time to find them. So, the essay on place (the third model of the fall term) went to my senior writing class (a class with whom my introductory writing students frequently exchanged letters); the review of student art (part of the first spring-term model) became a weekly program at the high school radio station; their experiments in impassioned and formal arguments (first winter-term model) were taped and played back for the class. Changing the audience helped make their writing a personal investment. Not surprisingly, getting a grade from me lost its traditional significance as the final word (I ended up writing letters to the students instead of grading their work). Their writing had more vital purposes. They were working for their own ends, not mine. I was another part of the process, a helpful editor.

Writing the Course (The Students and the Course)

Because the students saw so much of their work as part of a larger process, they came to view their work as part of the course material. In fact, their work replaced formal texts for the course (although we used — sparingly — *The Bedford Reader* (Kennedy and Kennedy 1985), *The English Competence Handbook* (Kalkstein, Regan, and Wise 1981), *Every Night at Five* (NPR Staff and Stamberg 1982), and *Time* magazine). Knowing that their writing was helping them and others toward successfully completing larger projects eased if not eliminated the pressures that are ordinarily associated with publicly critiquing student writing. For instance, the edit sheets we used in peer-editing groups and student-teacher conferences focused on examples of their writing that would later show up in one of the six style sheets I made up covering sentence structure, punctuation, agreement, paragraphing, expository essays, and writing poetry and fiction. Besides becoming part of the course material, their work influenced what the material would be. Two essays from the model discussed later in this chapter, for instance, led to our discussion of main and subordinate ideas in essays, paragraphs, and sentences.

Sometimes writing assignments became in-class assignments. For instance, late in the spring term, I asked the students to analyze a poem in a few paragraphs. Next, I asked them to write to the poet about the poem. After that, I asked them to compare the poem to another poem on the same subject. Comparing the three pieces became an assignment in itself about the way writers can emphasize different details to make slightly different points. In the winter term, I had students write poems about onions based on triggering images I gave them (things like "driving through the Dakota badlands, we came across a town called Onion"). Then, I had them write dramatic descriptions of scenes from 1968 based on similarly evocative images ("listening to the Beatles' White Album in a loft in San Francisco"). Finally, we talked about how this kind of information is useful in an essay like Lance Morrow's (1988) piece on 1968. In the fall term, I told students to make up stories about the subjects of their character sketches, based only on what little they actually knew from initial interviews. Then, they showed these pieces to the people they were studying. In each case, their writing became part of a lesson in writing. Sometimes, the writing they did was solely for their own eyes: a letter to a relative about an issue they had written about to me, a journal entry in which they released all their feelings about something they would have to consider objectively. Students began to allude to their own and others' writing in our discussions of grammar, style, and meaning in writing. Gradually, the course became a writing workshop in which students and teacher studied the written word together.

The models gave students the confidence to experiment with and study their own writing analytically. Though we always worked closely as a class, students discovered many of their strengths and weaknesses on their own, guiding me through the steps necessary to improve their writing. After a class reading of his most recent piece, one student noticed that his writing "froze" whenever he had to make an argument about a "real topic" (something that called for argumentation). However, whenever he was asked to write "about" something (an expressive as opposed to an expository topic), he came up with plenty of good sentences and detail. Reviewing several of his major writing projects, he figured out that his sentences were active subject/verb constructions in his expressive writing and passive constructions full of adverbial clauses in his expository writing. I suggested that he was anxious to state his argument in every sentence in the latter assignments rather than prove his argument through illustration and analysis. He agreed and added that he organized paragraphs in the "arguing" papers around vague ideas, whereas in his "personal" pieces he organized them more naturally around details.

The models turned the classroom into a kind of laboratory in which we were all curious tinkerers and fiddlers because much of the writing took the form of pre-writing. The students turned the first winter-term model — a series of informal and formal writing assignments — into an ongoing discussion of private and public voices in writing. As a class, we discovered that writers move to a neutral middle position when faced with the challenges of making a public subject personal or vice versa. We called writing that failed to bring the energy of personal conviction and the clarity of formal argument together "perblic" writing. The written work was the center of attention, not the teacher. After the first spring-term model — a series of art reviews ending with interviews of student artists — one of the students volunteered to bring in her own art, which the class reviewed. I was in charge of turning the pages in her portfolio. In the fall, the students had been intrigued with the idea of interviewing, so now they decided to conduct an impromptu interview of me. The atmosphere these models had created, in which the students felt encouraged to study their own writing, had turned them into their own teachers.

This subtle change in their relationship to the course was nowhere more apparent than in the way the models enabled students themselves to see the patterns in writing and thinking. The ease with which they could visualize large blocks of time organized around basic premises enabled them to think of the whole course, specifically their writing, as a living text. During a discussion about kinds of writing in the winter, one student alluded to the pressures of audience on voice when he wrote his first fall-term paper. Another student noted during the spring that his best reviews of art seem to have the same organization as his formal analysis of audio equipment, the only difference being the essay's tone. Late in the fall, a student discovered that the editing sheets gradually emphasized more formal aspects of writing. He concluded that these *formal* aspects in his writing were necessary to make his papers sound more *informal*, an observation he found extremely curious for the rest of the year.

The students discovered in their own writing all kinds of abstractions about writing itself: the relationships between subject, sense, style, and structure; the different kinds of information that can be brought to bear on a subject; the concentric fashion in which grammar and structure influence increasingly more abstract aspects of writing and ultimately meaning itself. They taught themselves this in part because they could see the patterns developing in a manageable body of longer writing. They remembered subtle concepts because they learned theory by practicing it first, not by hearing about and memorizing it before they could practice it. Because learning and writing became synonomous in these work models and because these work models encouraged students' active participation in the writing process, the students were active in the learning process as well.

To Each His Own (Teachers and Teaching)

Teaching composition with work models turns the teacher into a student and a researcher, and consequently a better educator. The models allow the teacher to schedule more conferences, peer-editing sessions, and in-class workshops. I found that I could use the flexibility of these models to my advantage in conferences. For instance, what I learned during in-class workshops informed what students and I discussed in conferences, which in turn influenced what we would talk about in class. I simply adjusted the schedule to accommodate any important revelations coming from classroom or conference. The relationship between conference and classroom greatly enhanced students' esteem (even their writing problems were contributing to a better course) and improved my understanding of writing as a complex, individual process.

The discussion of "perblic" writing in class resulted in a conference with one student about personal and public relevance in her writing, which in turn became the focus of class discussion the next day. After speaking with the student whose sentence constructions varied, I noticed interesting stylistic differences between students' expressive and expository writing in general. As we moved from narrative to analytical forms, several developments caught my attention:

1. Sentences moved from active to passive constructions. Specifically, complex sentences with an overabundance of clauses replaced shorter sentences with participial phrases.

2. Coherence developed from an image/action/voice emphasis to an outline/idea/audience emphasis.

3. Evidence became a matter of facts as examples, as opposed to events as examples.

4. Detail was no longer an end in itself. Rather, it was introduced solely as a means toward an end.

5. Tone became more formal, more serious.

6. Sentence variety appeared to be determined by the demands of ideas instead of action and pacing.

7. A vague authority replaced the peer audience.

If it hadn't been for that student's observations about his sentence constructions in our conference, I might not have focused on these differences at all (note that the majority of them have to do with sentence construction). Next year, I plan to pursue these differences in a model that focuses on them.

These one-on-one situations, impossible in a short-assignment format, turned out to be the best way to teach the mechanics of writing as well. In the winter term, I sat down with each student to talk about the principles of writing that their writing had demonstrated. Instead of lecturing the whole class about voice, audience, detail, or evidence, I was pointing out the subtleties of these issues in conferences and workshops that focused on groups of closely related pieces. Consequently, I was able to couch these discussions of audience and sentence variety in terms relevant to each student. How was sentence variety going to improve their final paper? Students knew that the ordinarily tedious exercise of grammar, for instance, was going somewhere. I could explain the mechanics of writing in ever-widening contexts. One student didn't understand how his rambling sentences were detracting from the meaning of his essay. In conferences I showed him how changing the pacing of his sentences changed the effect of his essay and how his run-ons revealed the trouble he was having organizing his ideas in his paragraphing and his overall argument. Another student did not understand the purpose of loop writing assignments on Kurt Waldheim. How could writing a "dialogue" between two people arguing about the war help her write "about" Waldheim? During a workshop, I started a debate with her during which we happened on two ideas: soldiers were frequently overwhelmed by the machinery of war and propaganda, and the war deeply affected the descendants of war criminals. Another student and I listened to recordings of her reading two pieces — one informal, one formal — so that she could hear the differences in her voice. She had a powerfully persuasive example of how and why sincerity is as important in arguments as it is in personal narratives. Not having to grade numerous assignments every night gave me the freedom to put the forms of writing in as meaningful a context as the content. More importantly, freedom from a short-assignment format's crushing dailiness allowed me to address each student individually.

The work models gave me the time to teach much of the grammar and usage that eludes young writers. In most introductory composition courses, the students represent a wide range of proficiency. Teaching dependent clauses to an entire class rarely succeeds. In fact, I've found that when I teach grammar this way, students have a tendency to make more grammatical errors, because they are trying to listen with my ears instead of their own. I've had much more success teaching grammar and usage with the models, because before the whole class I am able to present it as something genuinely relevant to the works in progress and with individual students I have the time to work out the logic of grammar, usage, and meaning in their prose.

The work models, therefore, helped me as a student of writing myself. The typical "daily" writing assignment is a five-sentence paragraph. How much can an instructor learn about grammar, organization, coherence, sentence structure, and verb tenses from such an assignment? If the assignment is focused, probably some useful things. How much can he learn about a student's ability to write? Not much. Writing is the sum of many parts, perhaps greater than the sum. That's how we teach literature. That's how we should teach composition. Using these models, I was able to follow students' work closely, discovering and testing patterns in their writing and thinking. In these longer writing projects, I could successfully encourage students to experiment with a collage of styles along the lines of Winston Weathers's (1981) theory about using a variety of stylistic options. Whereas short writing assignments can measure only isolated aspects of writing, longer writing assignments can measure kinds of writing, making the mechanics secondary (and therefore more intrinsic to the process of composition). In the fall, for instance, I loosely followed James Moffett's (1983) "I-You-It" approach to gradually more challenging writing, using models on personal experiences, character portraits, and description of place. Noting the students' developing attitudes toward the writing process, I more clearly understood Sondra Perl's arguments about recursive writing and retrospective structuring in "Understanding Composing" (1984). In the winter, I patterned the models after the author's relationship to the topic. Focusing on these general issues intrinsic to all kinds of writing gave me a way to study the real strengths and weaknesses in student writing, not just the symptoms.

It is simply easier to discern the real problems behind nagging grammatical and stylistic errors when looking at a handful of long writing assignments or a batch of shorter assignments designed to raise certain issues rather than teach rules in writing. I have found the models to be the best way for me to put Mina Shaughnessy's (1977) timeless ideas about errors as signals into practice. One student struggled with his expository papers because he always tried too hard to anticipate his audience's reactions, not because his papers were unorganized (though this certainly was the case). Another student repeatedly neglected to come up with any thesis statement despite the fact that his essays were rich with meaning. Focusing on the mechanics — lack of development, awkward sentences in paragraphs, repetition in the conclusion, irrelevancies — would have been useful by itself but would have missed the problem. This student, as became apparent when we compared his first fall-term model to his third winter-term model, lacked confidence in his writing. He knew the ideas were there; he simply didn't think them worth pursuing. In the same way that these models show students that writing is part of thinking, it reminded me that the mechanics of writing, while crucial and seductively teachable (like elementary math), are not what writing is ultimately about.

Grammar and usage aren't the only things the instructor can work on in the model approach to introductory composition. Anyone who is familiar with the volumes of superb theory and speculation about teaching composition knows that trying to apply, test, and revise these theories can be a daunting task for the instructor of composition. I have found that the extended writing project best serves the teacher who wants to use the classroom as a research tool and who thereby becomes a student as well. With the model approach, I have been able to experiment with the ideas of Nancie Atwell (1987), James Britton (1982), Janet Emig (1983), James Moffett (1983), and others. Paul Eschholz's (1980) ideas about using prose models in the process of writing informed my introducing prose models as a way to discover information about people in character sketches. Neil Postman's (1979) early ideas about education as a thermostatic activity responding to cultural phenomena gave me the idea to use the camera and microphone in my models, with filmed debates and broadcast art reviews. Janet Emig's (1983) discussion of the differences between talking and writing helped me in conferences and in designing oral and written editing sheets. I discovered interesting consequences for analytical reading when applying Arthur Stern's (1981) comprehensive review of limitations in traditional approaches to the paragraph to my class's use of *Time* magazine (first and second winter-term models). The work of fellow teachers—Gail Martin, Dale Lumley, and Amanda Branscombe (see Goswami and Stillman 1987)—encouraged me to have students choose their own writing, write about their writing, and share it with others. I tested Peter Elbow's (1984) theory about embracing contraries in my first winter-term model with great success. Numerous theorists and instructors have pointed out that no teacher should simply imitate the successful models of other teachers; rather, the instructor should adopt new ideas with every intention of adapting them to his or her style of teaching, the specific needs of that class, and the goals for that course. With models, I can put theory into practice in my own classroom in my own way. They are spacious experiments, which afford me the room to fine-tune the project as I discover ways the ideas will actually work for me.

Writers All (Teacher and Students)

Perhaps the most dramatic result of this works-in-progress approach was the changing relationships between teacher and students. I became more of a student in my class and the students became more like teachers. Changing attitudes toward their work and the course's content empowered the students. Discoveries in their work and in the course's design excited me. That students learned how to use their writing as a living text and the class as an ongoing workshop is, I hope, clear. However, there was one more dramatic way in which these works-in-progress permitted me to participate in the writing projects as a student. Because students worked slowly toward the completion of a longer essay over the course of two to three weeks, I often had the time to write the essay as well (especially since students were working on many smaller assignments along the way which I could compress or skip).

I discovered that when students know that a teacher is testing his or her own writing, they see that teacher as a colleague, as someone in the trenches with them. Teaching becomes a conversation about writing. Students can more easily see writing as a kind of thinking because the teacher can articulately share troubles as a writer with the class, showing students the way to think about their own writing as something they do for themselves to learn about themselves. Arguing that teachers should "write some of the essays we ask our students to write," Winston Weathers (1981, 332) goes on to say that such participation constitutes "an attempt to convince [the students] that composition, rhetoric, and style are things we really do, that they are part of our lives, that *we* are involved."

Students gained confidence editing my work. They critiqued my loop- and free-writing exercises. They analyzed a letter I wrote to the school newspaper in terms of audience and voice. After working on the personal experience model (see next section), students edited an essay I wrote following the same directions I gave them. Studying the teacher's writing assured them that they were not alone. For my part, there is simply no better way to understand what goes on with a writer than to be one yourself. In this new relationship, the class discussions were about shared experiences, not just assigned exercises and expectations.

The models, in short, reinforce the idea essential to any successful composition course: writing is natural. The following model demonstrates how many of the advantages of the works-in-progress approach to introductory composition worked during the first fall-term project. It is, in effect, an abbreviated version of my daily journal.

Model: I Was Drenched (Personal Experience)

In his essay entitled "Response to Literature" (1982), speaking of students' first encounters with literature, James Britton wrote that students and teachers should start with talk about people, places, situations in literature, and not with forms, conventions, devices, techniques. This thinking applies well to early writing assignments. I wanted to introduce students to writing in an unthreatening context. So, I created a model that I hoped would accomplish a number of goals:

- Allow students to explore their own experiences.
- Emphasize narrative/expressive forms of writing.
- Exercise an understanding of details, coherence, voice, meaning in the context of telling a good story.
- Introduce very basic ideas of analysis and synthesis.
- Suggest that writing well is frequently just seeing things more closely.
- Create an opportunity for them to study and think about their writing.
- Prepare them through experience for some of the things they would later understand through explanation.

This may seem like an overwhelming list of objectives for an introductory model, but the purpose of the models was to give the students an opportunity to learn things by doing, not by listening. This list represented my objectives. The students had one objective: write an interesting narrative about the last time they had a good time alone (an objective I deliberately expanded a few times). We rarely spoke of any other objective. Discussions of voice, coherence, detail, analysis and synthesis, and narrative all took place solely in the context of how to make this essay work for them.

Here is a brief sampling of some of my journal entries during the first fall-term model:

First Day

I told them three stories about embarrassing events in my life. They had to guess which story was true, which partly true, and which completely false. The class discussed real and public voices, coherence and detail, and meaning. I suggested to them that any good narrative ultimately relies on the relationship between its details and its objective — whether it be to inform, entertain, alarm, or argue a point — because details dramatize rather than state an idea or impression. Along these lines, the students discovered that carefully selected details create a coherence that is different from formal organization but no less effective.

Perhaps the most provocative lesson, however, was one I hadn't anticipated. Students were fascinated by the details I chose to "add" to the partly true story. Why did I choose those details? Did they make the story less true? Somehow more true? I would try to reinforce this lesson throughout the year in various models: that all writing is an essentially creative act. For homework, I asked the students to write nonstop for twenty minutes about the last time they enjoyed themselves alone. They were instructed not to worry about sentence structure, coherence, or grammar. Then, they were to read Annie Dillard's essay "Lenses" [1985].

Second Day

Two lists of details: those that seem relevant and those that seem irrelevant to what they want to say about the topic.

Third Day

I began the class with a series of questions about their details. Do the details change the meaning of their story? Might the irrelevant details add depth and color to their story? A student pointed out how details can generate ideas and ideas can generate details. We also studied some of the seemingly irrelevant details in the essay. The class tried to make their irrelevant details relevant in sentences about their experience alone, forcing them to see different meanings in their essay.

Fourth Day

I told the class to consider describing one aspect of their experience (the location, the weather, their mood, or their actions) in excruciating detail just to see what such an exercise would yield. Using Paul Goldberger's [1986] essay "Quick! Before It Crumbles!" (which I read aloud), I mentioned how having an angle, an attitude about your subject, can "uncover" details you may not have otherwise noticed.

In class, we reread "Lenses," Annie Dillard's essay about writing, this time focusing on the choices she made about the essay's "meaning." I pointed out that the author's intentions for a piece can also influence the essay.

I assigned the homework, which was to come up with another event in which they had a good time alone, with the intention of including this event with the first in a large essay. They will have to analyze what they have so far for meaning and then synthesize two experiences through the force of their detailed descriptions. It will provide still another angle on the first experience, presenting it now in the context of a slightly similar one.

Fifth Day

I broke the class into groups of three and had them edit each other's food pieces [homework from third day], relying on the following questions: What is the main impression the writer was trying to make? What is your favorite detail? Do all the details go together?

How many of the details have to do with your senses? How many details are about something other than what's immediately before you?

The students told me that they had discovered new feelings and thoughts about their subject when reviewing the various ways they've approached it. I told them that they discovered these things through writing and rewriting, that writing would be a way to order their experience. For homework, I asked them to write about their second experience as if it had happened to somebody else.

Sixth Day

I broke the class into groups of two. The partners read each other's first and second event and then wrote a sentence or two about how they thought they might go together. They considered questions about the relative importance of and relationship between the events. In their discussions, students were moving back and forth between creating and cutting, analysis and synthesis — varied relationships with their own work. For homework, I told the students to try putting the two events together.

Seventh Day

The same partners exchanged essays again, this time equipped with two edit sheets: one calling for written comments; the other consisting of questions designed to encourage focused discussion between writer and editor. ... The edit sheets reinforce various issues discussed during the project.

They are to generate a narrative based on personal experience that has as its point one of the truisms I gave them today. They are not to mention the truism anywhere in the essay. I'm hoping that this exercise will reinforce ideas we've discussed about the relationship between personal and general experience. Also, I think that it fruitfully mirrors the process they've experienced with their major essays because they have to let an abstraction inform the choice of event, the selection and organization of details, and even the style and tone of the piece (something like the opposite of what they're doing with the major piece).

Eighth Day

In class today we read two essays, by Black Elk [1986] and John Uplike [1986]: "War Games" and "The Playground" respectively. These were presented as examples of shadings of real voice. ... I told them that their essays would be presented to the English department in the weekly meeting and to my senior writing class. They, in turn, would be receiving copies of several essays from that class.

Because I have had plenty of opportunity to speak informally with each of them about their writing, they think of their essays in terms of personal challenges instead of formal rules to be followed.

Ninth Day

Today the class edited an essay I wrote on the subject of photography in Maine, in which there are two major incidents. They also interviewed me about the piece — What were the hard parts? Did I change the order or emphasis of any events? What point was I hoping to make? Why did I write this or that sentence?

On the subject of making a coherent impression or point through the selection and organization of details, I presented the students with comparisons between their food and truism pieces. In the first case, they had to impose some point of view on a random piece of food, coming up with a way to use the details before them; in the second case, they had to come up with the appropriate details about a personal experience to demonstrate the truism before them. We talked about which writing project was easier for them. When most thought the latter was easier, I suggested that creating details is easier than creating an idea. These two assignments illustrate how detail and meaning influence one another. They are to finish up their essays.

Tenth Day

In class, the students wrote at length about the experience of writing the essay. ...

Eleventh Day

Today we discussed Dave's essay, which led to an intriguing study of voice and the author's relationship to his material. Dave's varied sentences (particularly the differences between the two versions of one event) were quite interesting. I spoke about the close relationship between the grammar of sentences and the meaning of sentences. Dave's paper lent much credibility to our first discussion about grammar. Perhaps the most exciting result of this discussion, however, was the fact that Dave clearly learned something about himself as we spoke of his essay.

Jodie's second event in his essay is more like a collage of closely related events witnessed while sitting in the mall — seeing a mother brutally scold a child, watching a relationship develop between a guy and two competing girls, following a father affectionately carrying his son on his shoulders. Jodie reduced each of these scenes to one sentence so that their combined thematic effect was more important than any literal relation to the main incident.

These two essays dramatically illustrated how specific experience precisely evoked can lead to experience we all can share. They also showed how the relationship between main and subordinate ideas informs all aspects of writing, from sentence structure to an essay's tone.

In class two days from now, I will read two character studies — "The Blast Furnace" by Sally Carrighal [1984] and "The Woman

Warrior" by Maxine Hong Kingston [1987] — as examples of organizing main and subordinate ideas in sentences, paragraphs, and essays (prose models). We will also go over the first style sheet, which studies main and subordinate ideas, phrases, and clauses, in their writing.

Twelfth Day

Today we read and edited two essays from the senior class [they wrote on the same general subject]. I also had the class write letters to pen pals in that class about how they liked or didn't like this first model. In class, the students read my letters in response to their essays. While I devoted most of my time to the issues we studied while writing the pieces, I introduced concerns about sentence structure and organization, showing how their sentences frequently reflected their general intentions and how the essay's organization revealed subtle choices about emphasis and meaning.

When I compare what we did each day with what I had projected we would do, I find little similarity. The ideas are there, but the actual process took many surprising and, for the most part, rewarding turns. Because I had distant, but not too distant, goals in mind, I did not have to worry about specific assignments as ends to be achieved for their own sake. So, I had plenty of freedom to respond to the failures and successes of this particular class without forgoing any of the specific objectives I had for the model. In addition to those objectives, the model established a wonderful learning environment because it showed students that their own writing could be a useful tool towards further improving their writing (many students applied the writing exercises directly to their longer projects). They learned how to think about their writing as a clue to what they might really think, what they might really want to say. The following are a few excerpts from the essays and essays about the essays that illustrate this point:

Dave's Essay

The elements were in my favor: the running river sounded with a monotonous tone in continuous rhythm, drowning out any noise I accidently made. I could feel my foot break twigs and squish in the mud, but I could hear neither sound due to the rapid moving river. The day approached noon and the dew sparkled as the sunlight sifted through the trees. As I continued my search, I wandered through tall grass in hope of finding my prey. The long dewed grass left my feet wet and socks damp; the search continued.

At high noon the sun began to bake the tree protected forest and a steamy humid heat began to rise from the dampened ground. With the humidity arose a musty damp odor similar to that of a swamp-wet sneaker, semi-dried by the sun.

Dave's Essay on His Essay

In an effort to transport the reader I used an incredible amount of detail to describe events not that unusual. For instance, walking on the twigs over mud, the smell of the forest while the sun rises and walking on rocks while my sneakers were full of slime. I found it hard to remember exactly everything so I took another situation that had some of the same conditions. Maybe I could more easily remember walking home after playing football in the mud when my shoes were filled with slime. While hunting the rabbit I had forgotten about the mud, but while looking back on it I realized my shoes were full. Reflecting back on my shoes after playing football helped jar some memories and add some of the sensations I missed while hunting.

Nina's Essay

My arms were tired from holding the sail and my legs were aching. I was not as effective at keeping the boat flat, so, with every big puff, the whole boat would tip more and more to leeward. Eventually I flipped over, and several times at that. Each time, I righted the boat and continued to sail. I always enjoyed flipping over. It is sort of similar to falling off a bike, except that when you hit the water, you don't end out with cuts, scrapes, and bruises all over your arms and legs. All I could see was the shimmering water around me. I was lost in my own little world, flying so swiftly that water was shooting up in all directions. Finally, I turned the boat around and sailed back to the familiar coastline, watching as the houses seemed to get bigger, and leaving the sunset behind me.

The winter sun was rising up from behind the east face of the mountain. I wouldn't have to wear my wool hat today. ... We skiied to the trail to the far right: I forget the name of it now. Then I dug my poles into the hardpacked snow, and began my run. ... Then came the ice patch. My skis skidded and made that awful screeching sound, but I didn't fall, though. I regained my balance, put my skis together and was off again. The crisp wind was burning at my raw pale-pink cheeks, and the sun blinded my eyes as it reflected off of the white powder surrounding me. My hair was flowing behind me. Everything before my eyes became a blur of whites. I was gliding, flying down the mountain. With every quick turn, I could hear the swoosh of snow beneath my skis. I watched as the base lodge grew bigger and bigger. Soon enough, the ride was over and my friends were right behind me.

The water began to get shallow, so I pulled up the centerboard and hopped out of the boat. My shirt and boxer shorts were sticking to my skin. I was drenched.

Nina's Essay on Her Essay

I was always editing what I had written, especially after I wrote about the "second" experience. Images and feelings that I experienced seemed also to fit in nicely with the first part of the essay. The details from one part of the essay, I soon found out, were relevant in the other part, too. This method of comparing two experiences really helped me to write all of the details. It was really strange how I really seemed to improve my first essay simply by writing another similar to it. I had a lot of trouble with the essay the first day that it was assigned. The white page just seemed to stare me in the face, but after I wrote about the skiing, everything fit together, and my ideas flowed freely.

The following series of extracts demonstrates the kinds of conversations we were having about writing. First, here is Eric's essay:

The Orchestra and the Chapel

Laughing and playing, the Class of '86 wonders why we are here, why we are on this "stupid forest walk." Suddenly — "Shh!," we hear from the leader ahead, and twenty students fall silent — surprised, holding their breaths. We approach the trip leader, trying to figure out what he wants. "Listen!," he forcefully whispers. We all hear the flapping wings; the muddled sounds of hundreds of birds singing, one ringing out over the others like the highest piccolo note. The leader repeats the call of the piccolo, note for note. The bird hears the call as it comes closer to the trees directly above us. The chirp becomes louder as the bird is joined by relatives and friends. It sounds like an orchestra of birds, all playing the same note. I look around at the faces of my classmates — heads tilted back, mouths half open, silent.

After the birds left, the Class of '86 had no doubt why we were walking through the woods, and not a word was spoken the rest of the way.

Through this eighth grade field trip, I gained a fascination with nature. I became more attentive to bird calls, and I started to enjoy the damp, dense feeling that came from walking through the woods. The woods seemed to be a private place — unknown and uninhabited.

The following story tells of a time two years later when I chose the forest as a place to be alone. After two years as a camper and one as a CIT, I certainly knew how the system worked at Camp Lanakila. At 7:30 AM reveille blows and you are expected to be at breakfast by 8. Morning craft periods run from 10 AM – 12 noon, lunch is at 12:45, we have rest hour until 3 PM, and then afternoon crafts run from 3 PM – 5 PM. Dinner is at 6 PM followed by an evening activity and Taps at 9:30 PM. After three years of this regimentation at camp and a regimented lifetime at school, I suddenly had an urge during my year as a CIT to spend time alone — to jump outside of the regimented world into the world of no time, no voices, no people; the world of being alone.

One day, I slipped into the forest without notice during some free time in the afternoon. Walking slowly, I observed everything around me — the raspberry bushes and hill to the right, the stream and woods to my left, and the dirt and rock road that was under my feet. I knew that I would be heading for my favorite place in camp, the chapel-in-the-woods.

After about 150 feet of walking, I saw the chapel bridge to my left. I slowly strolled over the bridge, listening to the trickling stream underneath and then feeling my feet sink as I stepped off the bridge onto the chapel ground of dead, damp pine needles. I approached the circle of flat where trees were either chopped down or never planted in the midst of thousands of pine trees. I thought of the 220 people of the camp sitting in this circle — listening to nature, listening to the sermon, or passing the time away by making little forts out of pine twigs. It was like someone had taken an eraser and made them all disappear — for there was no one there as I stood staring at the empty grey pulpit and benches.

The benches were about my height in length, so I lay very comfortably there looking up at the circle of blue sky with its two white puffy clouds. Speechless, thoughtless, and motionless I lay, watching the tops of the straight pine trees brush the sky as they tilted back and forth in the wind. I heard the wind come in whisps — starting soft, getting louder, and then soft again. Absorbing the nature around me, I heard the birds chirp, smelled the damp fresh air, and noticed the crackled bark on the pine trees that rose forty feet into the sky like needles.

I savored the moment while it lasted, but knew it was time to go when thoughts started to rush into my head and I could hear the sound of campers' voices in the distance.

I wrote my general comments on students' essays in the form of letters. Close editing on each piece did not occur for several weeks. When the students completed two other major works, I sat down with them individually and reviewed everything in their pieces from pacing to paragraphing, coherence to commas. Students wrote in their journals a brief statement of their experiences and feelings while working on the essay. My response to Eric's essay follows, along with his journal comments and his subsequent rewriting of part of the essay:

My Notes on Eric's Paper

Eric,

There are fantastic sensory images in this piece, especially and appropriately when you reach the chapel-in-the-woods. I'd like to point out a passage which illustrates how nicely form and content go together in this essay. ... The description in the first paragraph starting with "Listen!" and ending with "silent" is a particularly good example. Notice how we move through the description quickly. Read it out loud. Despite the pace, your precise description heightens the anticipation. Every sentence begins with a subject and verb and ends with some kind of modifier: a phrase or dependent clause. The last sentence is set off with a dash. The modifier is slowed way down until we stop at "silent." So, each sentence starts out fast and fades a little. The style of these sentences anticipates the main event, a walk into the woods ending in complete repose.

I'd like to point out that you need to watch out for semicolons. They usually separate complete ideas. In this passage, the mistake isn't a big deal. However, later it messes up the way "the world of being alone" is supposed to work towards the bottom of page three.

One more thing about this passage ... notice how nicely you really keep the main idea in the forefront. There must be over ten allusions to sound in this passage, a passage that begins and ends with references to sound: "listen" and "silent." While I'm on the subject, however, I'm not sure that "muddled" is precisely the word you want at the start of this description. Look at it this way ... what is it exactly which changes this muddled sound into an orchestra in a few moments?

Anyway, some friendly comments:

1. That transition at the bottom of page two? UGH! Remove—not necessary. Your details do the talking. Just say something about the passage of time.

2. Same page ... is "uninhabited" the best word?

3. Do you think the eraser thing works? Doesn't seem to fit the mood here.

4. You need to work on the paragraph about the eighth grade ... give me an example that illustrates your developing appreciation.

5. Sometimes you'll list details which don't quite fit (the one about forts and the one about the hill on the right) either because they don't seem to be about the same thing or because they are much more or less specific than the other details in the list.

Lots of great writing here. Bravo. We'll talk in class.

Eric's Comments

When I was assigned to write the paper on my last time alone, I immediately thought of the camp experience. Knowing that "sometime" other people would read it, I started writing in the descriptive, story-like voice. My first paragraph described without too much detail the incident, and a bit of a reason for why I decided to be alone. The rewrite was completely different, using only one sentence from the original—"Speechless, thoughtless, and motionless. ..." I changed into the past tense, which seemed more flowing than the original present tense. The new draft seemed to be told like the story of Little Red Riding Hood, which did not satisfy me too much but I could not figure out another way.

I had trouble describing what I meant by "circle of flat," and I still do not feel satisfied with the sentence. I was not sure whether or not the schedule of the camp was too technical, but it seemed to help make my point about how regimented the life of a camper is. I really enjoyed some of the images created—the pine trees brushing the sky, the wind coming in whisps, and the erased campers and counselors. I also liked how I described the time alone as "a jump out of the regimented world into a world of no time," because so much of my life is centered around time—or should I say lack of time—I am constantly busy, and I think that was what made my time alone so special.

When asked to relate another story to the first, I tried to recall another experience in the woods. My final incident was actually a compilation of incidents of my childhood that all seemed to make sense together. I revealed the bad attitude of all of us, so used to the regimented school life that we had no appreciation of nature. The call of birds by the leader caused me to be more aware of nature and created a fascination of the woods—this seemed to be a perfect reason for my having chosen the woods as a place to be alone two years later. I decided to put the class incident in first for this reason as well as for chronological order. This story was more powerful in the present tense, so that is what I wrote it in. I think that I succeeded in showing instead of telling in this story, especially when I created the image of my classmates with their heads tilted back and mouths half open.

Eric's Second Draft of the Chapel-in-the-Woods Paragraph

Finally—time to get away. Time to get away from the campers, the work in the kitchen, and even the friends with whom I could spend a lifetime. Time to be alone, separate from everyone and everything involved in daily life. I think about the summer as a CIT—the ups and downs; the hard work and the relaxation; the friends, of course—while slowly strolling along the dirt road into the woods. I approach the camp's "chapel-in-the-woods" and decide to lie on one of the grey benches. Speechless, thoughtless, motionless I lie staring upwards, watching the pine trees brush the sky, waving back and forth in the wind. I feel like a log—depleted of energy, of life.

Making Sense of What's Around (Putting Things in Their Proper Place)

The works-in-progress approach raises the following logistical points:

1. You can condense or stretch a model. Frequently, what I list as the second or third day required more or less than one class period. Furthermore, our classes do not meet everyday. So, large blocks of time might separate consecutive class periods.

2. These models vary from class to class, year to year. I never teach the same exact model twice.

3. The extended time frames of these models invite the teacher to explore the potentialities of the teaching environment. Because work models do not stand or fall on the particulars, the teacher can easily involve the community or the school's facilities without jeopardizing the project's objectives. In fact, this kind of involvement enhances the works-in-progress.

4. The work models allow teachers to adapt ideas to their own style of teaching. After you get a few general ideas, you're off and running your own race (just like the students).

5. I find incorporating the excellent ideas of my colleagues much easier with longer writing models. How often have we wanted to try some successful writing assignment a colleague has designed only to realize that either we have no place to put it or we have to stop everything, try it completely out of any context, and then move on? The result, of course, is an awkwardly borrowed assignment. I have enough models during the year so that I can always find a useful place for someone else's fine exercise or idea. So, I can incorporate Peter Gilbert's ideas about writing with conviction in this model. Conversely, I could incorporate ideas from the models I use in the fall into a version of Ed Germain's extended writing exercise.

6. Most importantly, the work models free teachers from the time constraints associated with daily schedules. The teacher enjoys the flexibility needed to pause and focus on each student's particular problems. He can also pause and reflect on where his course is going.

As I've mentioned, major writing projects enabled me to apply exciting theories about writing to my own classroom teaching. Furthermore, students discovered some of these theories through experimentation with their own writing. In much the same way, I discovered and modified patterns in my course during the year. In fact, I had a much clearer idea of what I wanted to make of the whole course from September to June simply because I had fewer building blocks to handle.

Rather than struggling with dozens of disparate goals and finite assignments, I organized my year-long course into a series of ten to twelve models. Consequently, I could handle more easily the pervasive ideas of theorists who study writing in general. Like many high-school teachers, I was somewhat familiar with the current thinking about teaching composition, but incorporating the plethora of ideas seemed intimidating to say the least. With the work models, I had a way. I found that Peter Elbow's (1981) work with writing and revising and

Tim Donovan's (1981) article "Seeing Students as Writers" provided me with endless variations in my models. Moffett (his views [1983] on replacing formal textbooks with the living textbook of student composition) and Britton (his theory [1982] about the natural ways to develop a student's writing from personal experience to more public exposition) provided me with an overall view of how I wanted my course to work. Dewey's (1963) philosophy of experience and experimentation in education linked many of my models together, particularly in the recurring emphasis on the students as their own educators. Francis Christensen's (1984) studies of generative rhetoric influenced how I reintroduced grammar in each of my models throughout the year. I discovered that grammar could be taught to young, unsophisticated writers as intrinsically related to the subject, style, structure, and sense of what they were writing.

I identified each term with a major form of writing. In the fall we focused on expressive writing (narrative description). I introduced students to expository writing (formal argumentation) in the winter, and in the spring we studied literary writing (interpretive analysis). I tried to overlap these forms. I wanted to reinforce September's experiences with March's discoveries. I wanted to evaluate February in a November as well as an April light. I wanted to introduce the end in the beginning and develop the course from a center rather than a point on a line. Applying these grandiose designs in an introductory writing course would have been unmanageable had I not been able to hold the entire year, twelve models, in my hand and say, "This is what I hope to do." Surely, we all have organized our introductory courses in writing around sections based on mechanics and style (the formal organization of most textbooks makes these plans relatively straightforward), but how often do we have the time to organize them around big themes, theoretical ideas, experiments?

I think that the extended writing projects empower a teacher to develop a course in writing as an art to be acquired without sacrificing the basics that make art work. In fact, I think that teaching introductory writing this way renders the basics more vital than they can ever be in a more formal course. I found students more excited about dependent clauses, logical fallacies, and synecdoche when these served an end they could visualize because it was their end. These basics now served the creation and communication of their ideas about things in the world. They were an intrinsic part of the writing experience, not isolated exercises students march through for the sole purpose of avoiding clumsy errors. I found that I had to beat students about the ears when I taught the basics only as basics. Such students marched out of my course in an orderly manner, but I thought I saw chairs dropping on their heads. They could write competently, but their writing lacked the urgency and sincerity of my cry in Italian class: "For God's sake! Put down the chair!" My students may not march in the straightest line anymore, but they'll have all the necessary equipment and the freedom to use it any way they see fit. The only chairs I want them to see when they decide to write or read something are the ones they sit in.

Works Cited

Atwell, Nancie. 1987. "Class-Based Writing Research: Teachers Learning From Students." In *Reclaiming the Classroom*, 87–94. See Goswami and Stillman, 1987.

Black Elk. 1986. "War Games." In *The Little, Brown Reader*, ed. M. Stubbs and S. Barnet, 338–39. 4th ed. Boston: Little, Brown.

Branscombe, Amanda. 1987. "I Gave My Classroom Away." In *Reclaiming the Classroom*, 206–19. See Goswami and Stillman, 1987.

Britton, James. 1982. *Prospect and Retrospect: Selected Essays of James Britton*. Ed. G. M. Pradl. Portsmouth, N.H.: Boynton/Cook.

Carrighar, Sally. 1984. "The Blast Furnace." In *Prose Models*, ed. G. Levin, 11–15. 6th ed. San Diego, Calif.: Harcourt Brace Jovanovich.

Christensen, Francis. 1984. "A Generative Rhetoric of the Sentence." In *Rhetoric and Composition*, ed. R. L. Graves, 110–18. 2d ed. Portsmouth, N.H.: Boynton/Cook.

Dewey, John. 1963. *Experience & Education*. New York: Macmillan.

Dillard, Annie. 1985. "Lenses." In *The Bedford Reader*, 101–11. · See Kennedy and Kennedy, 1985.

Donovan, Tim. 1981. "Seeing Students As Writers." In *The Writing Teacher's Sourcebook*, ed. G. Tate and E. P. J. Corbett, 220–23. New York: Oxford University Press.

Elbow, Peter. 1981. *Writing with Power: Techniques for Mastering the Writing Process*. New York: Oxford University Press.

———. 1984. "Embracing Contraries in the Teaching Process." *College English* 45 (April): 327–39.

Emig, Janet. 1983. *The Web of Meaning: Essays on Writing, Teaching, Learning, and Thinking*. Portsmouth, N.H. Boynton/Cook.

Eschholz, Paul. 1980. "The Prose Models Approach: Using Products in the Process." In *Eight Approaches To Teaching Composition*, ed. Tim Donovan and Ben McClelland, 21–36. Urbana, Ill.: NCTE.

Goldberger, Paul. 1986. "Quick! Before It Crumbles." In *The Little, Brown Reader*, ed. M. Stubbs and S. Barnet, 110–13. 4th ed. Boston: Little, Brown.

Goswami, Dixie, and Peter Stillman, ed. 1987. *Reclaiming the Classroom*. Portsmouth, N.H.: Boynton/Cook.

Kalkstein, Paul, Tom Regan, and Kelly Wise. 1981. *English Competence Handbook*. 3d ed. Wellesley Hills, Mass.: Independent School Press.

Kennedy, X. J., and D. M. Kennedy, ed. 1985. *The Bedford Reader*. 2d ed. New York: St. Martin's Press.

Kingston, Maxine Hong. 1977. *Woman Warrior: Memoirs of a Girlhood Among Ghosts*. New York: Vintage/Random.

———. 1984. "The Woman Warrior." in *Prose Models*, ed. G. Levin, 15–17. 6th ed. San Diego, Calif.: Harcourt Brace Jovanovich.

———. 1987. "No Name Woman." In *The Compact Reader: Subjects, Styles and Strategies*, ed. J. E. Aaron, 374–86. 2d ed. New York: St. Martin's Press.

Lumley, Dale. 1987. "An Analysis of Peer Group Dialogue Journals for Classroom." In *Reclaiming the Classroom*, 169–78. See Goswami and Stillman, 1987.

Martin, Gail. 1987. "A Letter to Bread Loaf." In *Reclaiming the Classroom*, 165–69. See Goswami and Stillman, 1987.

McCarthy, Mary. 1984. "Uncle Myers." In *Prose Models*, ed. G. Levin, 24–26. 6th ed. San Diego, Calif.: Harcourt Brace Jovanovich.

Moffett, James. 1983. *Teaching the Universe of Discourse*. Portsmouth, N.H.: Boynton/Cook.

Morrow, Lance. 1988. "1968." Reported by Robert Ajemian/Boston, Anne Hopkins/New York, and Dan Goodgame/Los Angeles. *Time* (January 11): 16–27.

National Public Radio Staff and Susan Stamberg. 1982. *Every Night at Five: Susan Stamberg's "All Things Considered" Book*. New York: Pantheon.

Newfield, Jack. 1987. "Stallone vs. Springsteen." In *The Compact Reader: Subjects, Styles, and Strategies*, ed. J. E. Aaron, 191–98. 2d ed. New York: St. Martin's Press.

Perl, Sondra. 1984. "Understanding Composing." In *Rhetoric and Composition*, ed. R. L. Graves, 304–10. Portsmouth, N.H.: Boynton/Cook.

Postman, Neil. 1979. *Teaching as a Conserving Activity*. New York: Dell.

Shaughnessy, Mina. 1977. *Errors and Expectations: A Guide for the Teacher of Basic Writing*. New York: Oxford University Press.

Stern, Arthur. 1981. "When Is a Paragraph?" In *The Writing Teacher's Sourcebook*. ed. G. Tate and E. P. J. Corbett, 294–300. New York: Oxford University Press.

Toth, Susan Allen. 1985. "Cinematypes." In *The Norton Sampler*, ed. T. Cooley, 78–83. 3d ed. New York: Norton.

Updike, John. 1986. "The Playground." In *The Little, Brown Reader*, ed. M. Stubbs & S. Barnet, 340–41. 4th ed. Boston: Little, Brown.

Weathers, Winston. 1981. "Teaching Style: A Possible Anatomy." In *The Writing Teacher's Sourcebook*, ed. G. Tate and E. P. J. Corbett, 325–32. New York: Oxford University Press.

———. 1984. "Grammars of Style: New Options in Composition." In *Rhetoric and Composition*, ed. R. L. Graves, 133–47. 2d ed. Portsmouth, N.H.: Boynton/Cook.

Introductory Literature Courses

6

Readers as Writers/Writers as Readers

Lynne Kelly

Too often I'll finish reading a set of literary critical essays and be left thinking something is missing. The text in question appeals to all of us, class talks have been thoughtful and lively, but these essays ... Talk with colleagues has raised the question of how what we *ask for* when students write in response to reading has produced so much of what we and they don't like. In particular, "thesis" essays—by now nearly formulaic—have left students working within a narrow, literary, "school" genre that emphasizes combing a text for quotations to substantiate the validity of their assertion about a thematic motif, a character's motivations, or an author's intentions. Students, distanced from their material and themselves, may even find themselves arguing to defend a position they don't care about beyond its being defensible. When teachers talk with one another about such writing, it is variously described as impersonal and vague, trite and vapid, padded and authoritarian, and finally phony. We worry that we are moving students away from James Britton's double wish: that they "should read *more books* with satisfaction" and "should read books with *more satisfaction*" (1982, 35).

This essay is written not to argue against the virtues of the well-done literary critical essay or to urge that we stop assigning/teaching such essays but rather to suggest other ways of encouraging a literature class to respond to texts that are valid in themselves and might change the way students will later write critical analyses. I care most of all about more enjoyment and better results for more students.

Nancie Atwell (1987) defines "a reader" as "a habitual seeker after good book" (157). What does it mean to be hooked on reading? I begin here because we usually ask students to write *in response to* what they've read, and my question becomes a lead to what strategies teachers might choose from to extend the range of purposes for writing, and hence the range of responses students make when they write about a text. According to Atwell, "reading generates its most significant meanings when the reader engages in a process of discovery, weaving and circling among the complex of behaviors that characterizes genuine participation in written language" (1987). All of my own speculations about the appeal of reading have in common a grounding in paradox: I want to ascend and descend the rope of cause and effect in a novel's twists and turns, at once at home and yet surprised by the way plot keeps conflict in motion; I want to have my culturally determined expectations of a genre comfort and challenge me as they are satisfied and expanded, perhaps even thwarted; I relish giving myself over to another's version of reality, at once safe yet willing to be tempted — admittedly an easier surrender if the text supports what I already affirm. Most of all, I love the way a book keeps alive what I've come to call "all that affective stuff" — aesthetic delight, a breadth and depth of thoughtful feelings, the experience of having been an empathetic other, all of my own creative impulses.

Not much of my pleasure, of what has made me a reading junkie, is purely cognitive, although I'd argue if pressed that neither head nor heart is really working or worth much without the other. Although I no longer read primarily as a healthily narcissistic act of self-definition (as most engaged adolescents do), I'd feel shut down if I couldn't write to make some kind of fit with the author. In short, something of my experience as a reader responding in writing must mirror the creative process. I'd argue further that to feel impelled to remain neutral and objective in tone where the text/author demands involvement, even commitment, is worse than to "misread" — it's not to have read or written at all.

Along with this assessment of what draws me as a reader writing about literature comes the responsibility to transfer all I've learned from teaching writing as a process to teaching reading as a process. The "-ingness" of making meaning, of all we think and feel as we respond, is not lost when writers write as readers and readers as writers. How can we help this happen by the way we talk about books/ writing in class discussions and lectures, so that students experience how ideally broadening the *ways* of knowing finds its reward in an expansion of ideas? When students know that there is no set definition of what's worth saying, they stop censoring themselves and begin to become an interpretive community, confident in each voice. If this same sense of liberation is with them as they write, they have a better chance of experiencing E. M. Forster's faith in discovery: "How do I know what I think until I see what I say?" (quoted in DiYanni 1984, 2). With this provocative question, Forster suggests that he discovers meaning as the words appear; that he must read his way into what he has written to know what he means. The possibility of form finding idea is a novel thought to most students; I question whether they can have more than a cerebral appreciation for the organic unity of content and style — that is, for the way the two lick each other round — unless they have experienced this recursivity themselves as writers. Again, how can we help this happen?

I begin by trying to undo the notions students have about writers, texts, critics, teachers, and themselves (especially as "student writers"). They come to us sure of the absolute authority of authors, of the text as an inviolate island of meaning, and of critics as infallible decoders in a private club to which teachers secretly do or wish to belong. As long as students think of writers as magicians rather than agents and thinkers creating artifacts (how different from masterpieces!) out of their personal and cultural identities, they will write to pay homage to the authority of the perfect text, and responding to literature will seem a task to which they must prove unequal — worse, a task for which their "real" selves aren't wanted.

Real readers don't get shut out in the name of literary criticism if they are asked to explore the covert procedures that writers use to construct meaning and, in the process, explore their own. If reading, like writing, calls for the creation of meaning — this time in collaboration with a writer — students can't be passive consumers of "classics" whose inscrutability must be protected if these texts are to remain truly great. Active readers resist this conservative impulse and appropriate meaning for their own purposes. I've never read, say, Cynthia Ozick or Harold Bloom, for better or for worse, without being reminded of this. They and other so-called "creative" critics make no bones about throwing their experience up at the supposed "meaning" of a text; in fact, many would argue that that's what texts and readers are for, as readers in turn join the dialogue by responding to what they've read with texts — that is, voices — of their own.

The idea of readers having their own voices brings us back to those remarkably "affect-free" expository essays. How can we help students see themselves as makers of meaning when they read and write through the way they perceive their relationship to a writer's work? We might have students write about a situation they will encounter in their reading in order for them to have occupied the territory before the writer. We can also treat writers — *all* writers — first as agents and thinkers by studying early drafts or reading letters and journal entries about how their writing came into being at the same time that we are asking students to respond to each other's writing at different times in the composing. For the past two years in an introductory literature course at Phillips Academy, I've worked with students to find ways that writing about Joseph Conrad's *Heart of Darkness* would enhance their comprehension of the novel. Before I describe these assignments, how I handled them, and with what results, let me explain why *Heart of Darkness* was a strategic choice.

First, the narrative structure of the tale-within-the-tale demands that all of the faculties we use when we make meaning of and through language (reading, writing, listening, speaking) be tapped, and hence the novel provides a real linguistic workout that does not favor one kind of learner or way of knowing. Second, because Conrad's writing is so discriminating, it imposes, seemingly by osmosis, a like discrimination on its readers. Paradoxically, even as I learned through the students' journals and papers how much more than the features of this literary text — its many tropes and rhetorical devices — control making meaning, I also never stopped seeing proof of the power of Conrad's words to shape us into the very readers he wanted/needed to understand the complexities, especially the reticences, of his tale.

Not incidentally, I chose a canonized text — one with a wonderfully deceptive, starched appearance. The Phillips Academy faculty is struggling with the implications for teaching and learning that have grown out of its commitment to find diverse students and faculty. The belief that meaning is above all something to be found in the text (rather than in the production of individual reading/writing strategies shaped by temperament, preparation, and experience) profoundly shapes one's point of view about the issues diversity asks us to address: namely race, gender, and social class. I think I perceive, lurking like the text beneath the text, an undercurrent to some faculty lounge conversations regarding "touchy-feely" approaches — that is, expressive, student-centered, autobiographical writing assignments. (With *Heart of Darkness*, an example might be: "Describe a time when you 'stepped back.' What factors influenced your decision? What has having stepped back come to mean to you since the original action?"). Many question whether such assignments meet the criteria for rigorous thought set by all that the literary critical essay demands: coherence; a tightly focused structure, logically developed; consistency of voice and tone; ideas supported through direct quotation. I don't want our department to think in terms of "either/or" when "both/and," especially with careful structuring and sequencing, holds such promise. Also, I worry that inadvertently schools will divide titles of texts under the headings of "Canon" and "Other," with different pedagogical strategies to go with each column. While it is interesting to consider whether certain texts are more suited for certain kinds of compositional responses, concluding that the "Canon" demands one set of lessons and the "Other," another, suggests obvious biases. Above all I don't want any supposedly theoretical difference to become the germ of an insidious attitudinal one — namely, that such "touchy-feely" assignments work best, perhaps only, with lesser texts . . . and perhaps lesser students . . . and perhaps lesser teachers.

I chose three writing assignments for *Heart of Darkness* because each seemed to grow out of my first as well as my ongoing reading of Conrad's novel — for me a novel replete with doubles and voices (voices echoing, voices lying, voices silenced), told by a voice rendered as "speech act," defended by strategic omissions and "quick lefts" amidst disparaging if nervous interruptions from the Men of Empire. The signal is the adjective "inconclusive" used by Marlow's cronies to describe his style of telling; it is an invitation proffered early to take up the slack, to come along if not aboard. Because *Heart of Darkness* couldn't be more rhetorical and yet is never only rhetorical, no reader I've met stays outside the novel for long. The very understatement of Marlow's appeals invites empathy, and even subversion, as we sort out and take on each voice, left in the end to ask ourselves if we, like Kurtz, would have turned our back on restraint, or if we, like Marlow, would have chosen the consequences of restraint, especially the taste of death in a lie. And precisely because Conrad doesn't pretend to tell a story about "real" people among naturalistic objects and settings, he is able to bring off all of his rhetorical strategies by making one's perception of them seem identical to one's interpretation of his story. Since a reader is able to meet Conrad's text at the interesting levels of the literal, the symbolic, and the psychological, it is impossible to separate the craft of the telling from the story told. Students really do look at the writing interested in how all those conscious and unconscious decisions about words produced such effects — an intellectual undertaking, finally, and one that began with permission to find meaning where and how they might.

For the first writing assignment, entitled "Reader's Journal," everyone brings a new journal to class on the day I begin reading the first stretch of *Heart of Darkness* to them. (Before it becomes a reader's journal, they make an entry about their experience with diaries and journals, with free-writing of any kind.) I begin by hawking the journal as a place to catch the overflow of the pleasures of reading. As I talk I pass among them former students' journals and my own, calling these notebooks an unspoken log of responses, a record of goals, assumptions, contexts for reading and writing that trace the evolution from passive to active reader. Because what they write is a matter of their own effort and choice, I suggest they'll come to like the heat of recording uncensored what they think and feel as they think and feel it, even as slowing down reading by stopping to write allows for the cooler pleasure of reflection. Your journal, I say, is your record of the evolution of meaning made; to reread it is to watch yourself process a text and thereby to get to know yourself as a reader writing. In addition, it is a place removed from the pressure of a final draft and eyes that judge. Their autonomy is emphasized: they decide when to stop reading and write, how much to write, and what to write, although I do suggest they try a "column" method: the "lifted" text, comments and questions about it, and analysis of what accounts for their response. Since the journal is a place to find words for their thoughts — insights, questions, connections about the text — many see the logic of writing down the phrase, sentence, or passage that caused a response; the response itself; and any thoughts about how the writer/text had evoked this reaction in them (the invitation to scrutinize their own susceptibility to certain passages they find irresistible and valid).

Many students have indicated that their journal was the first place they began to sound like themselves *to* themselves, a melding of spoken and written voice. There are more utilitarian reasons for keeping a reader's journal: for use in collaboratively led discussions; for review before tests; for a record of selected quotations and the questions, insights, and connections that followed; for the chance to read my comments on what they've written. I also have my own teacherly reasons for urging journal writing. First of all, it's good training for staying in the text a bit longer than most students think to do. In addition, students who are not used to addressing questions about style end up thinking about it when they write about what has produced their responses. Because their responses are chronological (that is, recorded as they read), it's inevitable that eventually they come to see style as "context-as-arranged," to use Helen Vendler's (1984) words.

Furthermore, commenting on students' journals lets a teacher "be a person too," with endless implications for how class sounds and feels on a daily basis; but even before that dialogue with the writer, skimming journals yields insights that would make for a very interesting teachers' guide. By noting what features of the text students cite as meaningful, I intuit their processes of making inferences and finding questions and learn much about how memory, autobiography, and breadth and depth of reading experience become part of their recording purposes. In addition, I find the implications for how to structure class discussions are there in the patterns of relationships students form as they respond to the text. Study questions are dictated by what their journals show they are making, and not making, of the book. And students' journals do have common features: most readers don't question their own (or Conrad's) assumptions — indeed, don't see them as assumptions; they use a vocabulary wildly different from "lit-crit" or teacher diction, especially when they write about matters of style; they are more comfortable making statements than raising questions; they move to the level of implications frequently after assertions, rarely after questions; they write more about style after they have done the second assignment, the creative writing assignment — that is, when what they have written is, to them, as much the text as what is written in the novel.

In the second writing assignment (variously called "Lunar Gap," "A Chink in the Text," or "You Were There") the student enters the text and is given the chance to become an empathetic other on several levels (see Appendix 6−1 and 6−2). Each reader selects from among the many "scenes that weren't" hinted at in Marlow's telling: Kurtz's revels, Kurtz and the native woman, the Intended and Kurtz on the eve of parting, a feverish late-night dialogue between Kurtz and the Harlequin. It's made clear from the outset that the point of the assignment isn't to write like Conrad (if they or I should end up thinking they have, that's all right too); they are simply asked to enter actively into the creative process by making a chunk of text about something they want to imagine. In this way they have the opportunity to represent to themselves a complicated rhetorical situation in which a number of forces and constraints come into play. Asking them to do this assignment assumes a sophisticated level of understanding, happens late in the reading, and requires much in-class pre-writing if they are to feel confident. For example, they are asked to select a place in *Heart of Darkness* and list all of Conrad's options/choices at that point. Or they write about a "journey" of their own where the rules seemed to change en route or there were no guidelines at all. At least once, they come into class and start reading wherever they left off and ten minutes into it take over the text, just picking up the thread of the story in their own writing. All of these are dry runs for standing in Conrad's shoes.

Students who've entered the novel in this way can never again see *Heart of Darkness* as a given to be ingested unaltered. When they have done this assignment, many students see that they have refined their own analytical skills by indirectly passing judgment on a character or a situation, and therefore on Conrad and his novel as well — something that they couldn't do if they haven't understood what they've read. Few finish this assignment without feeling like writers. Additionally, becoming an empathetic other is meant to enhance their appreciation of the novel; because they find it more original and feel more intimate with it, many come to love it. And since there's no way to stand more immediately in a writer's shoes than to become a writer too, the exercise creates a bond that encourages students to read as writers and write as readers.

The last assignment entitled "Our Dinner with Conrad," takes place about a week after they have finished reading the novel, have gotten back their journals, and have heard one another's "lunar gaps."

When we've done a week's worth of talking in class, mostly based on their questions, I reserve a large living room with comfortable couches, and we meet at four on a Sunday to eat dinner and listen to a seamless group reading. Each of them has practiced reading eight or ten pages aloud. A chair and a light is placed at either end of our oval, and as each passage draws to a close, the next reader takes the empty chair.

Normally we read according to our own purposes, stopping if we get hungry or sleepy or psychologically uncomfortable; but this reading demands that all of us submerge our purposes and give ourselves over to a stimulation and a unity at once large and other, with the intention of understanding it all once more (in writing parlance, "re-vision"). The eerie combination of déjà vu and awakening passing over their faces testifies to Britton's remark (1982, 32) that reading a novel is like remembering an experience you haven't had. For almost four hours we are all aboard the Nellie, alternately listening and narrating, and so sensitized to hearing our voices become the voice of the story that every faculty for apprehending through language is tuned. The silence at the close of the novel is so loud and so full that inevitably someone compares it to "the heart of an immense darkness."

We do not meet for the next class; the time is used to work on the papers purposely vaguely titled "Reading as Reperception." (See Appendix 6−3) We talk before the reading about the ways hearing the novel whole may bring some passages forward as others recede, about the human voice's capacity to give words a privileged dimension, about the shifting weight of lines heard again, about how the tale by moving uninterrupted from voice to voice becomes like the river. The emphasis is on process, in that their papers are "about" what happened to them as makers of meaning as and after they'd heard *Heart of Darkness*.

When we come together again, it is to read what we have written. (I'm a reader and I do the assignment too.) Someone starts and another writer, hearing a connection, picks up when the first finishes—another seamless reading. At the end someone always says that we should have taped both readings, and that someone is always shouted down. Most insist that hearing secondhand wouldn't—couldn't—be the same. In their insistence I hear how experiencing Conrad's novel firsthand and figuring out what to make of that experience has made it their own. Because of this, it is almost impossible to answer the question of what kind of essays they write; there are as many kinds of essays as there are writers. Someone will select an image and let it become an emblem; someone will hear something he or she hadn't really heard before—the repetition of word "nigger" or the similarities in the descriptions of the Savage Woman and the Intended—and speculate about their reasons for previously resisting the text. Someone else will leap the text by using an idea about Empire to go back to a former text—Camus' *The*

Stranger, say — to look again. Many write about what became more clear, sometimes including an account of why it became so; a few students write about where Conrad seems to be Marlow, where he doesn't, and why. The essays I've included with this paper are analytical essays despite not being assigned as such. For me, the question of what accounts for the detached tone of so many critical essays is brought front and center again: students who are given the choice of finding their topic and their means of addressing it are given the double privilege of autonomy and control. They write believing that what is important to them *is* important.

For the three weeks we read and write in response to Conrad's *Heart of Darkness*, the emphasis is on the ways literature affects "real" readers and how these effects shape what we know. Here "real" is in quotation marks to question the notion of an "ideal" reader, a corollary to the concepts of an ideal literature and an ideal way of working. And if more ways of knowing are accessible, then content, meaning, the known — call it what you will — expands as well. In addition, when students work through writing assignments intended to blur the line between creative and expository writing as well as between reader and writer, any discussion of theme or meaning leads back to authorial intention, or what is inherent in such stylistic choices as diction, syntax, cadence, and grammar. As students become more aware of a writer's selecting presence by experiencing their own, they inevitably move from inward (expressive, personal) to outward (conceptual, analytical) concerns. In other words, their interest has enabled them to read and write about literature in the way that the few students we describe as engaged and original and attentive to language now write when assigned a literary critical analysis.

Appendix 6–1
Student Essay
"A Chink in the Hedge"

"I did not intend to inquire as to why the old doctor never saw the patients when they returned, of if they returned at all, for fear that his answer would be unenticing. It seemed to me that everyone around me, especially inside that office building, understood more than I concerning my cloudy duties as an agent. He often glanced over at me, always emitting a laughing, knowing, curious air. I think he wanted to climb inside my head and take on my thoughts for a while. To find out why I was going 'out there.' The reason for measuring my skull, I suppose. Nevertheless, how were the changes inside expected to affect the outside, and how were these changes going to be measured with nothing to compare them to? I would have dismissed him as a half-brained scientist working for a Nobel prize, but his omniscience was too uncanny. There was a missing piece . . . a chink in the hedge. He knew he was right, and I think that's what bothered me the most about him. It was *his* theory and everything we did was going to prove it. We were the guinea pigs of the experiment. There was something unusual that we would be exposed to in Africa. It would have been interesting to speak with him after my journey now that I consider it. I believe his theory may have been proved right. His reaction to Fresleven and Kurtz would have been interesting . . ."

He paused, lost in thought, again, except this time with an almost imperceptible grin. Whoever this Kurtz was, I think Marlow was either fond of him or received him with substantial awe, and Marlow is not someone who is led easily. The dark night air was silent, and enveloped us all. The stars, by now, were absent from the sky, and only the stars on the horizon, one for each citizen of that magnanimous town, could be spied. Marlow began again, startling even me, probably one of his more devoted listeners.

"Well, being curious about this doctor's specific intentions and theory, I observed aloud, hoping for a reaction, 'You seem to know quite a bit about these agents, as I suppose you call them, considering you do not see them when they return.' I received a reaction completely different from that which I expected. He glared coldly and repeated, 'I'm not such a fool as I look, quoth Plato to his disciples.' As you see, trying to get information from the doctor was like extracting permanent teeth. I suppose I should have given up, but I had to know. I felt as though I was about to step into a corridor darker than night and, the door shut and locked behind me, I would be left to grope inside forever. Not a very comfortable feeling, I assure you, and yet the doctor was completely unwilling to shed any light on the situation. 'What is your theory, and how will we prove it?' I asked, being candid in the hope that he would respect my frankness and enlighten me. 'In the interest of science,' he started, and I already knew what he was going to say. But I didn't want to hear that, I wanted to hear of the changes inside, to be forewarned. On any other voyage I would have leapt without looking, but this was an exception. Everything pointed to severe danger, but danger of what? Not of the natives, but of the mind, I thought. I became impatient, 'You are not Plato,' I said under my breath. He heard, and lost his resilience. 'You have proved yourself to be atypical; however, I cannot quite say exactly what I am looking for. I only know it's there. You probably will not be as affected as the others.' He spoke softly as if I knew what he was talking about. But I did, in a way. I understood his feeling. We had both the same intentions . . . not to outdo, but climb inside and move around in each other's skulls. He then proceeded to warn me. These warnings gave even more reason to trust in him as I hadn't, not five minutes before. What was even stranger was that he had understood me and knew what I understood. We thought very much alike, he and I. Still, I don't think he knew what 'his' discovery meant. He would have to live it to truly know."

Zenzi Gadson

Appendix 6–2
Student Essay
"Inside the Mist: Fleshing out the Apparition"

... from right to left along the lighted shore moved a wild and gorgeous apparition of a woman. She walked with measured steps, draped in striped and fringed clothes, treading the earth proudly, with a slight jingle and flash of barbarous ornaments. She carried her head high; her hair was done in the shape of a helmet; she had brass leggings to the knee, brass wire gauntlets to the elbow, a crimson spot on her tawny cheek, innumerable necklaces of glass beads on her neck; bizarre things, charms, gifts of witch-men, that hung about her, glittered and trembled at every step. She was savage and superb, wild-eyed and magnificent; there was something ominous and stately in her deliberate progress. And in the hush that had fallen suddenly upon the whole sorrowful land, the immense wilderness, the colossal body of the fecund and mysterious life seemed to look at her, pensive, as though it had been looking at the image of its own tenebrous and passionate soul.

She came abreast of the steamer, stood still, and faced us. Her long shadow fell to the river's edge. Her face had a tragic and fierce aspect of wild sorrow and of dumb pain mingled with the fear of some struggling, half-shaped resolve. ... She looked at us all as if her life depended upon the unswerving steadiness of her glance. Suddenly she opened her bare arms and threw them up rigid above her head, as though in an uncontrollable desire to touch the sky, and at the same time the swift shadow darted out on the earth, swept around on the river, gathering the steamer into a shadowy embrace. A formidable silence hung over the scene. ...

She turned away slowly, walked on, following the bank, and passed into the bushes to the left. Only her eyes gleamed back at us in the dusk of the thickets before she disappeared.

Joseph Conrad, Heart of Darkness

Opening, arms so wide across the sky, as a falcon spreads its black wings, if only to fly over this bitter water to take you from your land—but I remember again and again: excitement, and I am the sky, the black canvas from which you draw your strengths, excitement builds between us and my blood stirs thick with unspoken memory I am river, the heart of the jungle so dense, steamy, and like my jungle I choose to veil myself with beauty that hangs and trembles. My heart is the beat of the drums at night and I grew up one of my people not knowing that you existed. But when you came we all worshiped you. Now you leave us! I hate the stench of your white sweat that is theirs, they who reclaim you for your, their, land, even as I lick the salt from your face . . .

Remembering . . . *at night, a ring of fire, in the close red light the men sing and clap, clicking their tongues in pulsating time, shadows leaping and falling upon their flesh; women trill fiercely somewhere deep within their throats, rattling strands of shells. The meat turns inside the flame, smoke clouds the sky, hovers over us protectively. The rhythm is so huge and constant that soon our hearts are leaping into it . . . and the jungle undulates in our veins, swelling with fervor and contracting and releasing again. We throw ourselves into the dance, singing the words you taught us, and even when the warm rain begins to fall we dance and dance; faster, and the smell of the meat burning pervades our senses. The night is with our music and the rain invisible, only felt and heard sizzling and crackling in the glowing pyre, and the hidden shadows are sultry, swaying, like vines that slither silently and twist around us. And you sit in the center, the core of the dance, the great circle, and from your greatness we expand into the cyclic chant . . . around you the tribe, it all opens out springing from your seed . . .*

Now I am a carcass, spitting in the flame. I am so gutted and scorched under this skin, all my adornments weigh heavily upon the outside, and though they glitter and sparkle like the waters, they are spearlike protection against the curse brought upon us all. The rattle of my ornaments speak as I have forgotten what to say to drive the dark spirits away, those who have come to reclaim you, our light. Once I loved you with something that was not love, with my breath, with my abdomen, with my bony ribs, with the mud of the grass and the drip of rain too. In the beginning everyone wanted you to notice them. That was all I wanted too. But then when you saw me it was not who I was or who I now know I am; it was the creature that you created for your own pleasure as you created all of us, created of the black mud, of your twisted creepers streaming green black sweat, your mind embodied by a dark white spirit. Calling back to the spirits of my ancestors, the heartbeat has skipped a beat when it merged with yours and the circle was broken, and the seed does not unfold slowly green until it becomes more of the soil from which it sprouted — now people die and the earth is not replenished, only burned as I have been inside, and if the seed of creation was within me surely it would wither and die.

Remembering hunting . . . Do you know the smell, the thick taste of blood? You found out soon and our eyes glinted nakedly as one pair when we tore the skin of our game. Their heads meant nothing but a token of our triumph, though your remembrance is different than mine: I remember such things like the sound of the rain upon each thirsty eager leaf, as we turned our faces to your voice. Things happen and you leave them behind you, but I live every breath that was taken before me every moon of life. Now I have betrayed the secret of life, and who knows if the sun will return?

Lisa Levy

Appendix 6–3
Student Essay
"Nobility and Degradation: The Soul in *Heart of Darkness*"

"His soul was mad. . . . Being alone in the wilderness it had looked within itself and, By heavens! I tell you, it had gone mad." Marlow marvels at the horrible change which Kurtz had undergone, a dehumanizing change extending into his very soul and warping it. It had "no restraint, no faith, and no fear, yet struggling blindly within itself." The sheer degradation of Kurtz is both terrifying and incomprehensible, yet one of Conrad's main questions in this tale is, I believe, whether Kurtz was unique in his potential for self-ruination or whether indeed this terror could come upon any man. In other words, does every soul possess a darkness like Kurtz's, brooding deep inside and needing but the incessant whisper of the wilderness to emerge?

In many ways, this entire book is an exploration of darkness and light, or blackness and whiteness, both outer and inner. Throughout we see contrasts of both men and symbols in black and white: the white string wrapped around the neck of a starving black boy, the black background of Kurtz's painting, from which light emerges, the white spot on the map of Africa, which turns out to be the physical heart of darkness, the stark contrast of the black and white men themselves in the story. The last contrast is two-leveled, since it is the white men who possess the black souls and the black men whose souls are innocent and "white." The conflict between the dark and the light is evident everywhere in the book, in the constant struggle between the races, and the larger attack of the civilized world of the whited sepulchre upon the wild power of the Congo. But there is an inner and deeper conflict as well, concerning the divisions of one's own soul and the fight against the darkness therein. For this is the greatest danger of the heart of darkness: the terror and corruption it works upon the soul.

"Acrophobia of the soul" the disease is called, and the phrase is well-used. The "falls" that the degradation encompasses are such that one is not swept unwilling into the abyss but rather runs there with great desire. The manager and others have leapt in headlong. Kurtz fell unwittingly as he rushed forward, in blindness and greed. The wilderness, as a symbol and essence of the vengeful power in this place, traps the foreigners who dare to violate it. Marlow describes in the introduction to his story, "the savagery, the utter savagery, closing in." The circumstances in which a white man finds himself are so utterly foreign and totally different from the "civilized world" that no custom or defense learned there will be of any avail. A person must adapt to survive there and not try to conquer, because one may believe one has conquered, like Kurtz with his deadly ivory, or the manager with his position, but in reality the wilderness itself has triumphed. No white man who comes in contact with the place departs it unchanged, because of the "savagery" and because of the power which it possesses over those invaders who are not of the wilderness, not in tune with it as the natives are. In their reality as an extension of the forest's power lie their innocence and immunity to degradation; it is only in contact with evil whites that black people degrade themselves, as with their worship of Kurtz, sicken and starve, as symbols of their land, and endanger the passion and nobility of their culture. Though the white invasion is a laughable folly in one sense, it is also a cruel evil because it brings nothing but harm to both sides: the white men fall from misguided colonizers and traders to avaricious and ruthless racists, the most prominent and most fallen being the general manager.

Kurtz's fall is so dramatic and so drastic because he falls so low from such a height. A gifted scholar, talented artist, brilliant musician, most eloquent speaker, and a man of genius and nobility with great ideas and unbounded potential, he was nevertheless a man who was left alone in the utter depths of the darkness of the forest with the darkness of his own soul and its lust for wealth. He had to "take counsel with the great solitude" which had "whispered to him things about himself which he did not know" and this "irresistibly fascinating" whisper "echoed loudly within him because he was hollow at the core." Beneath the exterior civilized brilliance of Kurtz lay a fatal flaw with which the months of living alone and unaided hearkening to the insidious murmurs of the land about him drove him slowly and surely mad. In the awful solitude of his unprotected soul the transition was probably horrifyingly easy.

A terrifying creature is Mr. Kurtz when we and Marlow meet him, so completely is he degraded and inhuman. But Conrad does not allow us even the comfort of believing him a unique evil because we see so clearly his fall and Marlow's teetering and the brooding forces responsible that we must realize that Kurtz does not fall because he is uniquely corruptible but because of the circumstances he was under. The inherent flaws found in all men are human qualities which merely emerge when "civilized" men are placed in an alien situation so totally threatening to their conditioning and mentality. Marlow does *not* fall, uniquely among white men, not because of his restraint or purpose or self-examination, though these qualities aid him considerably, but because he perceives the path Kurtz has taken before him and hence was "permitted to draw back [his] hesitating foot" at the very edge of the abyss. It is a slim victory, but Marlow wins it because of Kurtz.

Thus the theme found in this discourse is that the potential of degradation or nobility exists in every soul. Lives of faith, truth, and restraint help one to resist the darkness, but each man bears light and darkness in his soul, needing only shocking and drastic circumstances to bring the darkness out in abominable magnification. Kurtz fell even as Marlow would have fallen if Marlow had come first: each man's unique darkness, which might never be felt if he did not set foot from his comfortable and sterile world into the unknown, must be wrestled with in this journey of self-discovery. Marlow achieves his own enlightenment and resists his darkness through Kurtz's succumbing, through the view of his summation of "sombre pride ... ruthless power ... craven terror, and intense and hopeless despair," through his final terrible and perfect whisper: "The horror! The horror!"

Liza Ryan

Works Cited

Atwell, Nancie. 1987. *In the Middle: Reading, Writing, and Learning with Adolescents*. Portsmouth, N.H.: Boynton/Cook.

Britton, James. 1982. *Prospect and Retrospect: Selected Essays of James Britton*. Ed. G. M. Pradl. Portsmouth, N.H.: Boynton/Cook.

DiYanni, Robert. 1984. *Connections: Reading, Writing, Thinking*. Portsmouth, N.H.: Boynton/Cook.

Holland, Norman. 1975. *5 Readers Reading*. New Haven, Conn.: Yale University Press.

Vendler, Helen. 1984. Lecture on Wallace Stevens's "The River of Rivers in Connecticut." Cambridge Massachussetts. August.

7

Writing Across the Aims of Discourse
An Approach and a Method for Teaching Literary Composition

Kevin O'Connor

Toward the end of our discussion on *The Scarlet Letter*, I began to feel the class meetings were becoming a little predictable. The Phillips Academy class members, mostly eleventh graders, had been carefully tracing certain literary images and themes as we read through the novel together. These students, interested but not especially excited, were probably already anxious about the expository paper that I had assigned them. For most, this was their first real literature class, and they were struggling to master the rudiments of "critical writing." Because I wanted to stir the class's emotion, I decided to begin class one day by reading them a passage, which I found both brilliant and comical in its excess, from D. H. Lawrence's *Studies in Classic American Literature*:

> Hester Prynne was a devil. Even when she was going around so meekly as a sick nurse. Poor Hester. Part of her wanted to be saved from her own devilishness. And another part wanted to go on and on in her devilishness, for revenge. Revenge! REVENGE! It is this that fills the unconscious spirit of woman today. Revenge against man, and against the spirit of man which has betrayed her into unbelief. Even when she is most sweet and salvationist, she is her most devilish, is woman. She gives the man the sugar-plum of her own submissive sweetness. And when he's taken this sugar-plum in his mouth, a scorpion comes out of it. After he's taken this Eve to his bosom, oh,

so loving, she destroys him inch by inch. Woman and her revenge! She will have it and go on having it, for decades and decades, unless she's stopped. And to stop her you've got to believe in yourself and your gods, your own Holy Ghost, Sir Man; and then you've got to fight her, and never give in. She's a devil. But in the long run she is conquerable. And just a tiny bit of her wants to be conquered. You've got to fight three-quarters of her, in absolute hell, to get at the final quarter of her that wants a release, at last, from the hell of her own revenge. But it's a long last. And not yet. (1964, 93–94)

The class reacted excitedly. I had predicted the feminist debate, the defense of Hester and womankind in general, that the Lawrence excerpt would evoke, but I was surprised by the student's unanimous enthusiasm for the *kind* of essay Lawrence had written: passionately polemical, unabashedly personal and subjective, grossly generalizing and opinionated.

"Why can't we write essays like that?" one girl challenged me directly. "Wouldn't you grade us down if we did?"

I can't remember the details of my apology for emphasizing the more conventional expository essay form, but I don't think it was particularly convincing — for them or for me. The girl that asked that question was later accepted into Harvard, where my traditional emphasis will probably stand her in good stead, at least as far as her grades are concerned. But her question still nags at me and has given birth to recent experiments in my classroom as well as to this essay.

It is true that in teaching literary composition for the last twelve years I have valued qualities that markedly contrast with the Lawrence piece: precisely qualified interpretive generalizations; concrete textual support for these generalizations; coherent, discursively analytical prose. Certainly these are qualities to be admired, and, like most teachers of introductory literature courses, I have been gratified when those special students write originally insightful critical essays that sometimes equal the work of the best graduate students. Certainly critical writing can enhance the reading experience, encouraging students to read more closely and appreciatively. But more often than not for the majority of my students, these exercises in the New Critical thesis essay, still emphasized by most comp-lit teachers, have done little more than to introduce them to a very narrow genre of writing and to improve certain skills in the expository mode. The following is an excerpt from a paper I assigned on Heathcliff's character development in *Wuthering Heights*:

And innocent and kindhearted Heathcliff enjoyed a pleasant childhood roaming the moors with Catherine. The pair developed a supernatural love, which made little sense to narrator Nelly Dean, who commented, "She [Catherine] was much too fond of Heathcliff. The greatest punishment we could invent for her was to keep her separate from him; yet she got chided more than any of us on his account." Catherine and Heathcliff would often steal away in the morning and frolic in the moors behind Wuthering Heights, not to return all day. The punishment endured by the children for such misbehavior did not hinder either of the two. "They forgot everything the minute they were together again." Further proof of Catherine and Heathcliff's everlasting love is provided in Chapter Nine when Catherine articulates to Nelly the feelings which Heathcliff, much to his dismay, does not believe exist. "Nelly, I am Heathcliff. He's always, always in my mind: not as a pleasure, any more than I am always a pleasure to myself, but as my own being."

This was not one of the better essays in the class, but the writer was certainly making an earnest effort here to write an effective expository essay with the methods I had introduced to him. He has made interpretive generalizations about the behavior of the characters, and he has supplied concrete references to the text, including direct quotes, by way of support. Still, the faults in the piece are obvious enough: the paragraph lacks coherence around one idea; he falls into running commentary and summary at points; the chronological context of his generalizations is not always clear. But these are problems of expository "skills," which can be remedied through editing and revision. The deeper problem lies in the writer's detachment from the material, his lack of creativity as well as of personal and emotional investment. Any interpretive commentary laced through his prose (e.g., the mystical nature of the love and Nelly's earthly incomprehension) has been recycled from our class discussion. Both his abstract and concrete statements are equally matter-of-fact and tonally flat: the writer's point of view and his sense of an audience are hardly discernible. Though not the most imaginative reader, the writer was someone I knew to be enthusiastic about literature and passionate about people as well as ideas, and so I wonder in retrospect if the form of the essay assignment itself was partially to blame for his lackluster performance.

I am increasingly convinced that too much emphasis on the primarily analytical aim of the expository thesis essay may distance students from the literature at the very time in their development (say from the ages of fifteen to eighteen) when they should be investing themselves more personally and emotionally in it. Arguing for the primacy of "feeling" in artistic symbolization and against its false opposition to "reason," for the rational intellect viewed as just a higher form of feeling, Susanne Langer asserts that "a highly developed mind grows up on the fine articulation of generally strong and ready feeling" (1967, 147). In his essay entitled "Response to Literature," the English educator James Britton succinctly describes the potential for the neglect of feeling in the antinomy between literature and critical response: "The principle of organization of a critical statement is cognitive; that of a work of literature is in the final analysis, affective" (1982, 34). Students indentured to the critical essay by prevailing educational attitudes are deprived not only of an opportunity to apply insights from "literary" experience to their "real life" experience but also of an acquaintance with a whole variety of other legitimate literary responses, of other "aims" and uses of discourse.

If the reading of literature and the writing about literature can be validly spoken of as "skills," I want as a teacher to help students develop these skills. Reading and writing critically are "useful" activities in college, at work, in one's personal life. But like most English teachers, I am an idealist, and retain the liberal-humanist notion that in reading and responding to literature my students can experience moral insight, imaginative liberation, emotional empathy, and self-discovery — in short, they can become better human beings. One small pedagogical step in serving both these utilitarian and idealistic ends is to loosen what James Britton has referred to as the "stranglehold" of the expository essay and to reshape our concept of what constitutes a valuable literary response (1984, *vii*).

In his book *Literary Theory*, Terry Eagleton challenges the assumptions of traditional canonists by arguing that neither "literature" nor "literary criticism" exists in definable terms. Making a persuasive case for the social responsibilities of "criticism," Eagleton's book is primarily an attack on the proliferation of competing critical "schools" that have lost sight of the practical goals of their endeavor. But the implications of his argument are especially relevant for secondary and college teachers of introductory composition and literature. Eagleton demystifies the notion of criticism and broadens it to include "any kind of talk ... about an object named literature" (1983, 197) and laments that the active enjoyment of literature tends to be encouraged for younger students while the older students are faced with the "grimmer business of analysis" (1983, 212). In making a radical proposal for substituting a "theory of discourse" for the illusory notion of a "theory of criticism," Eagleton invites English teachers to reconsider their emphasis on the expository critical essay. James Britton supports Eagleton's perspective when he claims that "the kind of discovered knowledge that an expository essay might demonstrate and present to the public is more likely to be arrived at by using forms of discourse that are not in themselves expository" (1984, *vii*). The remainder of this essay will consider ways in which Eagleton's and Britton's challenge to conventional "critical" writing and pedagogy can be met.

In reading through various new theories of rhetoric and discourse, I have been particularly excited by the practical application of the ideas of James Kinneavy, outlined in his *A Theory of Discourse* (1980), and James Britton, presented mainly in *Prospect and Retrospect* (1982) and *Language and Learning* (1970). Though the theories of Britton and Kinneavy diverge at crucial points (which will be discussed later), they are very similar in that they both define types of discourse in terms of their *purpose* — Kinneavy discusses the "aims" and Britton the "functions" of discourse — and conceive that these types exist on a spectrum of sometimes complementary and overlapping purposes. I think the conceptual categorizations of Kinneavy and Britton can be useful to teachers of literature and composition by helping them clarify the purpose of their writing assignments and consider a broader variety of purposes.

Instead of focusing on the traditional rhetorical modes (narrative, descriptive, persuasive, expository), Kinneavy's taxonomy, as summarized in his essay "The Basic Aims of Discourse," distinguishes kinds of discourse according to aim:

> If one represents the communications process as a triangle composed of an encoder (writer or speaker), a decoder (reader or listener), a signal (the linguistic product), and a reality (that part of the universe to which the linguistic product refers), then the focus on one of these tends to produce a specific kind of discourse" (1980, 95).

Kinneavy's triangular theory (1980, 19) is diagrammed in Figure 7−1.

According to Kinneavy's definitions, discourse dominated by subject matter (reality talked about) is called "referential discourse." Discourse that focuses on eliciting a specific reaction from the decoder (reader or listener) is "persuasive." When the language product is dominated by the clear design of the encoder (writer or speaker) to discharge emotions or achieve individuality or embody personal or group aspirations, the discourse tends to be "expressive." And finally, when the linguistic product (signal) calls attention to itself, to its own structures as worthy of contemplation in their own right, this discourse is "literary" (Kinneavy 1980, 95, 97).

There are several practical benefits of Kinneavy's taxonomy for the writing teacher. First, it can help a teacher clarify the purpose of writing assignments and consider a more comprehensive range of purposes. Second, for evaluation of these assignments, it helps establish clearer criteria based on the particular "aims" of the discourse. Third, because Kinneavy's taxonomy of discourse is not hierarchical, it reinforces the importance of writing across *all* the aims of discourse: specifically, it undermines the notion that "analytical," "expository," or "theoretical" language products are in themselves more highly evolved and more important forms of discourse. Furthermore, the unnecessary opposition between the goals of a "composition" course and a "litera-

Figure 7–1
The Communications Triangle

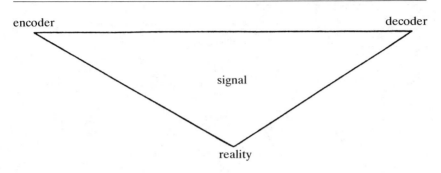

"ture" course is averted, given that the written responses to literature will span all aims and modes of discourse. Finally, the communications triangle that Kinneavy employs is similar to the conceptual diagram (see Figure 7–2) that M. H. Abrams uses to classify elements of critical theory in his *The Mirror and the Lamp* (1953, 6). Hence, for the teacher concerned with a rationale for literary response writing, Kinneavy's schema serves as a bridge between a theory of discourse and a theory of literary criticism.

In *A Theory of Discourse* (1980)—in which the nature, logic, organization, and style of each of the four categories of discourse are examined in detail—Kinneavy provides specific examples of each type of discourse. I have selected examples from each category (and subcategory) and shown how they might be applied as classroom assignments in response to literature:

- *Expressive discourse*:
    1. *Individual*: the teacher might assign a literary journal or diary, in which an individual student articulates personal reactions to texts.
    2. *Social*: in an attempt to embody the feelings and aspirations of oneself or a group, a student can write a manifesto or declaration using literary examples.
- *Referential discourse*:
    1. *Exploratory*: a student can offer a tentative diagnosis or definition of or solution to a literary problem; other forms of exploratory discourse might be characterized by a dialogic approach, in which two opposing points of view are presented but not resolved.

Figure 7–2
Elements of Art Criticism

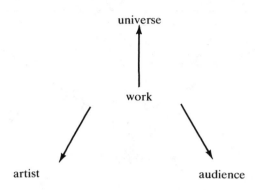

2. *Informative*: summaries, précis, background information on author, historical period.

3. *Scientific*: most traditional "critical" writing would be included in this category, such as explications and literary arguments based on evidence and logic.

- *Literary discourse*: depending on the "aim" of the assignment, a student could be assigned to write his or her own literary text in response to the reading text. Such a composition could be an imitation; a parody; an addition, extension, or revision of the reading text; or simply any original literary product inspired by the reading text.

- *Persuasive discourse*: a student might be assigned to defend/criticize a literary character's actions or attitudes from a legal, moral, or political perspective; or to defend/criticize the book's (or author's) presentation of a controversial issue.

It is clear how different literary responses fulfill different aims of Kinneavy's anatomy of discourse. It is more difficult to relate these various forms of discourse to the principles of traditional literary criticism.

As previously mentioned, Kinneavy's communications triangle is similar to the triangle Abrams uses to define different elements of critical theory. According to Abrams, an aesthetic theory that explains art essentially as an imitation of aspects of reality is "mimetic." Any theory that views art primarily as an expression of the unique sensibility of the artist is called "expressive." When a theory of art emphasizes the intellectual or emotional effect it has on the audience, it is "pragmatic." And when art is analyzed as a self-sufficient entity and judged solely by intrinsic criteria, the theoretical presupposition is "objective" (1953, 8–29).

The correspondences of Abrams's diagram to Kinneavy's coordinate points of encoder, decoder, signal, and reality are obvious enough. Furthermore, both Kinneavy and Abrams maintain that the text itself reveals the predominance of one purpose over another. Yet, Kinneavy (1980) does not discuss the implications of the similarity. One important implication for teachers of literary composition is clear: just as students need to practice a comprehensive variety of discourse types according to their different purposes, they also need to approach literature from a comprehensive variety of theoretical perspectives.

As for the direct application of Abrams's diagram, I suggest that the crucial issue in regard to literary response has to do with when a teacher's writing assignment asks students to identify with the author of the text they are reading and when it asks the students to approach the text as "critics." Because it is my assumption that in many English classrooms students are asked to approach literature primarily as critics, I need to stress James Britton's insight that "critical-expository" purposes are often served by modes of discourse not in themselves "critical-expository" (1984, *vii*).

Furthermore, in presenting examples of writing assignments based on Abrams's four categories of criticism, I want to highlight how both writer-based (expressive and literary) and reader-based (objective and referential) assignments serve similar purposes. Thus, in each of Abrams's theoretical categories, I suggest first an assignment in which the student identifies with the writer and the creative process of the literature under study, and then an assignment in which the student approaches the work as a "critic":

- *Expressive theory*:
  1. By identifying with a goal or problem of an author, students face the same stylistic, structural, and thematic concerns in their own creative writing; hence, the students are able simultaneously to express themselves creatively, to develop writing skills, and to enhance their appreciation of the original text. Charles Moran has written convincingly of his own classroom experiments in his essay "Teaching Writing/Teaching Literature" (1981).
  2. As a critic objectifying the text as a revelation of the author's sensibility, students can analyze the *tone* of the work, where style, structure, diction reveal authorial feelings and attitudes.

- *Pragmatic theory*:
  1. Student are asked to write about their *feelings* toward a character or event; if the students are writing about a developing character or about an evolving event, they could describe and narrate how their feelings changed during the course of reading.
  2. Once the students have articulated their own feelings as responsive readers, they can analyze how and why the author's text appeals to feelings in its audience.
- *Objective theory*:
  1. Students may be asked to write their own text, in which its self-referential image pattern, symbol, theme, or structural device is crucial to the meaning of the text.
  2. In this category, the students would be asked to write the traditional New Critical essay, in which the student are discouraged from relating the text to their own feelings and experiences in the world; rather, the keys to the meaning of the text—symbol, image, theme, structure—are discoverable within the text itself.
- *Mimetic theory*:
  1. The students may be asked to depict a character, a scene, or an event with a "realistic intent"—that is, to communicate an aspect of the world's condition as is, where the index of truth and value exists beyond the text itself. In a longer piece, the students could write an essay or narrative about a social issue, such as racism.
  2. Students can evaluate how "realistically" events, characters, and issues are presented in the novel. Since such a discussion will point out toward the world rather than in toward the text, it is inevitable that students will also be writing "expressively," about their feelings and attitudes toward the natural and social world, rather than about the world itself.

For students, as for professional critics, the categories will rarely remain pure and will always be overlapping to some extent. Yet, the clarification of purposes and theoretical presuppositions in literary response are valuable for both teacher and student. The teacher can change evaluative criteria according to different assignment purposes. Moreover, the student's "subjective" identification with the creative process is a valuable prelude to "objective" appreciation and analysis.

In the context of this dichotomy between "subjective" identification and "objective" appreciation, James Britton's discourse theory is similar to Kinneavy's. Britton's "functions" correspond roughly to Kinneavy's "aims." He posits both "expressive" and "poetic" categories similar to

Figure 7−3
Function Categories of Language

Kinneavy's "expressive" and "literary." However, Britton's theory differs in two respects. First, his system includes a "transactional" function, which is used to "get things done, language as a means" (1982, 107) and which seems to include aspects of both Kinneavy's "persuasive" and "referential" aims. Second, as classified by David Foster in *A Primer for Writing Teachers*, Kinneavy's system is textual whereas Britton's theory is "relational" in that it involves the dynamic interrelationship of speaker, speech, and listener (1983, 47−55). Hence, both the speaker's "intentions" and relationship to what he or she says are more important for Britton. Whereas Kinneavy would find evidence of the "expressive" in the text, Britton defines his "expressive" in terms of the writer: it is "language close to the self" (Britton 1982, 106), "utterance at its most relaxed and intimate, as free as possible from outside demands, whether those of task or audience" (Britton 1975, 82).

Britton (1975, 81) depicts his functions of language as a sliding scale with the "expressive" at its center moving either toward the "transactional" or the "poetic" functions (see Figure 7−3). Underlying Britton's threefold division of function categories is his theory of language roles. In the transactional function, we use language in the role of "participant." In the poetic function, we use language in the role of "spectator." (The expressive function can move toward either pole.) Britton defines these roles as follows:

> When we use language to recount or recreate real or imagined experience for no other reason than to enjoy it or present it for enjoyment, we are using language in the role of spectator; when we use language to get things done, we are in the role of participants (participants in "the world's affairs"). The latter role includes the use of language to recount or recreate real or imagined experience in order to inform or teach or to make plans or solicit help or to achieve any other practical purpose (1975, 91−92).

Especially relevant to literary response in these role definitions is Britton's concept of "contextualization" (1982, 107−8). Because language in the role of participant is less concerned with its formal construct than the desire to achieve an end, the reader is at liberty to contextualize what he or she finds relevant, selectively. For instance, the reader of *Moby Dick* may be interested primarily in how to harpoon a whale. But because language in the role of spectator is concerned with the creation of meaning as a verbal artifact, a formal construct, the reader resists piecemeal contextualization and engages in what Britton calls *global* contextualization. After contemplating *Moby Dick* as a poetic construct, the reader's worldview may be changed.

Teachers of literature want their students to *read* and appreciate literature in the role of spectator for "one is somehow able to savor feeling *as feeling* in a spectator role in a way one isn't able to savor it in a participant role" (Britton 1982, 105). However, too often students of literature are asked to write exclusively or primarily in the role of participants—that is, to write expository compositions intended to inform, instruct, persuade their audience. Hence, a gap exists between the reading process, engaging a text on the poetic level, and the writing act, engaging the audience of their essay on a transactional level. Expository writing of this kind does not reflect the reader's gradual process of emotional and intellectual discovery, his or her creative interaction with the text; rather, it effectively asks the reader to communicate a meaning already determined.

In this regard, it is important to consider the central place of the expressive function on Britton's scale. This "writing close to the self" is able to move freely from one role to another. For the purposes of specific applications to curriculum, one is tempted to move sequentially out from the expressive. In "Literature and Exploratory Writing," Karen Pelz describes her own original experiments with such a sequence. Pelz's sequence moves along the expressive-to-transactional line; it "begins with the particular (personal experience) and moves to the general (the world of ideas)" (1984, 61). Teaching *Walden*, Pelz begins a series of assignments by asking her students to write expressively about a natural place they have experienced; she ends the series by asking students to address Thoreau's use of figurative language and to discuss literary concepts such as symbolism. Though Pelz applies aspects of Britton's discourse theory brilliantly, her sequence does not directly address the expressive-to-poetic spectrum of his conceptual framework. It is this end of the scale that Britton believes has been dangerously neglected in the classroom.

I propose another sequential application of Britton's theories to literary response. Instead of moving from the particular to the general, or from the personal to the abstract in linear progression, writing assignments could also be categorized by their "quality of experience." That is, Susanne Langer has termed art a "virtual experience" to distinguish it from firsthand experience (1953, 215); likewise Britton (1982, 102–10, 208–11) has demonstrated how literature can be responded to from both the "participant" and "spectator" perspectives. It is natural and legitimate that we sometimes read literature as "participants": we react to and make judgments about characters and events *as if* we were experiencing them firsthand. Thus, I suggest a sequence of assignments that begins with "real-life experience" (mostly expressive), moves to "virtual experience" (where the discourse can shift between roles of participant and spectator), and culminates with "literary experience" (mostly transactional).

Following Britton's conceptual model, this is a relative and horizontal movement, not a progressively hierarchical one (as is the curricular sequencing of James Moffett in *Teaching the Universe of Discourse*). Though it comes last in the sequence, transactional-expository writing about literary experience is not necessarily "higher" — nor is it more complex, highly evolved, or important — than poetic narrative writing about personal experience. The experience written about and the written product are merely categorized according to different qualities of experience. Britton does not conceive of development in relation to modes but sees the expressive function as the matrix from which differentiated forms of mature writing are developed (1975, 83). Whereas in terms of my own (and Pelz's) sequence for literary response, it is probably more effective to begin writing expressively about "real-life experience" in order to make writing about "literary experience" more natural, such sequencing does not imply judgments about the value of these qualitatively different experiences.

The following series of assignments illustrates how my sequential concept might be applied to a reading of *Wuthering Heights*. Each category (theme, characterization, image) contains three possible assignments relating to qualities of experience: "real-life experience," "virtual real-life experience," and "literary experience."

- *Theme*:
    1. Write about an instance of class conflict or classism in your own life.
    2. Defend or attack Cathy's marriage decision as classist. (Cathy is written about as if she were a volitional real-life person.)
    3. Write about some aspect of Brontë's view of class conflict in the novel. (Cathy and Heathcliff are discussed as literary creations.)
- *Characterization*:
    1. Write about someone you know (or yourself) who has experienced problems similar to Heathcliff's.

2. Rewrite or invent a scene in the novel from Heathcliff's point of view; compare/contrast Nelly's and Cathy's view of Heathcliff.

3. Write about Brontë's view of Heathcliff's character development.

- *Image/symbol*:

1. Write about how some aspect of the physical environment affects your behavior.

2. Write about how some aspect of the physical environment plays a crucial role in the action of the story. (The environment in the novel is discussed as if it were real.)

3. Write about how Brontë uses images of the physical environment symbolically in the novel.

Though the above sequence is based on different qualitative experiences, the assignments can be revised to serve both writer-based and reader-based purposes (as discussed in relation to Kinneavy and Abrams) — that is, writing in the role of both spectator and participant (as discussed in relation to Britton).

I believe that creative, and especially narrative, writing assignments can serve critical-expository purposes. If effective, these kinds of writing assignments help bridge the gap between the process of discovery in reading and writing — what Ann Berthoff has referred to as "the making of meaning" (1981) — and the attempt to communicate meaning as if it were a predetermined product. Narrative holds undiscovered potential as a mode for the presentation of process in literary response.

One of the most illuminating moments in my continuing education occurred several years ago in the seminar classroom of the poetry critic Helen Vendler. Though she had proven herself capable of overwhelming the class with brilliant exegeses of the poems, she occasionally took a different tack. On one occasion in particular, I remember her explaining how she came to certain conclusions about the meaning of a sonnet. In short, she gave us a chronicle of her own misreadings, rereadings, and reinterpretations of the text. Such a demonstration taught me more about how to approach a poem than any of the same teacher's finished essays, in which the process of her discovery could only be imagined. Students in introductory literature courses could derive a crucial benefit from similar pedagogical techniques and from writing assignments that emphasize meaning as a process of "what we half create/and what we perceive" (Wordsworth 1977, 360) in reading literary texts. Furthermore, as Susanne Langer suggests, because intellect may be just a higher form of feeling, the evolution of the reader's feelings in reading and rereading a text is essential to any eventual intellectual judgment, moral or aesthetic, by the reader (1967, 149). Thus, I suggest three kinds of assignments, basically narrative, to reflect the process of "the making of meaning":

- *A chronicle of rereadings*: Working in a notebook, write a spontaneous critical reaction to a poem or short story (it may be focused on any element of the poem or story, such as character, theme, image, place); repeat the exercise on successive nights; write a story or chronicle of your rereadings, noting changes, mistakes, discoveries in the process.

- *Personal narrative about literary experience*: Tell a story about how a literary experience changed your perceptions or attitude about something.

- *The evolution of feeling*: Working from a notebook, make entries expressing your feelings toward a character, an issue, an event, or a place as you read on in the novel. When you have finished the novel, reread the entries and write a chronicle of how your feelings changed. This assignment is a natural prelude to an expository essay on character development.

A final word also needs to be said about how creative writing assignments (Kinneavy's "literary" and Britton's "poetic") can serve the manifold aims of literary response. When students enter the interstices of a text — by reimagining a scene, inventing a new stanza, speaking through the point of view of a character — they must use a number of faculties simultaneously to accomplish several interrelated purposes. In order for their compositions to cohere thematically or aesthetically, they must understand what the author has already written: they are readers and explicators. Furthermore, by acting as collaborative authors, they must tap their own expressive and imaginative potential. Finally, by revising or extending the text, the students are making critical judgments upon it. Hence, this kind of assignment helps bridge the gap between the process of creative reading (the collaborative "making of meaning"), where the text is an open-ended series of creative choices, and the culminative critical act, where the text is a static repository of meanings waiting to be discovered and communicated.

Though the discourse theories of Kinneavy and Britton highlight the narrow range of much literary response writing, in applying these theories I do not mean to question the value of the conventional expository essay but rather to put it in clearer perspective with other aims of literary response writing. These discourse theories ask us as English teachers to give equal attention to the various aims of discourse, all of which are valuable. These theories further enable us to break out of the increasingly hermetic and self-referential world of "literature" and literary writing. The debate between the teachers of composition and the teachers of literature about respective goals has been aroused by a false dichotomy. Literary experience can and should be valued for itself, but it can also serve well as a natural starting point for teaching writing across all the aims of discourse.

Works Cited

Abrams, M. H. 1953. *The Mirror and the Lamp*. New York: Oxford University Press.

Berthoff, Ann E. 1981. *The Making of Meaning*. Portsmouth, N.H.: Boynton/Cook.

Britton, James. 1970. *Language and Learning*. Middlesex, England: Penguin.

——. 1982. *Prospect and Retrospect: Selected Essays of James Britton*. Ed. G. M. Pradl. Portsmouth, N.H.: Boynton/Cook.

——. 1984. Foreword to *Courses for Change in Writing*. Ed. C. H. Klaus and N. Jones. Portsmouth, N.H.: Boynton/Cook.

Britton, James, et al. 1975. *The Development of Writing Abilities (11–18)*. London: Macmillan.

Eagleton, Terry. 1983. *Literary Theory*. Minneapolis: University of Minnesota Press.

Foster, David. 1983. *A Primer for Writing Teachers*. Portsmouth, N.H.: Boynton/Cook.

Kinneavy, James L. [1971] 1980. *A Theory of Discourse*. Reprint. New York: Norton.

Langer, Susanne K. 1953. *Feeling and Form*. London: Routledge & Kegan Paul.

——. 1967. *Mind: An Essay on Human Feeling*. Vol. 1. Baltimore: Johns Hopkins Press.

Lawrence, D. H. 1964. *Studies in Classic American Literature*. New York: Viking Press.

Moffett, James. 1968. *Teaching the Universe of Discourse*. Boston: Houghton Mifflin.

Moran, Charles. 1981. "Teaching Writing/Teaching Literature." *College Composition and Communication* (February): 21–29.

Pelz, Karen. 1984. "Literature and Exploratory Writing." In *Courses for Change in Writing*, ed. C. H. Klaus and N. Jones, 59–66. Portsmouth, N.H.: Boynton/Cook.

Wordsworth, William. 1977. *The Poems*. Ed. J. O. Hayden. New Haven: Yale University Press.

8

Exhausted Student Writing Exhausted Haiku
Introducing Literary Analysis to High-School Students

Carole Braverman

They say that for ex-smokers, the critical point of recidivism is coffee in a good restaurant or a divorce. For me, who can afford those temptations only rarely, it was my innocent perusal, when I started teaching high school English in 1979, of my first stack of essays in literary analysis. I picked them up with a short-lived casualness that now corresponds in my memory to Laius's visit to Delphi after the birth of his son. These essays were, in fact, about *Oedipus Rex*, and class discussion, to my delight, had been going great. After several minutes of puzzled reading, however, I began tapping the side of my head with my palm, the self-dramatizing gesture I've picked up from sitcom characters in confusion who want to make public their need to realign their brain. The sentences for the most part weren't ungrammatical; I recognized the words and most of the syntax; the language was clearly English. That so much of it didn't make sense made me feel as if I had momentarily lost my mind or happened late in life on a latent but profound dyslexia. The new challenges that literary analysis presents to high school students — formulating, expressing, and connecting abstract ideas — were skills I learned gradually, and my compassion (for myself as well as them) encouraged me to experiment with a variety of helpful suggestions on the problem of convoluted prose and ideas. But amid the considerable joys of the teaching profession—a class discussion so unexpectedly exciting it startles us into community, kids who climb through windows bearing gifts of driftwood or lunch remains, students who considerately make their breath-taking discoveries of literature or self while I am their teacher—evaluating and grading their essays in literary analysis have remained, for me, the yeoman's work of teaching.

I have tried (and continue to use) lessons that emphasize form and structure: thesis and topic sentences, one central idea per paragraph, concrete examples, transitions, precise and lively verbs and adjectives. I have mixed analytic assignments with journal writing (which invites dialogue rather than evaluation and has proved very valuable in their exploration of feelings and ideas in a nonpressured and nonjudgmental space). I have included more formal subjective responses (those that also explore the relationship between literature and their own experience and values, but where the stimulus is more specific, more closely tied to the text, and the response more vulnerable to my "alerts" about vague or lazy writing). I have developed creative exercises (the most successful of which not only free their imagination and playfulness but give hands-on experience with form and theme). And I have managed, with hit-and-miss results, to personalize interpretation.

An assignment that has successfully combined their articulation of personal values and feelings with a critical interpretation of text is the following: "Write a personal letter to the blind Oedipus as he leaves Thebes tapping the world with his cane. What are your feelings about his present condition and the choices that precipitated it? Were his actions wise? What has been gained and lost by his decision—for him, for his community, for you? Be honest (he's no hothouse flower when it comes to the truth), but give your feelings credibility by showing him you are no casual writer of condolence notes but a person well acquainted with the relevant details of his story." A creative exercise that has worked well with this play (and travels well to others) is to ask students to write a missing scene from it (anything in myth that either precedes the point where Sophocles picks up the story, or occurs offstage), using the style and dramatic conventions of Greek theater. They then present the scenes in chronological order in their own Greek theater festival.

While the hard-core stuff of "critical argument" still gives me intermittent attacks of desk phobia—the dread of even getting near the place where their essays are piled for marking—I still believe in the value of its goals, repeating them to myself from time to time like a long-winded mantra: to help them understand how a work is put together, the relationship of form and content; to help them clarify, sharpen, and organize ideas; to clarify the distinction between personal feelings and perceptive interpretation by testing their responses against the author's intent; to empower them with a precise and lively vocabulary for talking about literature; to develop skills of argument and persuasion; to encourage the view of literary criticism as a creative form in its own right, one that requires as original a voice as the writing of personal essays or short stories.

Helping students to analyze an author's vision of the world, and then to test that vision against their own values and experiences is another important objective for me in teaching literature. I've found John Updike's short story "A & P" (1989) very helpful in introducing students to this dual perspective. Sammy, the first-person narrator of the story, quits his job at the store after the manager publicly embarrasses three girls who were shopping in bathing suits. A vigorous class debate is inevitably triggered between those who think the gesture is heroic, an instinctive inclination on Sammy's part to be true to himself and his values, and those who think his action is immature, self-righteous, overly dramatic, and self-serving. I then ask them to write an essay that focuses on what Updike feels about Sammy's decision. They must detach themselves from their own values and responses, referring to the text to support their conclusions. What they choose to look at in the story to formulate their conclusions, as well as what they overlook, leads to rich, lively discussions on discovering the author's point of view, particularly in first-person narrative.

Along with the incantations and the healthy mixture of writing assignments, the frequent sharing among my colleagues of approaches that work well has proved effective in warding off desk phobia. In that spirit, I share one approach with you that I like a lot: an introduction to poetry for tenth graders that combines the writing of poems with the writing about them. My description of the process is oriented toward practical implementation — the classroom discussion that provides the context for the writing assignments, their progression, my handouts and the variety of ways students respond to them (my thanks to the students whose examples I use in this essay), suggestions for pacing, personal preferences for handling workshop edits, and specific and overall goals.

In the last term of their tenth-grade year, our students take a literature course focusing on poems and short stories. When the focus of the course shifts from fiction to poetry, some of my students brace themselves for boredom and incomprehensibility. On a list asking them to brainstorm the question "How do you tell the difference between a story and a poem?" the observation "it's harder to understand" appears frequently, second only to "it looks different on the page." Starting with a poem's visual impact as the most agreed upon and obvious difference, I ask them to "find a poem" (this exercise was suggested to me by a former colleague, Mike Lopes, and I thank him for it). They find a short piece of prose from anywhere — textbooks, newspaper articles, advertisements, classified ads, course descriptions, dorm rules, a letter from a friend — and experiment with rearranging the lines into something that *looks* like poetry, selecting the rearrangement they like best to share with the class. They then get together in small groups to choose from the masquerading poems the ones that best "pass." The whole class then reconvenes to discuss the selections and the effects the line manipulations have had on prose copy. The following "poem" was adapted from a newspaper article about the Alaska oil spill in 1989:

> It has been compared with Hiroshima
> and Chernobyl
> but the Exxon Valdez may prove to be
> the Good Ship Lollipop
> for thousands of
> jobless workers
> lawyers
> environmental consultants
> boat captains
> and
> company representatives
> flocking to the disaster scene,
> hoping to cash in on
> the
> most
> expensive
> oil
> cleanup
> in history.

The following lines are a rearrangement of an advertisement for a deodorant:

> Be confident with Sure Wide solid.
> Sure's Special Formula
> Glides on dry
> Helps keep you dry
> Provides all day protection
> Sure's wide package
> Fits comfortably in your hand
> Takes just a few strokes to apply.

How has the student adapter of each piece, by isolating the words, affected the emphasis of the idea, forced us to pause, savor, speed up? Are the rearrangements arbitrary, or has the imposed emphasis deliberately affected tone and point of view? What lines, inherent in the prose itself, have helped it "pass" as poetry? Why are rhythm, rhyme, repetition, assonance, alliteration used particularly heavily in advertising copy?

Most of my students, in response to the question "Is it poetry yet?" still don't think most of the pieces really "pass." Though they're not sure why, at least initially, their instincts usually escalate into insights once discussion gets rolling: "It just wants to sell me deodorant"; "It's not true"; "It just has something to say, but it doesn't say it in an interesting way"; "It doesn't spill over into anything"; "It doesn't stay with you"; "It doesn't touch my emotions."

The first "real poems" we read are Japanese haiku. Sensual, intensely compact, formal in structure, short, they serve as effective models when, later in the week, I ask students to write their own poems and give them only one night to do it. The variety of personal expression achieved in so tight a form also bears good witness to the generosity, efficiency, and sheer "mileage" of words and images, that magnificent discrepancy in poetry between size and resonance — how little need be said, if said well, to evoke how much is meant. Also, if poetry is what is "lost in translation," translation is a good place to begin, especially if you can provide students with a few different translations for the Japanese original. Here are two translations of a poem by Matsuo Bashō (1644–1694). The one on the left is by Earl Miner, the one on the right by Bobette Deutsch (Perrine 1977, 228).

The lightning flashes!	A lightning gleam
And slashing through the darkness,	into the darkness travels:
A night-heron's screech.	a night heron screams.

Disagreements about which translator took a better crack at it yield lively discussion. When opinions are challenged by classmates who don't share them, vague, prepackaged explanations — "It sounds better"; "It flows better"; "It's vivid" — sharpen into more honest and precise observations: "*Slashes* is a better verb than *travels*, it makes you hear what the poet hears"; "It connects better with the visual abruptness of flashes"; "Heron's don't scream, they screech"; "What the poet wants you to experience is the quickness, the fleetingness"; "But he's talking about the afterglow of lightning, you're not supposed to see the heron, only hear it after it disappears in darkness"; "The second keeps the end rhyme"; "The first keeps the syllable count."

We talk about similarities among all the poems — the form, the sharp brief images, the appeal to the senses, the reflective resonance, the natural setting. We imagine what haiku might look like if written by Eskimos or Bedouins or stockbrokers. I then hand out haiku written by former Andover students and ask the class to read through them, choose their favorites, make notes on those they think might have been written by the same poet, and explain why. The goal is to increase and sharpen their vocabulary for talking about poetry before they start writing about it. The selections in the handout are a deliberate mix—in quality, style, setting, tone.

Students' responses the next day are lively and fun. They try to detect gender, temperament, the triggering stimulus of the image. Did the poet see something, hear something, taste something, remember something, fudge it five minutes before class? Are the images conventional, fresh, weird? Even generally reclusive students are instigated into opinion. Connections and contrasts between poems are protean in their realignments: the playful and the solemn, the realistic and the romantic, the literal and the figurative; those that appeal to the senses and those that reflect on inner life; those that use poetical devices (rhyme, onomatopoeia, personification) and those that read like prose; those with hidden metaphors and those that wear them on their sleeve; grotesque images and mundane ones; the violent and the pastoral; the immediate, identifiable world of petty grievances and the idealized images of nature; the observant and the introspective; the predictable and the surprising; the visual close-up, the medium shot, the long shot.

Once the discussion has established a fairly lush vocabulary for describing their responses, I ask students to choose one poem and write about it for ten or fifteen minutes. Those who want to, read their responses aloud, and the class comments. While the verbal liveliness of the dialogue doesn't always transfer to paper at this point, vague and lazy responses ("the poem is vivid," "it has a definite style," "it's flawless and beautiful") are fewer because such remarks have already been challenged by their peers in discussion.

Having to write quickly has its disadvantages—it short-circuits critical judgment and the resonance of considered reflection. But it also usually short-circuits pretentious and convoluted prose, encouraging playfulness and spontaneity. It sometimes also produces deliciously far-fetched explications—especially in response to poems that are symbolic or rich in connotation—but our unpersuaded laughter usually becomes an excellent object lesson in balancing spontaneity with textual awareness. Responses are also often imaginative, witty, vibrant, and written with a natural voice, lending credibility to one of my primary objectives: that they experience literary analysis as a creative form. The "why" as well as the "how" of literary analysis—its power to illuminate a text, the collaborative nature of reading, the way our voices can bring the page to life—have also, though more rarely, been an experience in this exercise. On one handout there was this haiku:

> Blue, I asked for blue
> I needed to taste blue
> I got red instead.

It had only one admirer, but his lonely and empathetic defense of the underappreciated poem was so insightful, it deepened the understanding of it for many in the class, including me.

> In this haiku, the poet seems to be whining or complaining about the fact that he did not get what he wanted. . . . The double use of "blue" illustrates this whining because it sounds as if he is demanding something. "I asked for blue, I needed . . . blue." In this haiku, the stressful conditions are hinted at through the use of connotative words. When he uses the word blue, as in "I asked for blue," it seems as if he wants to get away from anxiety (probably caused by school worries), because blue has a cool, soft, mellow connotation. In the second line, the fact that he "needed to taste blue" might mean that he wants peace from a stressful world, and to get away from the "red." The "red" in the third line contrasts the "blue," and this red connotes anger, frustration, friction, and heat, in a figurative sense of the word, and overall, stress caused by teenage life.

Because I don't have a great ear for work I haven't read yet, many of the kids have a better knack for extemporaneous commentary than I do, so I usually butt out at this point, preferring to defer my own input until I've read their work and organized my thoughts on what I want to target. I'll then type up examples from their written work focused on particular problems and particular successes. Negative examples are a valuable teaching tool; "wordiness," "convoluted prose," "lack of specific example" are continually waved before them like ropes of garlic. But they are never selected from a student in the class where they're discussed, unless they are burying something wonderful.

After their first stab at writing a response to a student haiku, students are asked to write five of their own for homework. When they bring them into class, I have them copy them over on a sheet without their names, then distribute these randomly to the class. Each student chooses three from the "body of work" of the anonymous writer and writes a critique. They're asked first to regard the three poems as a whole, developing conclusions about their resemblance to each other (or lack of it) — reoccurring themes, stylistic patterns, quirks, moods, settings — and then to analyze each one in detail. (There's a certain amount of luck of the draw in this process: that some kids have more to work with than others is one of the drawbacks of the assignment.) Their rough-draft group-editing session deliberately separates critic from poet, who are then paired up on the day they hand in their final drafts. The poets add their own responses in writing to the evaluation of their work, but there's also a lot of informal giggling and shouting across the room while they're reading. While there are occasionally defensive murmurings and marginal scribbles detailing the annoyance at being misunderstood, in general they love reading about their own creative process, ranking this assignment (in the end-of-the-term evaluations of the course) high on the list of ones I should keep. It lends stature to their work, validity to private feelings, a sense of power and delight at the shocks of recognition and the pleasures of being understood, sometimes better than they've understood themselves.

> Charles' interpretations were really cool. Sure, I made up the haikus and all, but I didn't really think about them, having them analyzed is a new feeling. I especially liked his view of the Nuke one (which I put in purely as a joke). I never thought of the person being a politician. But I like that interpretation a lot. I think Charlie did really well and came pretty much on the mark for all three haiku.

One girl in my class last year had an impressive gift for metaphor. Anything she composed — whether exposition, narration, description, analysis, or even research — overflowed with comparisons that were startling and original, usually magnificently apt, occasionally obscure. When she wrote her haiku, she was hesitant to turn them in, because the images, rich and evocative, were a little frightening and impenetrable, puzzling even to her. Here are three examples:

> Grass green with the life
> On a hill, the slope goes deep
> a pile of shit speaks

> Thin, ruddy black skin
> Caverns hills swampy fog folded
> in veins of ruddy blood

> Strong supports held up
> escaped beaming smiler
> Teeth striding the dark

This is an excerpt from a classmate's extended evaluation of these poems:

> Grass green with the life ... is at first pleasant ... making the reader feel warm, carefree, happy, and soothed. ... But the second line begins the shift of emotions. ... The "slope goes deep" arouses suspicion because it disrupts the peaceful setting ... to create a falling mood. ... The "pile of shit speak[ing]," quite unexpected in a poem about green grass, completes the shift and accurately conveys the meaning — this is not a neat, orderly stack of shit, or a small dump, but a pile; no other word could fit ... or give the feeling of sudden disgust "shit speaks" so easily gives.
>   [In the second haiku] the image one first sees is of a person with "thin, ruddy, black skin," but then, it seems that the first line is a metaphor of the "caverns" and "hills" mentioned next. The reddish color of the caverns and hills is compared to a thin layer of skin, and

really lets me visualize the scene, because the color seems almost tangible . . . even the fog being blown around has the same reddish tint. By using "ruddy" in both lines, the poet is taking two different scenes . . . and linking them by color. . . .

The third haiku is the most mysterious. The first line is odd because "held up" rather than "holds up" . . . denotes that the supports are being held up rather than doing the supporting . . . and makes one wonder if something happened to the "strong supports" that usually connote so much security. Another curiosity is the implication of a man-made structure, rather than the objects of nature in the other two poems. The second line may first strike one as humorous because of the (possibly unintended) pun of "beaming," with "strong supports." The image conjured up by this line may be of someone who is proud to have escaped from something so secure. This image is continued into the third line, in which you can only see the teeth of this "smiler." The use of the word "dark" links with "escaped," and they both contradict the sense of security in the "strong supports" of the first line. "Striding" is very descriptive, yet unusual to describe teeth. This personification works to sharpen the picture of the smiler, who is smug in his escape. . . .

The link between these three poems that seems to define the poet's style is her use of mysterious, startling images . . . that catch her reader off guard. She chooses her words carefully, so that they all seem necessary. None of these poems could be read as a sentence, which makes them very enjoyable to the reader who likes bizarre poems ending with a twist.

This is an excerpt from the writer's reaction to her classmate's analysis:

This evaluation, especially on the second poem, brings out new meanings for me. The ways I wrote it signified a personal feeling of myself, my race, my family. Yet in this evaluated version, images that I shut out in my narrowmindedness were presented. Thank you for your fresh analysis and for opening my views.

The writer of the essay, reading this response to her critique, experienced personally the power of sensitive interpretation.

As suggested earlier, the dialogue between poet and critic is occasionally less appreciative, making the interchange different, but not without value. One critic found a classmate's haiku full of "oppressively trite phrasing. . . . a morass of weak, overused phrases and images . . . that I had to slog through, and if I wasn't writing this paper, I wouldn't have bothered to do it." He singled out particular offenses:

The worst problem was "My life flashes before me." Not only is it not the author's image by any stretch of the imagination, it's one that wouldn't even have occurred to him if there weren't ten generations of authors who say that's what happens when you die. And although there are only so many concepts of death, "darkness and silence" isn't one of the more original ones either.

He later tempered his remarks somewhat: "The second poem is a much better piece. I've heard 'waiting for death' before, but the line 'His gaunt look horrified me' is very immediate and visual and does convey a horror to the reader." Nonetheless, the essay heated the poet into a passionate defense of his intent. He used up all the margin space (wholesomely curbing my own excesses in that narrow area of commentary) and still had plenty of explanation left over for a final "coup de grace" summation:

> I used these phrases because they were direct, blunt, conveyed the meaning I intended. ... This is my view of death. It is nothingness. They may not be eloquent or beautiful, but they are flatly abrupt. This abruptness captures for me the essence of death.

While the defense of his own choices here is not totally separated from defensiveness (who likes to hear that what they've written strikes others as trite or cliché-ridden?), the author of the poems was moved to reassess, to clarify his purpose and intent. The necessity of pointing out clichés and prefabricated writing to students is one of my least favorite responsibilities. When classmates themselves do it, it has the virtue of being both easier to accept *or* reject, to see where writing has not communicated effectively to another person, to consider the reasons, and then, in revision, to rely on one's own judgment.

I have found the progression of this exercise — students talking about poems, writing quickly about them, writing some themselves, analyzing each others' work, and then responding to critiques — one of the most effective introductions to writing about poetry I've ever used. It has an immediacy, a sense of personal contact, and follow-through that really engage students. When I return final drafts, they maintain an interest in the destiny of their classmates' essays that extends beyond the usual "What did you get?" It also encourages an original voice. The results are often playful and fun to read, as well as perceptive and detailed. The experience gives credibility to the point and effectiveness of literary criticism at its best, a credibility that motivates students to take on the challenges of more complex tasks.

Works Cited

Perrine, Laurence, ed. 1977. *Sound and Sense: An Introduction to Poetry*. 5th ed. San Diego, Calif: Harcourt Brace Jovanovitch.

Updike, John. 1989. "A & P." In *The Norton Anthology of Short Fiction*, ed. R. V. Cassill. New York: Norton.

9

Making It Yours

Thylias Moss

Part 1: Possessiveness as Virtue

In the case of love, the rule is to avoid possessiveness, but as deeply in love with something other than her own words as the writer may be, engagement with the writing process means quitting that other lover until the pen runs dry or available disk space is used up. Be possessive when you write or run the risk of dishonoring writing's short bible that consists of one commandment set down by perhaps the most famous writer of all: "To thine ownself be true."

This endorsement of possessiveness is not without assumptions, one of which is that your purpose in writing is to express your ideas and opinions as opposed to the ideas of someone else. Actually, good as that purpose is, it alone is irrelevant unless a presupposition about your relationship to your ideas is true: namely that you respect your own opinions and ideas enough to take them seriously. After all, there's no substantial reason to possess flimsy, watery ideas that you're eager to purge from a mind obese with trivia that cannot be made significant. Be possessive if what you're being possessive about has meaning, which is to say, can make a lasting contribution.

Perhaps the second best reason to make an idea yours is that you're less likely to lose interest in a personal belonging that has value to you, which is to say, that makes a lasting contribution to you. If the idea is just a motel you've checked into for one class period, you've little incentive to take that idea to its limits or anywhere else. On the other hand, if you give birth to it, and if that baby looks like you (meaning you've possessed it so thoroughly even an exorcism can't separate you), then you'll likely be more willing to love it even when it spits up on you, more willing to sit with it through a colicky night, more willing to wipe its behind, to praise its smallest accomplishment as if nothing greater has yet occurred in the world.

Consider the rather bleak consequences of failing to possess; a teacher offers a passage of prose touted as being an example of great writing, something you wouldn't be bad off emulating, maybe even the source passage of that first-paragraph quote. The goal, that teacher might imply, is to write like that rather than, improve upon the way you express yourself. I hope that no one ever tries to write like me; they aren't me; leave my writing style alone. Get your own. Oh sure, study what I did, even speculate about why you think I did what I did so that you derive some idea of the possible relationship between a writing style and the life/personality of the writer. Learn to discuss the structure of my essay, my poem, my story so that you can learn to discuss your own, so that you can better look at your own writing and understand what you did. Just don't try to mold your experience, your voice into mine. Don't try to figure out how I would say what you have to say, but do learn from how I manipulate words, how meaning is affected by language, sequence, syntax. You are not me; why then should you write like me? If you cannot exist without writing like someone else, then be sure you pay that someone else royalties. If you can prove in a court of law that you are me, then feel free to go ahead and write like me, even type my name in the byline; but without such legal precedent, leave my writing to me; I don't need that kind of help. Don't misunderstand; the world could use more observation from other points of view, more trying on of someone else's shoes — especially when those shoes are moccasins like mine — but putting on those shoes does not change your identity; as yourself, you gain new and powerful perspective, but you must write of these gains as just that, not as if you actually are the person. Write of the insights those shoes brought to you. Thus, you are not restricted to writing *about* yourself, just *as* yourself, as the authority on what you learned by trying on these shoes. Create whatever character or persona you want as the vehicle for these ideas, but the ideas *must* be yours, not someone else's.

That distinction between writing *as* yourself and *about* yourself cannot be overemphasized. So many would-have-been writers succumbed to that killer notion *write about what you know*, because these victims knew that they didn't know anything but couldn't live with the embarrassment of writing about their lack of smarts. One problem with that write-what-you-know rule is that it implies that knowing is finite, that you know all you're going to know. Write about what you now know, not about what you learn. And at what point does learned information become knowledge anyway? When does casual acquaintance become knowing? Contained in writing-as-yourself is the instruction to try on new perspectives, to "learn". Quite simply, if you encounter a teacher who insists you write exclusively about what you know, then run try on some shoes — assuming you don't already know much — and get yourself some knowledge to possess.

It would be unfair for me to continue without explaining just how it is that possessiveness and I became so close. The root of this relationship probably is in a pair of patent leather shoes worn only on Sundays, shoes that for fifty-two (more if I hadn't outgrown them) weeks were Vaselined and larded to newness. Not having much equity, much that would make decent collateral, made me value each object that I could call mine without having to share it with others in my family, others in my community, others anywhere in the world. Every time I breathed, I was aware of possessing spoonfuls of air that were entirely mine. My body thrived off the air my body inhaled; no other body could possibly be sustained by my air.

Such feelings gave me the sense of self-worth and self-importance (fine, even necessary as long as that sense of self stops short of arrogance) essential for believing in the value and validity of my own ideas. I was the only expert on what I thought, so if the thoughts were to be accurately revealed, only I could oversee the revelation.

That was the secret right there; once I accorded the status of expert to myself, I wasn't intimidated by the seemingly more learned, more powerful, more legitimate voices. Who was I that my ideas mattered? Where were the earned and honorary degrees affirming the worth of my words? Who died and made me king? But that's the point isn't it; no one made me king; but many died, Africans in my past, Cherokees in my past. Someone in my past was disinherited from a throne, a high place in society. And that disinheritance is fuel burning importance into my voice. What and who I am is something not duplicated in this precise form anywhere else on earth; something supposedly true for everyone, even twins who despite receiving identical genetic gifts do not occupy the same space at the same time so cannot therefore have the same experience. Your fuel may be something else, but don't be afraid to ignite it; don't be afraid of having a fire inside that will burn you up if you don't douse the flame with words. My fingers are torches when I write.

Possessiveness in writing is not without practical advantage; it can help make the grade you receive one that you don't mind. Would that this were a perfect world where student writers were always forced or permitted to develop their own writing topics in individual ways. Most student writers, however, must sometimes write about an assigned topic that is as unappealing as rutabagas. At such times, the student's own disinterest in the topic, rather than anything inherently boring in the topic, causes frustration, pushes the fledgling writer into a hatred of what could prove to be salvation. You must be able to transform any topic into one that empowers your voice and ideas; you must take possession of it, sculpt it into a replica of yourself.

Rutabagas, for instance, are something I probably could not recognize in a store out to trick me with deceptive labels in the produce section. I recall being served a rhubarb and strawberry pie at the house of someone trying to be my friend, and I was grateful that rutabagas weren't also under the crust, though considering my dislike of the pie, rutabagas may well have been under that crust indeed. I trusted the would-be friend as she rattled off the ingredients that if rutabagas were there she would have told me; she was that kind of woman, one unable to keep secrets for moral reasons that were logical if you listened to them, so I didn't listen whenever she explained because I didn't want to have to give up keeping secrets.

I've never knowingly tasted rutabagas. My prejudice against them certainly must seem like the worse kind. I haven't given them a chance. Maybe I just want something else in this society to know what denied opportunity feels like; so many poor have felt it; so many blacks, Indians, boat people. What's shocking is that I can logically explain my objections to them although I haven't even taken the trouble at least to read about them in an encyclopedia. I know nothing about harvesting them. About their seeds. About their neglect if many reject them as I have. I know my kids do and will. They aren't going to order rutabagas from any menu, and unless it is an ingredient in McDonald's special sauce, they will never taste rutabagas in my lifetime.

The word *rutabaga* itself assaults me; it sounds like something that must scuffle, that scoots around in alleys, accepts whatever is thrown at it, makes few demands upon its environment, fewer upon itself which is its primary environment. It deals mostly in dirt, doesn't it, and seems a pickaninny model, a hambone model, a Southern hurtful denigration migrating North. It's got hundreds of braids on its head, little short patches of hair that look like watermelon seeds. Rutabaga is such a lynchable word that I leave it alone because I can't deal fairly with it; I want it to fight, to cast off this image, but it just shuffles back onto the supermarket shelf where it's sprayed like Civil Rights persisters. Hard to believe that the same man who so wisely advised his readers to be true to themselves also spouted the more ridiculous "A rose by any other name would smell as sweet"—ridiculous because it's all in the rutabaga's name. Greenberg knew what it meant to prune the *berg*. He knew just what he'd lose as well as precisely what he stood to gain. Sure he hacked away at his family tree, but a stump makes a better footstool. Marking the white box on a form rather than the black box is different. And some people in this country still believe that that difference does indeed involve the different ways the races smell, meaning both how the races use their noses, sniffing out business, for instance, and the odor of the races.

Pecola in Toni Morrison's novel *Bluest Eye*, was a rutabaga in a place where no one had acquired a taste for them, where people chewed them up and spit them out. A rutabaga. Something perishable, something on a shelf—because Pecola made herself available, arms outstretched all the time, a scarecrow scaring away those from whom it wants love. Something passed over so many times it struggled to love itself. A rutabaga is its own scarecrow, as is Pecola who scared herself away from herself, out of her rutabaga blackness into a cauliflower whiteness all in her mind. A rutabaga inspired that Temptations song *"Ain't too proud to beg."* And pride is just what a rutabaga needs. It's not proud enough to defend itself from this diatribe. I can say whatever I want without worrying about rutabaga retribution. It won't become angry but will believe my words are justified.

I don't hate the rutabaga; I feel sorry for it. It is what the Dick and Jane books wanted me to be and what Pecola felt comfortable in becoming when she read those books. It is what I could have been had I not had the fortitude of my own voice. Pecola let societal voices and voices from high yellow throats and all-American commercials drown out hers. The rutabaga is what I could have been had I not believed that the space I occupied in the world was sacred. No rutabaga can grow where I stand; there is too much power in the ground beneath my feet. I would lift it up but that would feed my power; no, I will curse it and curse it until it reaches its limit and strikes back realizing it has no other recourse unless it breaks, which it won't want to do because it won't want to depart the earth without having experienced something even remotely like triumph.

Perhaps what I've shared isn't what the teacher wanted, but all the teacher should want is for you to speak clearly and passionately as you say that which is important to you about the topic, no matter the source of that topic. Hence, if I order you to write about doors, you should not complain, but should examine the idea of doors until the idea becomes your idea.

Some offer brainstorming as a means of possession, but brainstorming for me is in the rutabaga category; I don't want any storms in my brain. I want good weather for my thoughts. I don't want my ideas to lose their purpose and direction by having to run away from the heavy rains that will make their straightness kink up. Storms are too potentially destructive. They are not allowed in my brain. If it can rain cats and dogs, why not rutabagas as well? Now how would that be for me, the rutabaga-hater queen, to have clouds pouring out rutabagas in my head? I can't take such chances.

Instead, I ask one two-part question of every topic I must confront: what is important (to me) about whatever and why? With rutabagas, it was important that I didn't eat them, and you should know by now

why I avoid them. Writing for me is simply answering questions. I start
with that basic question of what/why and then deal with the subquestions
that evolve right through revisioning.

Revision too can be an act of possessing; when I revise, I'm trying
to help a piece become more authentic, more accurate in revealing
exactly what I want to say. I use revision to remove the training wheels
from my ideas. Revision is where I stop force-feeding a piece. Not
until I can look into the piece as a mirror (of my idea) do I stop
revising. Revision is where what I hatched leaves the nest and hopefully
flies. I let go and the piece has a life of its own, is subject to all that
can befall a life — the sadnesses, the joys, the successes, the failures —
but if I did a good job raising and nurturing that idea, faith takes over,
and eventually (sometimes after more revision) the piece rises above
rejection, above conflict, and is published.

Part 2: The Lowdown (In Which the Author Assumes the Voice of Her Student and Lets Her Say Her Piece)

To anyone who might be listening, I would like to rebut some of that
"making-it-yours" jive just laid on my mind — and I did say *my* mind. I
do own my mind if not a stitch more than that. Now the primary
objection to that little discourse is that it suggests too much that there
is a need to go forth and possess. Behind that suggestion is the
implication that whatever is already possessed is somehow deficient,
not up to the high standards of someone riding high on the horse,
someone tall in the saddle. And within that implication is a few grams
of discrimination against those of us who are pedestrians. Those of us
with an ongoing personal relationship with the ground. Those with not
only hands-on experience but feet-on experience as well. Those totally
immersed in the life, not high-stepping or trotting on it.

Down here on the ground, we have ways of communicating that
don't rise to the higher altitudes. Our way of being is heavy, a phrase
that is the polite way of saying that pigment has weight, and the more
melanin inhabits your skin, the more cargo you carry around. Now
that melanin obviously, then, is the most precious possession you've
got, because you never set it down or leave it with someone; you don't
even trust it to a bank's safe deposit box; you carry it and never take a
rest from its weight. Two things can happen: either the weight can beat
you down and become your tombstone or you derive strength from
that lifelong weight-training program. Though this rebuttal may seem
heading down a colorful path, color is but the frame for culture; the
ground-level culture itself is colorful — full of curves, relaxed, uncor-
seted, unmanipulated as opposed to the forced straightness of the
other culture, a straightness that molds, shapes, and therefore inhibits

expression when through its language restrictions I must try to be true to a self that doesn't translate directly into that language.

It's like the difference between being harnessed or going braless. The difference between being mass-produced and being original. The advice was always to write as myself, but it is downright doubtful that the author intended to extend the invitation to write that way to certain selves whose natural modes of expression contain some elements the standard would disallow seeing as those elements come from the ground and not the sky, just as some melanin is best described with colors drawn from various types of dirt, and other waits for the sky to send snow before it is named.

At the source of my words is an oral tradition. Our intention is to retain the music, the rhythm of our tradition in our movement, in our speech, and in our writing, which is a visual record of the tradition. I am setting down a musical score without using conventional musical notation. Words instead of quarter notes, treble and bass clefs. This tradition is mine; this tradition is what I must be true to — the alternative is to present a false self, thereby honoring the request of most teachers who would rather not deal with my music cause of its tendency to veer away from the standard rather than towards it. As long as I know that I can sing teacher's tune when (or if) I want to, then I don't worry — neither should teacher. What I want is the option, the permission to choose to present some ideas in my own music. Some topics are better off left in the idiom, better off if don't nobody whitewash them. Take Sojourner Truth's famous "Ain't I a woman?"; now that line would lose all impact had it been passed through the generations as "Am I not a woman?" or even worse, "Am I not a member of the female species?" "Ain't I a woman?" has force, indicates that she wasn't about to take no mess off nobody; look at how pointed the vowels of "ain't" are; how they cut.

Let me put together another example. The destruction of Pecola in Toni Morrison's novel made me cling to the idiom like a religion. I declared myself (there wasn't anybody else to do it) a highest priestess of that religion and swore (the privilege of the highest priestess) that when the assignment arrived to write about the novel, I was not about to shelve the idiom in my mind, but would instead shelve the Queen's English (cause it wasn't Nefertiti whose crown and scepter mattered). Then came the task of dealing with Maureen Peale, the "high yellow dream child," who was a rutabaga for me. Now those kinds of dreams, those American kinds of dreams (some of which used to be called quadroons and octoroons while we darker nightmares were called baboons), are what killed Pecola; you might as well go ahead and say that one of those dreams was her mausoleum (some of which are bigger than those cold-water flats and apartments we have to live in sometimes). She was totally surrounded by that dream; there wasn't no suitable air for that child to breathe. So when the assignment came, I did just what the teacher instructed us to do; I wrote about what I knew, and I knew that Maureen was a house, I knew that when Pecola gave her address, she said, "Maureen Peale"; when she tried to fit any key into any lock, I knew she was trying to open a door to treasure, to a future of beauty, wealth, and prosperity, all of which had a Maureen Peale price tag on it. As a tribute to Pecola (and every nappy head ever called ugly, every flat nose ever called ugly, every wide behind ever called ugly, every thick mouth ever called ugly, every ebony face ever called ugly), I wasn't about to watch my p's and q's, my semicolons and my commas; if black was ever going to be completely and thoroughly beautiful, then more than physical attributes had to be prettified, but the language — the entire way of being, seeing, and doing — had to be devilified as well.

Here is the paper I wrote (Exhibit A):

The Real Estate Value Has Gone Up[1]

Once upon a time, there was this homeless girl named Pecola. Her fairy godmother was good as dead seeing as how she moved to the suburbs where she got paid for her services though those suburbanites was the last ones in need of some services.

Now this is a fairy tale although Pecola was the real thing, made of bone and corpuscle and such, but a lot of folks act as if the homeless don't exist so I had to make Pecola something that everyone could understand. Of course I must admit that something existing that everyone understands is a fairy tale itself. You know, like how just about everybody and his brother understands that this is the land of opportunity and is satisfied with stopping right there at understanding; ain't interested in going no further, say at least to putting understanding into action — because understanding ain't saying nothing until it is put in that place. Just going that little bit of distance could have saved Pecola's life.

In this never-ending search for blue eyes (she wanted them not just for cosmetic and aesthetic purposes, but also for the changes the entire world would undergo when viewed from privileged eyes), Pecola always came across the proverbial no room at the inn aka redlining. Then she happened upon (happened upon because the child plainly had no sense of direction and even if she had had one, she had picked for herself an inappropriate destination, one that would require her to deny herself, to torment her identity, to stop being who and what she was. She had no self to esteem so went looking for one that she knew was worthy cause this girl didn't have no time to make even one mistake); she happened upon an establishment with a vacancy, the Maureen Peale Arms. It was perfect. For a fire escape, it had Rapunzel-length "lynch ropes," wavy and tied at the ends with ribbons that kept coming undone when she sat on them.

Hair so long it smacked her butt when she walked — and that's the closest even in the slaving times that she and her milky kind ever came to a horse whipping. Pecola checked in. She knew nothing bout that caveat "let the buyer beware." She didn't look at the fine print, just at the fine texture of Maureen's hair. Pecola had been miseducated. Prince Charming, Dick and Jane, Snow White. There was no Kettle Black in her books, just in her mirror. Even the Ugly Duckling that she was about to trust and call her ally turned out to be a traitor when it put her down to go about its lily white swan's business. She didn't even realize that the Maureen Peale Arms were so welcoming to her because Pecola was the necessary contrast to lift heightened beauty even higher.

Those better armed, meaning better informed, knew that if Maureen Peale were a house, she'd be a condo smack-dab in the middle of a ghetto. Her electricity bills would be a bitch though; Lord knows it takes a lot of electricity to shine a spotlight 24 hours a day on your brand new aluminum-sided-two-bedroom-three-bath-with-gazebo-in-the-yard. A spotlight that was so *bright*, so *intense*, a passerby could plainly see that the floors were so immaculate you could do more than eat off of them, you could sow, grow, harvest, cook and *then* eat off of them. But you'd have to bring your own food cause her cupboards ain't stocked with no blackeyed peas and ain't no johnny cakes on the stove (just as her face don't give nun, she don't want no part of life to present signs of darkie past). Her cabinets contain boxes upon boxes of Oreo cookies (her efforts at confession) although Vienna fingers are her favorite (cause the outsides are lighter), flour, sugar, rice, instant potatoes (she plays bridge with Mrs. Crocker).

If you do decide to subsist on her staples, and then get sick (the overwhelming whiteness of her food can do a job on you), the bathroom — what I call it; she says all she has is a "powder room" — is just down the hall a piece; mind, you don't step on the new bone-colored carpet with those dirty shoes of yours. She don't have no such a thing as a medicine cabinet cause she ain't got the need nor the desire — why would she? She has no illness — her color and fine sandy ("almost blonde" as she puts it) hair done cured her of all ills. She don't even need space for no bergamots or pressing oils or bleaching creams. All she need is a big mirror, one of those wall-to-wall babies, for she is a living testament that some privileged people don't have to do all of that "wanna-be" nonsense to themselves. Her bathtub (not that she in her purity ever needs to bathe) has no ring around it because dirt don't hardly fall on her skin (though I know it is devil-deep in her hincty ways). If anything, her bathtub got a halo around it and choruses of cherubim and seraphim. Ivory soap. Of course. 99 and 44/100 percent pure — we know just what the rest is.

But my; you should see her bed. It looks like it ain't never been slept in. Maybe cause it hasn't been. She don't sleep; she just lies flat and closes her eyes so she won't have to see no ugly, no tell tale darkness all night, her toes pointing accusingly at her closet as if it's all her clothes fault that she's so perfect.

As the sun goes down, her picture window becomes pictured —
the horizon always looks better glimmering off the surrounding
tenements.

When the time comes to correct this essay (although the teacher
probably wouldn't allow me to label — much as the world likes labeling —
that piece of writing an "essay"), the teacher could have herself or
himself a red-pen field day and return to me what looks like a pre-
schooler's study in red. So much to change, to eradicate, to purge from
my sassy and disrespectful paper. I might even get to hear "sacrilege"
or "blasphemy," words I am not fortunate enough to hear everyday. I
will have made the topic mine, I will have written as myself, but the
teacher will not be satisfied, maybe gently explaining to me that if I
want to make it (she'll say "succeed") in the white (she'll say "this")
world, I have to conform to the standard of excellence. But I insist that
this paper on Pecola must not under any circumstance conform because in
this case, that conformity would be sacrilegious; that conformity would
be blasphemous. Pecola went berserk, died for want of such perpetually
denied conformity. There was no way that girl could assimilate; she
was always going to stick out like a sore thumb and that thumb would
get sorer and sorer as the hammer of abuse and discrimination continued
to fall upon her. She was stuck, hammered into that spot between a
rock and a hard place. But check this out: I would be adamant, I
would take that C or that D; I would not renege on this principle for to
do so would be to reject the very life of me, would be to cast myself
down as a Pecola shadow. There has been too much struggling and
striving since the middle passage for me to turn the clock backwards
just to please a teacher who is narrow. I am wide.

Really, this should not even be written; you should listen to this on
a cassette because all this is oral; it's written down for everyone's
convenience. So try to hear and not just read. Try to get yourself
involved with and dancing to the rhythm of my sentences.

Strictly for the sake of argument, I will present a revised version
(also a deception) of the essay (Exhibit B) in which I follow some of
the teacher's suggestions.

A Meditation in Which Toni Morrison's Maureen Peale Is Considered via the Metaphor of House

Because Pecola sought her identity in someone other than herself,
that person effectively housed her, sheltered Pecola from the harming
effects of both herself and the world. Communication was severed;
Pecola essentially ceased to exist. Hers was an act of self-sacrifice in
which no one was saved, hence no heroism may be awarded to her
act, just tragedy.

Morrison uses sets of polarities to entrap Pecola tragically. Black
vs. white, ugly vs. beautiful, kinky vs. straight, poor vs. rich, dirty vs.

clean. Pecola's inability to view herself in the world as ever crossing the barrier that makes opposites of these pairs may be understood as the fault of Pecola's own eyes. How skillful Morrison was in selecting eyes as the vehicle for her social commentary, for the way in which people are seen, perceived, viewed is responsible for the attitude towards them. This significance of vision being established, Morrison then uses society's racially discriminatory eye as Pecola's mirror, for this is where Pecola looks when she tries to see herself. She sees the same stereotype that they see but in a more exaggerated form, for society's eye is distorted as is a funhouse mirror.

The juxtaposition of Maureen Peale and Pecola allows the reader to define the problem more clearly; while both girls are technically black, Maureen will always enjoy an acceptability and accessibility that Pecola cannot, simply because Maureen more closely approximates white society's view of itself. Maureen is not the opposite of the peaches and cream standard of beauty as is Pecola. That Maureen and Pecola have a friendship, no matter the motives, is easily explained by a scientific law: opposites attract and through that attraction define each other. Since they are opposites, each girl may look at the other and by naming the other know herself to be whatever the other is not. They are the equivalent of the tandem night and day.

Like an insect, Pecola's dark existence craves that lightbulb that she circles, dances for, yet cannot possibly enter. From the lightbulb's perspective, it is worshipped and entirely guiltless, for all it did was exist, was shine in its god-given right and glory. The bug came to it; it did not solicit the bug. Interestingly, however, the bulb does not consider turning itself off or lowering its wattage or extolling and admiring the benefits, privileges of darkness. As long as the bulb is able to shine it will, like the sun, Pecola satellites orbiting, held by a gravity-tight force. The sun does all the living, all the leading, all the controlling. The door is locked. Pecola herself was once the key, but the fascination with that strong light has blinded her; she sees nothing but the flash. Her optic nerves have been burned to uselessness, yet to gaze upon her, her eyes seem to blaze, not with the rage that could lead to a reclaiming of self, but with the cold reflection of the sun's fire. The moon appears white, appears to shine, but it has no light of its own, cannot maintain life anywhere in the universe. It lives in a house constructed of the sun's gravitational tug.

Although possible to view Pecola's housing of herself in Maureen Peale and what she symbolizes as an act of defiance, as an example of the triumph of the human will in that this dejected, rejected, useless-both-to-herself-and-anyone little girl refused to maintain the homeless status assigned her, to do so would be resorting to trick photography, magic and optical illusion. There is no beauty in the image of Pecola ramming a post from Maureen's white picket fence through her heart, killing only her child's body, not the ugliness that fuels the world.

The argument ain't about which one of these exhibits is the better essay; that determination is gon' vary according to subjective whim and according to audience. Exhibit B is meant to be literary, to exist only on a piece of paper, whereas Exhibit A is supposed to be all the way live. Exhibit A is supposed to have more urgency about it, and that urgency comes across in the voice, in the speaker. Now I done made my point that I can write in that other way, but on occasion, my for real mode of expression has to take charge so I can ram the point home. Ain't nothing wrong with Exhibit A — couldn't you read it, couldn't you understand it, can't you see why I insisted that A be allowed to exist because if it didn't, I'd be locking Pecola into a house on top of a house when I'm here to break down the steel doors, open the steel windows, and get some fresh air in there to revive the girl who will never live as long as she has to depend on Maureen Peale by-products. See, I didn't have to make this rebuttal mine; it was mine already. I ain't about to suppress it all the time, pretend all the time like it don't exist just to be acceptable to a society that don't want to accept me, just a darker (within reason) version of itself. It is sho nuff bad enough that I relax and hotcomb my hair just to fish for some compliments and approving eyes from the majority, so in this case, at this time, I ain't budging one inch. If Exhibit A ain't your cup of tea, don't fret none; Exhibit A ain't no cup of tea no how — it's me, and whatever I am, that's what Exhibit A is too.

Note

1. Adapted from an essay by Kirsten Saunders written for Thylias Moss's Competence class, April, 1989, Phillips Academy, Andover, Massachussetts.

10

The Ends in Sight

Craig Thorn

We need to reevaluate the way we use two teaching tools — New Criticism and rhetorical models of paragraph development. Both are tantamount to grammars of writing and writing about literature. As with grammar, they have become too important in our teaching methods. As with grammar-oriented introductory writing courses, introductory literature courses that rely too heavily on basic New Critical tools and traditional methods of organization separate students from what they are writing about and even from their own voices.

New Criticism is the grammar of early studies in literature. Most of us teachers were trained as New Critics. We read Cleanth Brooks and I. A. Richards; we studied Maynard Mack; we knew something about great literature as a kind of science of language featuring networks of imagery and allusion, parallels in characterization, and studied patterns in plot development. Initially a response to the rarefied academic approaches that kept the study of literature at the university level, New Criticism opened literature to anyone by focusing on the text. It promised, in short, that one did not need a profound education in Western culture, literary theory, or traditions to understand a good book or poem. Because teachers can easily conduct class discussions about literature using imagery as a basic vocabulary, the extended image, the parallel scene, and the foil have become the means by which most of us convey meaning in literature to our students. Unfortunately, discussing literature in these valuable but limited terms enables students to respond to literature without really having to understand it. Blood imagery in *Macbeth*, Oedipus's various foils, parallel scenes in Paris and Pamplona in *The Sun Also Rises* are intrinsic to each work's meaning, but taken by themselves require only a technical appreciation of the work. Examine the following essay topics, all of them relatively sound, on three of Shakespeare's plays (cites are to *William Shakespeare: The Complete Works*, edited by Alfred Harbage, New York: Penguin/ Viking, 1969):

Topic 1

Or shall we play the wantons with our woes
And make some pretty match with shedding tears,
As thus, to drop them still upon one place,
Till they have fretted us a pair of graves
Within the earth; and, therein laid, "there lies
Two kinsmen digged their graves with weeping eyes ..."
(III, iii, 163–68)

Show how the imagery of tears, moaning, and weeping contributes to the portrayal of Richard II.

Topic 2

But these sweet thoughts do even refresh my labors,
Most busiest when I do it.

   His spirits hear me,
And yet I needs must curse.

Ferdinand seems fairly content in the first passage (III, i, 14–15) whereas Caliban seems fairly bitter in the second passage (II, ii, 3–4). Though their situations, past and present, bear striking similarities, they react differently. Why? And what do these differing reactions suggest about the play?

Topic 3

Why, the wrong is but a wrong i' th' world; and having the world for your labor, 'tis a wrong in your own world, and you might quickly make it right. (IV, iii, 81–85)

Show how Emilia's reasoning represents the kind of world all the characters live in and the kind of people characters must be to survive in Shakespeare's *Othello*.

All these topics could lead students to dramatic discoveries and strong convictions. Note that each question offers the faint possibility for intuitive, personal responses to Shakespeare. The students might make some provocative assessments of character in responses to these "problems." However, the phrasing of the questions encourages students to see the characters as literary devices that convey literary themes. The student flips through *Richard II* looking for words like "weep" and "tears." He or she is immediately forced to think of Caliban and Ferdinand as symbols for ways of thinking about life. Emilia is part of Shakespeare's play, not part of the student's world. In this context, the phrase "the kind of people characters must be" summarizes the very problem with New Critical approaches to teaching literature. I struggled with these kinds of essay topics for years until I finally asked myself: "Am I talking solely about characters when I speak to students about literature or do I hope that they may see people somewhere in those characters?"

The historical context, the social significance, the biographical information, the psychological possibilities, and most importantly, the manner in which these fictional lives may speak to the students' lives are topics that the introductory course in literature may inadvertently shortchange. Both Kevin O'Connor's and Lynne Kelly's chapters offer alternative ways of looking at and writing about literature that allow students to see the work from a variety of perspectives and express what they see in a variety of voices. New Criticism often examines only the scaffolding of the building; in fact, it sometimes knocks out the scaffolding and erects its own. Students see only the skeleton of a place that contained rooms with elaborate appointments and moving people. Even worse, what was once a populist response to what many academics perceived to be elitist literary criticism has itself become an intellectual orthodoxy, a language of authority to which students are expected to adhere. The New Critical approach to literature can reaffirm the students' sense that literature is precious and unreal. Thylias Moss's piece on the authority of the individual's voice addresses some of the unfortunate consequences of New Criticism. Teaching writing from the prose-model point of view and literature from the New Critical point of view results in writing as an exercise of sterile rules rather than a way to discover and communicate meaning. New Criticism stands between students and the living text. Prose models stand between the student and their own unwritten texts.

Prose models — rhetorical approaches to writing such as cause/effect analysis and five-paragraph arguments — appeal to students' limited trained abilities when they are presented as ends in themselves: they are imitative, mechanical, formulaic. As with New Critical tools, prose models are extremely valuable as a means toward more successfully achieving an end, but taught as examples students must follow in specific assignments, they are static exercises. Asking students to write about the differences between the state and local police using the a-b-a-b-a-b method of comparison/contrast does not encourage a desire to make the topic interesting to them and their readers (to make their own music as Thylias Moss might put it); rather, it asks them to show you that they know what the a-b-a-b-a-b method of comparison/contrast is. Here, for example, are some relatively sound writing topics that are hindered by their emphasis on method rather than the information:

> Downtown, there are two places to have your hair cut: Joe's Barbershop and Sheik Araby. They are very different places which I want you to

compare and contrast. Try to use as many details as possible and to follow closely the rules for comparing and contrasting.

It seems that every year where and with whom you sit in the dining hall says something important about you. Try to classify the various groups that currently exist in the dining hall. Remember to have a consistent principle of classification.

There does not seem to be any clear formula for success when it comes to making a hit television show; yet, every year there are television shows that everyone watches. Picking a popular show ("Wise Guy," "The Cosby Show," "Rosanne," "Cheers," "Thirty-Something"), explain what causes the show to be so good. Remember not to confuse effects for causes. Also, be sure that you clearly state what the principle causes for the show's popularity are.

The topics themselves have much potential. They are interesting to students. They may even be part of their personal experiences. However, the emphasis is on how they say what they say. In fact, students are likely to alter their opinions to fit the formulas expected of them. Needless to say, the students' real voices will not be heard. As with New Critical approaches to literature that discount any other way of looking at or writing about literature, these kinds of prose-model assignments implicitly devalue the students' opinions, experiences, even their observations on occasion.

Why not simply ask where the students would rather go for a haircut? Then, suggest where appropriate that the students might want to write/rewrite the piece using some of the tools available in the comparison/contrast model of developing a paragraph. Ask the students whether or not they think the dining hall promotes exclusive cliques. Then, point out that they might be more persuasive if they outline what kinds of cliques exist in the dining hall if they think that it does promote them. Ask them to analyze why they enjoy their favorite television show so much and urge them to clarify their conclusions by trying to think of what causes them to enjoy it so much. If we want students to care about these important means of organizing information, then we have to encourage them to feel strongly about the information they are organizing. Deemphasizing prose models and formal arguments as ends in themselves makes them more valuable and interesting to the student writer. Compare, for instance, these two day-by-day outlines for a short essay:

Outline 1

A. Introduction: State the subject, the process by which it will be approached, and your attitude toward and thoughts about the subject.

B. Presentation of Main Evidence: Summarize the kind of evidence you will present and state the thesis partially or fully.

C. Background Information: State the facts of the case or history leading up to the point to be discussed.

D. Main Argument: State and argue the thesis.

E. Summary of Evidence: Organize and present information that supports your point of view.

F. Refutation: Answer opposing arguments.

G. Conclusion: Restate the original appeal to the reader, make new arguments, and perhaps summarize the proofs of your argument.

Outline 2

A. Consider starting with one of the following: an anecdote that captures for you the main reason why this subject is interesting; a quote from someone about the subject that gets your attention; a detailed description of an appropriate setting that introduces some of the feelings you have about the subject; a brief description of how you came to be interested in this subject that you think might be useful or interesting to your reader.

B. Consider any or all of the following approaches when presenting your argument, the background, and the proof:

1. Photographic approaches: "Snapshots" of dramatic moments having to do with the subject or putting together lots of related images to create a collage effect proving a point.

2. Historical approaches: Getting opinions of what others had to say about the subject and how the subject has developed; reading magazines, books, and newspapers.

3. Setting: Does your subject indicate a trend or attitude? Where does the subject take place?

4. Rhetorical approaches: Can your subject be compared or contrasted to other subjects? Does breaking the subject down into parts or classifying the subject as part of something larger yield important information about the subject? Is the subject caused by something, or is it causing something to happen? Can you come up with examples that demonstrate something about the subject?

5. Anecdotal approaches: How has your subject affected actual people? Who is personally involved in your subject?

6. Creative approaches: Make up an imaginary dialogue on the subject that reflects opposing views; make up an absurd argument and try to defend it; make up an imaginary scene, characters, or story that might illustrate your point; make up a scene from a play, novel, poem, or song about the subject; write in a voice or in a style that is clearly not your own to defend your point; address a very specific audience on the subject; make up many different ways of looking at one detail; list all the possible biases you might have on the subject.

C. Conclusion: Consider ending with a question, an update on what is most recently happening, a striking detail or story, a restatement of your main argument, or a dramatic quote.

While I have deliberately exaggerated the differences between a strictly formal and a more varied, informal approach to the essay (in fact, I used to give students the first outline with only some embellishment), the differences bespeak subtle attitudes about what constitutes acceptable information. The first implies that whatever knowledge the student has to offer—in the form of personal experiences, feelings, and conclusions about observations—is not relevant to a considered discussion of the subject. While in some kinds of writing our personal involvement in the subject can be problematic, we certainly do not want our students' first experience with expository writing to be devoid of personal experience and conviction. On the contrary, we may wish to encourage creative contributions to an argument if only as effective pre-writing techniques in which the student has the opportunity to make the subject his or her own.

As Thylias Moss dramatically demonstrates in Chapter 9, insisting on one kind of writing about one kind of information can effectively result in all students speaking with one bland voice. I would argue that while the second outline certainly makes the teacher's job more challenging (consider all the possibilities to be shared with your students), the results will be much more rewarding. Furthermore, the essay will have to be more subtly organized than one following the first outline, since the kinds of information and voices presented will be more varied. Ironically, more essays in magazines like *Time* and the *New Yorker* follow the second outline than the first. Prose models, unfortunately, can suffer the same fate as New Criticism, becoming a language of authority that denies students access to their own voices and cuts them off from information they might have discovered in other ways, whether this be information about police forces or *Wuthering Heights*. Do prose models adequately explain the power of essays by Franklin, Bacon, Didion, Angelou, or Naipaul? Does New Criticism adequately illuminate Frost, Atwood, or Llosa? Both New Criticism and prose models are peculiarly Western in that they insist on strict forms of logic, surgical and scientific dissection of experience, and thinking as a linear process. Try teaching Ishmael Reed from a New Critical bias. Try explaining why most writing in the *New Yorker, Boston Globe, Time*, or the *Wall Street Journal* has little to do with the precise way we are all prone to teach classification/division paragraphing.

The New Critical and prose-model approaches to reading and writing emphasize the written word as the product of technique. Basically, teaching expository writing using prose models is like teaching poetry according to literary terms: "Read 'Ozymandias' as an example of an ironic situation and identify metonymy in at least three of the assigned poems by Emily Dickinson." As with rules of grammar, New Critical tools and prose models can stand between the student and what he or she wants to say. The grammars of New Criticism and prose models emphasize form over content; they concentrate on the finished product, not the process. The crowning irony of our attention to these grammars is that students think of them as anything but vital in themselves precisely because they are too often taught as mechanical tools that are ends in themselves.

When New Criticism is taught as a *way* to understand more about the author and his or her work, when prose models are taught as a *way* to discover meaning in what a student has chosen to say, then the student sees both grammars as a means toward achieving a desired end: communicating what *he or she* wants to say about the subject. In Chapter 8, Carole Braverman alludes to the traditional methods of organizing an analytical essay, but she invites students to identify with literature in creative, highly personal ways by introducing them first to the process of creating literature themselves. As Kevin O'Connor mentions at the end of Chapter 7, such an assignment exercises critical and interpretive tools as well as traditional analytical reading.

Both New Criticism and prose models are absolutely essential grammars for the student new to literature and to writing. They are popular with teachers because they provide some measurable language in a discipline that is highly subjective. They are useful with students because they give them a language that enables them to approach the more refined, formal techniques of good writing, fiction and nonfiction. In fact, this essay's intention is to ensure that students recognize the genuine importance of these new languages in achieving the goal teachers want their students to have: to write well about what they want to say.

Advanced Writing and
Literature Courses

11

In Defense of Film
Teaching Film and Writing
Ada Fan

We are living in a land where we do not know the language. Film and video have become our society's most visible means of communication — and yet they are not studied in our schools; they may be entertaining audiovisual aids, but they are hardly the stuff of a serious curriculum. Instead, we in the academy scoff, regarding film as fluff and video as some vile by-product of our television sets, which we view as a necessary evil: a purveyor of news, popular culture, and PBS. But we are consigning our students to a dangerous ignorance. In this age of computer literacy, we should be embracing film and teaching it in the classroom, to ensure that they learn to control the visual media, that they are not simply manipulated by it. Just as prose must be anatomized in the classroom to invest students with the power of language, film must be anatomized and understood. Students need to be learning — and using — the grammar of the visual language that assails them continually; they need to be reading film critically, writing about it analytically, and trying it out creatively.

We forget that the novel was not considered a serious literary genre when it first appeared, was considered nothing but popular entertainment; Dickens's novels, serialized in magazines, were not analyzed for their critical, much less curricular, potential but were pored over for their comic and suspense value. Even after critics and reviewers began articulating the complexities of the more sophisticated novels, canonization was a long time in coming, as was acceptance into the curriculum.

With all our talk about the literary canon, film must be taken more seriously. Film is, after all, literature: it has become our preferred mode of narrative, of storytelling. We go to the movies on Saturday night as a matter of ritual, to steep ourselves in our cultural myths; and we sit around the TV watching videos the way our ancestors sat around the hearth telling stories. The mythic power of the *Star Wars* trilogy is obvious, and our cultural fixation on certain stories and characters is evident in the number of sequels some films have generated. (Which is not to say that we should study the most popular films; we do not necessarily study the best-selling books. There is, however, an argument for examining those works with the greatest popular appeal: they represent our society's psychic and visceral needs.)

Because our students read film closely — and often the same film repeatedly — they are easily induced to discuss both the issues and the techniques of film. Classics like *The Wizard of Oz* (Fleming 1939) and more recent favorites like the *Star Wars* trilogy (Lukas 1977, Kershner 1980, Marquand 1983) and *E.T.* (Spielberg 1982) offer rich mines for analysis, to be studied traditionally, in terms of genres, themes, symbols, characters, settings. These particular films lend themselves to mythic interpretations, focusing as they do on the orphaned hero(ine) and a rite of passage to be performed, assisted by magical helpers and blocked by wicked authorities. The genres of these films — musical comedy/ fantasy and sci-fi/adventure — make for illuminating comparison and contrast with other film genres, such as cartoons, the western, the horror film, domestic comedy, farce, drama, and the suspense film, especially when examining the functions of storytelling and ritual (easily linked to literary theories like Aristotelian catharsis and psychological theories like Bettelheim's on the efficacy of fairy tales in ego development). As with written literature, these films supply substantial material for critical papers.

But it is not really enough to teach film as traditional literature. Because film is primarily visual, we must pay close attention to the visual aspect, to the images chosen and to their handling, discussing all this in technical, cinematographic terms. We need to notice if the camera is moving or still; how the shots are framed; what angle, point of view, and image size are used; how the subjects and settings are lit; and how the sequences are paced, paying attention to the duration and number of the given shots and to the logic of the cuts. As in theater, the significance of directorial choices and acting — the actors' movements and facial expressions — and the effects of setting, costumes, makeup, and props also deserve attention. Insisting on visual analysis sharpens the students' powers of observation and amplifies their understanding of characterization, setting, images and symbols, narrative, and the communication of a message. Ultimately, the focus on visuals enables the students not only to view film more critically but also to read literature much more closely. And once the students have observed closely, the gathering of concrete evidence to support a thesis or secondary point follows as a natural consequence.

Because I have taught film in two separate courses over the past few years (making plenty of blunders along the way), I make bold to point out several approaches to incorporating the teaching of film — with writing — into a literature class. But anyone who begins teaching film in English classes can develop the approach best suited to his or her style.

The most obvious approach involves screening the film version of an assigned novel or story: like Steven Spielberg's *The Color Purple* (1985) after reading Alice Walker's novel (1982).[1] The transformation of an epistolary novel preaching the gospel of Africa into a Hollywood film imitating a Dickensian rise from rags to relative riches makes for a fascinating study. Here, it is essential to discuss not only some obvious changes in the film version — Spielberg's drastic compression of Nettie's African experience and his invention of Shug's preacher father, both for dramatic focus (though the first undermines Walker's edifying intent and the second sentimentalizes Shug's background) — but also the smaller directorial modifications — like Albert's larger physical stature (a sign of visual strength, to replace the mysterious power of Mr. ____) — to show how directorial decisions, both additions and deletions, reshape the story in the translation from mental to visual medium.

The film *The Color Purple* is ruled by visual drama, which is provided by camera angles (extremely low on Celie's stepfather and Albert, to exaggerate their dominance), the invention of the sisters' patty-cake game (to link them in a shared action and so intensify their attachment), and the shaving sequences (to introduce tension and to link Celie's story cinematically to that of Nettie). Students learn that the internal, psychological dimension enjoyed by novels, especially those with first-person narration, is lost to film, which is largely confined to external appearances, to that which can be depicted visually. (First-person narration in film usually sounds hopelessly contrived.[2]) The propensity of Hollywood films to sink into superficiality and insubstantial — but pervasive, dangerous — romanticization becomes apparent.

An exercise helpful for anyone interested in narrative, both students and teacher, is to list all the episodes in the film and all the episodes in the novel side by side and then to consider the reasons behind the deletions and additions in the film. Obviously, all that occurs in a novel cannot be compressed into the time frame of a film, so the scenes and incidents included become especially significant, serving several functions: to advance the plot, to develop characters, to present a theme. In many ways the film follows the rules of the modern short story: every detail wields a significance that resonates throughout the work.

Thus Nettie's story, especially the ritual scarring of the children (rendering a cultural ritual into violent barbarism), becomes a foil to heighten the tension between Celie and Albert instead of serving as a new, broadening perspective. Similarly, Shug is given a father, so that the eventual reconciliation with her father can provide an upbeat counterpoint to Celie's disastrous relationship with her stepfather. (Note that the father's identity as minister legitimizes Shug and turns her into a merely naughty, good-hearted daughter, a shift from her original, more subversive role as a rebel who abjures society, rejecting woman's traditional responsibilities.) In film, one or two encounters serve to establish a relationship: so Celie and Shug's sexual relationship can be conveniently dispatched in a single embrace and a cutaway to wind chimes. (And so the theme of women helping and healing women, in a world dominated by men — and of a woman's thriving on her very physical love for another woman — is virtually excised.)

Short writing assignments work well here, focusing on *one* difference in plot or characterization introduced by the director and discussing the reasons behind it, its cinematic treatment, and the significance of the change for the film as a whole. In traditional terms, this piece might involve example, description, cause and effect, and evaluation, with a comparison-contrast perspective. Comparisons between cinematography and the prose of the original — especially contrasting the director's handling of the opening, the climactic scenes, and the ending — might be emphasized. Spielberg's lovely, lyrical opening in *The Color Purple* — the two sisters romping in a field of flowers, to a grand, high Hollywood score, cut short by a low-angle shot of the towering, ominous father — is something of a leap from Walker's opening — the italicized imperative, "You better not never tell nobody but God . . . ," followed by Celie's terse accounts to God about her desperate condition. The fluid cinematography and elegant composition (e.g., the juxtaposed images in the window, when Albert comes to ask for Nettie's hand; Albert's house and children, upon Celie's arrival) romanticize, if not sentimentalize, Walker's stark, fragmented, first-person narratives. The film's impressive technique calls attention to itself, thus diminishing the emotional effect (for example, Albert's pursuit on horseback of Nettie, the camera tracking Albert through the trees).

Screening films that drastically rework literary classics yields even more dramatic rewards. Here the comparison-contrast mode dominates: the modern perspective, usually more cynical and bleak, is opposed to the perspective of a former age, usually more hopeful, if not optimistic. Francis Ford Coppola's *Apocalypse Now* (1979), popular at Andover as a partner to *Heart of Darkness* (Conrad [1902] 1986), invariably intrigues students with its parallel story line, with its nihilistic inversion of Conrad's theme. Its Vietnam setting and hallucinogenic atmosphere attract most (though repel some) students. Its consciously mythic over-tones — the keys for which are provided in Coppola's shot of Kurtz's books, Frazer's *The Golden Bough* ([1922] 1963) and Jessie Weston's *From Ritual to Romance* ([1920] 1957), — and its quotation of T. S. Eliot's "The Hollow Men" ([1925] 1971) (which, of course, takes for its epigraph the cabin boy's "Mr. Kurtz — he dead") offer built-in oppor-tunities to discuss the rise of myth and the fall of Christianity in modern literature. (There is room, too, for a segue here to Eliot's *The Waste Land* ([1922] 1983), which also pays homage to *From Ritual to Romance*.) After a briefing on *The Golden Bough* — on scapegoats, the sacrifice of divine animals, and the priesthood of Diana of the Wood (in order to become priest, one kills the existing priest) — students can make sense of Coppola's ending, perhaps writing an explication of it: on the intercutting of the ox sacrifice with Willard's assassination of Kurtz (which sets up Kurtz as the Army's scapegoat); on the curious reverence given Willard after he kills Kurtz (since he is seen as Kurtz's successor); and on the final close-up of a crucified Christ (which ident-ifies both Willard, whose face is similarly framed in the beginning and end of the film, and Kurtz, the slaughtered, godlike figure, with Christ).

The potential for comparison-contrast writing assignments is bound-less: Conrad's Kurtz, a heroic figure who stumbles, through warped idealism, but who redeems himself through self-revelation, versus Coppola's Kurtz, a military hero destroyed by his own delusions and by a morally corrupt imperialism; Marlow, who saves Kurtz, preserves his image, and cherishes the "saving illusion," versus Willard, who kills Kurtz, destroys his stronghold (ordering the massacre of his followers), and believes in nothing (except perhaps following orders); Conrad's women, whose idealized world offers hope and meaning, versus Coppola's women, the American beauties who misuse their power and the Asian waifs who are utterly powerless; Conrad's surreal allegorical abstraction and commentary on European imperialism in Africa versus Coppola's harsh, hallucinogenic realism and attack on American exploi-tation in Asia; and Conrad's dense, tortuous prose, especially involving Marlow's delayed realizations (the arrows, his blood-soaked shoes, the heads on posts), versus Coppola's disorienting cinematography and editing (the bridge scene, the severed head, Kurtz's washing his bald head), as well as Conrad's device of a narrator repeating Marlow's story versus Coppola's use of objective and subjective camera.

The modern film treatment of myth or folktale draws on the undeniable power of the original story and works as a haunting, collective dream. Polanski's *Chinatown* (1974), an outstanding example (and one of the perfect films of our time, I think), elegantly elaborates Sophocles' *Oedipus* trilogy ([429–25 B.C.] 1939) in modern terms. But when students view *Chinatown* after reading *Oedipus Rex*, they are usually baffled; beyond the incest motif they see little. Here is the teacher's great chance to play magician. Initiate discussion by asking students to find the common ground shared by the two works, guiding them gently to consider not only the nature of the incest but fate, the role of the hero, the function of vision/eyesight and water. Convince them of the conscious intent, by writer Robert Towne, to transpose the myth to a modern context by pointing out certain details that do nothing to advance the plot but that recall the oedipal myth: the strange appearance of sheep and shepherd in a Los Angeles courtroom; the Grecian columns beyond Mulwray's tidepool; the unnecessary, momentary limping of Jake Gittes when he loses his shoe (with close-up), alluding to the piercing of Oedipus's ankles; the gratuitous slashing (by Polanski himself) of Jake's nose ("Do you know what happens to nosy fellows? They lose their noses"), which parallels Oedipus's blinding himself for his lack of vision; the emphasis on vision itself (Venetian blinds, binoculars, car mirrors, camera, broken tail-light, broken sunglasses, bifocals, a wife's black eye, Evelyn Mulwray's being shot through the eye). Bring out the significance of Oedipus's sleeping with his mother in total ignorance, as opposed to Evelyn's sleeping with her father with perfect willingness (classical innocence versus modern decadence); a divinely ordained prophecy, as opposed to an outcome controlled by the society's corruption, as embodied in Chinatown, which represents Jake's past (godhead and order versus godless chaos); a heroic protagonist directly participating in the incest, as opposed to an anti-heroic protagonist entering the scene as an outsider (involvement in crisis versus alienation from action). There is also the use of water: in *Oedipus* it is an essentially invisible presence, but one that is felt (especially in *Oedipus at Colonus*), an instrument of the gods; in *Chinatown* it is central, with life-giving water being diverted for selfish ends, as life-generating sexual energy is also diverted from its rightful channel for selfish and, ultimately, destructive ends. I usually assign a comparison-contrast paper on Greek versus modern fatalism, hoping for a thesis articulating the Greek's belief in fate, absolute *a priori* values, and an ultimate peace that comes with the acceptance of the gods' will, as opposed to our modern belief in free will and an existential condition, with the sense of underlying futility.[3]

In my Images of Women senior elective course, I use the immediacy of film to explore various literary genres and themes, as well as to stimulate personal writing in a journal. A few classic films work well as a modern foil for traditional love poetry and poems written in admiration of women. *The Philadelphia Story* (Cukor 1940) — with the erection of Tracy Lord on a pedestal and the subsequent demolition of her goddess stature by R. Dexter Haven — and *Casablanca* (Curtis 1942) — with its shimmering images of the beautiful Ilsa Lund, inspirational and brave but ultimately dependent on the men around her — can be joined with Elizabethan sonnets, Cavalier lyrics, Romantic/Victorian lyrics, and modern poetry (especially, for *The Philadelphia Story*, Shakespeare's "My Mistress's Eyes Are Nothing like the Sun" ([1609] 1983), and for *Casablanca*, Byron's "She Walks in Beauty" ([1814] 1983) and Yeats's "When You Are Old" ([1893] 1983)). High society films of the forties, with their showcasing of beautiful women in beautiful clothes, lend themselves to examinations of woman as objects of art, as beings whose worth lies in their physical appearance. Close-ups of women, through filtered lenses, and lengthy shots recording their expressions and their movements abound in these films; and these images correspond to the catalogues of woman's physical charms contained in traditional love poetry.

We examine the death of women (always a more romanticized subject than the death of men) in Ingmar Bergman's *Cries and Whispers* (1972) and James L. Brooks's *Terms of Endearment* (1983). In Bergman's film Agnes's surreal agony, which disturbs and distances us, illuminates the nature of several types of women — mostly negative — with Agnes emerging as the standard of the good woman. In her death we find, ultimately, a reaffirmation of life. In Brook's film, Emma's realistic suffering from cancer, which draws us in and evokes our sympathy, establishes the relative strengths and weaknesses of her domineering mother, her unfaithful husband, her loyal best friend, her angry son, her sympathetic lover — with Emma canonized as the feisty young woman, blunt and true. In her death, however, we feel mostly loss. Both films set up the dying woman as brave, admirable, and full of faith, one a religious faith and one a human faith; and both raise the question of why the woman must die to be heroic. The assignment here is a comparison-contrast paper on the treatment of the two women's deaths, with consideration of these questions: Why is the male director so interested in the woman's death, the ultimate defeat of woman? Why is the death of a woman more romantic, more dwelt on in literature and film, than the death of a man? What are the separate purposes of the two directors; and how does each achieve his aim? Because Bergman's film is so difficult, many students balk at this; but the request to reconcile the disparate approaches stretches them healthily.

Concentrating on one director is akin to concentrating on a given writer: students learn to recognize what elements make up a director's style. An acknowledged giant, like Alfred Hitchcock, offers the most possibilities. In my Images of Women course, Hitchcock demonstrates vividly man's simultaneous admiration and loathing of woman. Much has been made of Hitchcock's penchant for blondes, usually troubled, aloof, and strangely vulnerable — all of whom are threatened and tortured bodily, if not murdered—and students are greatly intrigued by this assault on the beautiful, this coexistence of worship and misogyny. While all the Hitchcock classics (with blondes) should work well, *Notorious* (1946) and *Psycho* (1960), with their shared configuration of victimized blondes, controlling mothers, and troubled sons, suggest an excellent comparison-contrast opportunity. Hitchcock's noted economy of style bears comparison with poetry, especially poems like Browning's "Porphyria's Lover" ([1836] 1989) and Hecht's "To a Madonna" (1978), both of which deify and desecrate the beloved woman.

Besides focusing on one director, I have chosen to study particular actors (nee actresses), like Katharine Hepburn, Elizabeth Taylor, and Jane Fonda, who can serve individually as the subjects of essays. The course of their careers reflects the changing—and unchanging—images of women in our time. Katharine Hepburn always plays bright, spirited, indomitable women, from the strong-willed romantic lead who is nonetheless subject to an imposing male who can break down her guard, in classics like *The Philadelphia Story*, *Adam's Rib* (Cukor 1949), and *The African Queen* (Huston 1951), to the crazed, Cassandra-like figure in *Long Day's Journey into Night* (Lumet 1962). Elizabeth Taylor's career has spanned the two poles of woman as romantic object: the sweet young virgin in *Father of the Bride* (Minelli 1950), and more sensuous but utterly self-sacrificing in *Ivanhoe* (Thorpe 1952); the femme fatale, sultry and sensual in *Cat on a Hot Tin Roof* (Brooks 1958), and more aging and vicious in *Who's Afraid of Virginia Woolf?* (Nichols 1966). Always the high-strung and vacillating young woman (at least for a decade) who acts courageously, Jane Fonda has run the gamut from sex kitten in *Barbarella* (Vadim 1968), to troubled prostitute in *Klute* (Pakula 1971), to ambitious writer and anxious friend in *Julia* (Zinnemann 1977), to submissive wife transformed to liberated woman in *Coming Home* (Ashby 1978); in so doing she has exemplified the rise of women's stature in contemporary society. Writing on an actor who has played a series of roles, the student must reconcile the general and the specific, characterizing the actor's approach and manner and focusing on specific performances and scenes.

The efficacy of journals in the teaching of writing has already been established. When it comes to teaching film and writing, journals become particularly valuable, especially in courses studying primarily film. The personal response to movies can be so immediate and visceral that students need a place to express their feelings; and directed discussions and critical analyses are usually not appropriate forums. Students also need to try out ideas, sometimes using a journal for brainstorming or pursuing half-formed theories, occasionally soliciting the instructor's response. Because students are not very well versed in film technique, they often feel shyer about voicing their thoughts in front of their peers and so welcome a journal. It also helps to encourage them to consider other memorable films they've seen and to try to analyze how and why those films have affected them. And self-analysis and self-knowledge, of course, usually inspire more sophisticated articulation of thought.

Viewing and studying films invites imitation. Just as creative writing forces students to think like writers and to look more closely at plot, structure, description, characterization, dialogue, language, and all the elements of fiction and poetry, writing a fragment of a screenplay deepens students' understanding of film and narrative development. I usually assign as a final project a three-page film treatment (summarizing plot, characters, setting, general approach), which is based loosely on autobiographical material, and a seven-plus page script of a climactic scene (including dialogue, action, bare description of cinematography). The results are always gratifying, to both writers and readers.

I do not necessarily recommend any background reading on film: what is most important is that the teacher become trained in viewing film from a more technical standpoint. A course in filmmaking is an effective introduction or reference to general works on filmmaking (whatever is available). There is always the wonderful old classic still used by professionals and film schools, Joseph V. Mascelli's *The 5 C's of Cinematography* (1965), which provides a thorough grounding, even when skimmed. But it is possible simply to sit in front of a television and to watch actively, looking for cuts, image size, camera movement and angles, lighting, and so on. Ultimately, the development of a more critical eye relies on the close viewing of films, videos, and television.

Appendix 11−1
Suggested Procedure for Teaching Films (With Writing)

N.B.: I refer to the video cassette format since this is what is generally available, but I cannot urge strongly enough the adoption of video disc technology. With video disc, we have instant access to whichever scenes we designate (with instant repeat viewings of those scenes): an absolute necessity in analyzing film. With VCRs, we lose momentum, time, and student attention as we clumsily fast-forward or fast-search to the next scene.

1. Choose a film related in theme or plot to a literary work studied in class. It must be a film that can stand up to repeated viewings, preferably one that you particularly like. Reserve a copy of it in advance (from a library or store) to ensure its availability; or you may want to purchase your own copy.

2. Watch the film once straight through, for plot and your own entertainment.

3. Screen the film again, at least once, preferably twice (or more), on a VCR with a footage meter, setting the counter to 0000 at the beginning of the actual film (to maintain accuracy when using other copies of the film) and keeping remote control and pen/pencil in hand. Try to be aware of the technical at every turn: moving (panning, tracking, hand-held) or still camera; camera angle (low, high, point of view); size of image; depth of field; lighting; editing (watch for every cut; practice counting the number of shots in TV commercials whenever you watch). Take notes on whatever strikes you, recording the footage.

4. Have the students view it once straight through, outside of class, as homework, at an arranged time in your classroom or audiovisual center. The simplest approach is to assign a film (or program) scheduled to appear on TV. (You might even work your syllabus around the TV calendar — for example, *It's a Wonderful Life* (Capra 1946) around Christmas; *The Wizard of Oz* upon its annual showing.)

5. Choose a very few scenes or sequences for class viewing, ones that encapsulate themes and/or involve crucial turns of plot and at the same time include telling cinematic choices (such as angles or close-ups that favor certain characters or that dramatically affect the viewer, and revealing cutaways).

6. Before reviewing your selections in class, take care to set the counter to zero at the beginning of the film. Then cue up your first selection. These preparations are best done before you begin class; keep both set-up time and subsequent searching time to a minimum, as the class's attention will disintegrate whenever the picture disappears. (It would be better to set the VCR to revert to a TV channel rather than have the screen go blank; at least your students' eyes will continue to be focused on the screen.)

7. View each scene once straight through, making general observations. Afterwards, ask questions or make a few more comments. Then screen the scene again, making your points and using the remote-control "pause" button to freeze the frames in question. (If you anticipate lingering over a point, mute the monitor when you pause the tape; or be prepared to mute.)

8. Assign a short paper (or even a paragraph) comparing or contrasting some specific point or aspect in the film with the related equivalent in the given literary work. Ideally, the students should view the film again (or a selected scene or scenes, if you decide to limit the assignment — which makes for greater convenience, as you can

easily set up another screening of a few scenes in class). You may want to give the assignment before your students view the film, instructing them to take notes as they watch. Or you may want to assign a more general topic to be written on before in-class analysis, and then assign a rewrite afterwards. Emphasize the importance of supporting theses/points with concrete evidence from the film.

As students become more practiced at analyzing film, their evidence will become increasingly cinematographic and technical. Suggestions for other writing: personal responses (alias journal entries); rewriting a given scene in the film, adding another, or remaking the whole film (ask them to play writer-director and write up treatments for a remake); adapting an assigned text for the screen; inventing their own films, either in treatment or script form, or both.

Notes

1. A study of Roman Polanski's *Tess* (1979) after Hardy's novel, *Tess of the D'Urbervilles* ([1891] 1979), is particularly recommended, with attention paid to the openings of each work, the cuts between scenes (especially involving knives), the treatment of Alex (kinder in the film), the use of unifying motifs (like the milk cans upon Tess and Angel's engagement and upon their reunion).

2. Karel Reisz's *The French Lieutenant's Woman* (1981) based on the novel by John Fowles (1969), shows how drastic the changes can be between novel and film: in order to preserve the sense of self-referential narrative manipulation performed by a modern author fabricating a Victorian tale, Harold Pinter wrote a screenplay that sets up a film within a film, modern actors constructing a Victorian romance.

3. Classes are easily impressed with another oedipal tidbit from the more recent *Back to the Future* (Part I, 1985), directed by Robert Zemeckis. When discussing in *Oedipus Rex* the place where three roads meet, bring out the Freudian interpretation (of father, mother, child, in a yonic configuration), then draw the figure Y on the board and ask if anyone recognizes it from the movie; then, when some clever student calls out, "the Flux Capacitor — which makes time travel possible," smile and remind them of the oedipal story line in *Back to the Future* (Zemeckis 1985). That film can also be incorporated into discussion as a comic and romantic resolution to the oedipal situation.

Works Cited

Ashby, Hal, dir. 1978. *Coming Home.* United Artists.

Bergman, Ingmar, dir. 1972. *Cries and Whispers.* Cinematograph — Svenslea Filminstitutet.

Brooks, James L., dir. 1983. *Terms of Endearment.* Based on the novel by Larry McMurty. Paramount.

Brooks, Richard, dir. 1958. *Cat on a Hot Tin Roof*. Based on the play by Tennessee Williams. MGM.

Byron, George Gordon. [1814] 1983. "She Walks in Beauty." In *The Norton Anthology of Poetry*, 3d ed., 589. New York: Norton.

Capra, Frank, dir. 1946. *It's a Wonderful Life*. RKO.

Conrad, Joseph. [1902] 1986. *Heart of Darkness*. In *The Norton Anthology of Short Fiction*, 3d ed., 240–311. New York: Norton.

Coppola, Francis Ford, dir. 1979. *Apocalypse Now*. Suggested by Joseph Conrad's *Heart of Darkness*. Paramount.

Cukor, George, dir. 1940. *The Philadelphia Story*. Based on the play by Philip Barry. MGM.

——, dir. 1949. *Adam's Rib*. MGM.

Curtis, Michael, dir. 1942. *Casablanca*. MGM.

Eliot, T. S. [1925] 1971. "The Hollow Men." In *The Complete Poems and Plays: 1909–1950*, 56–59. San Diego, Calif. Harcourt Brace Jovanovich.

——. [1922] 1983. *The Waste Land*. In *The Norton Anthology of Poetry*, 3d ed., 1000–1012. New York: Norton.

Fleming, Victor, dir. 1939. *The Wizard of Oz*. MGM.

Fowles, John. 1969. *The French Lieutenant's Woman*. Boston: Little, Brown.

Frazer, James George. [1922] 1963. *The Golden Bough: A Study in Magic and Religion*. Reprint. New York: Macmillan.

Hardy, Thomas. [1891] 1979. *Tess of the D'Urbervilles*. Ed. Scott Elledge. 2d ed. New York: Norton.

Hecht, Anthony. 1978. "To a Madonna." In *The Hard Hours*, 18–19. New York: Atheneum.

Hitchcock, Alfred, dir. 1946. *Notorious*. RKO.

——, dir. 1960. *Psycho*. Paramount.

Huston, John, dir. 1951. *The African Queen*. Based on the novel by C. S. Forester. Twentieth Century–Fox.

Kershner, Irvin, dir. 1980. *The Empire Strikes Back*. Twentieth Century–Fox.

Lukas, George, dir. 1977. *Star Wars*. Twentieth Century–Fox.

Lumet, Sidney, dir. 1962. *Long Day's Journey Into Night*. Based on the play by Eugene O'Neill. Embassy.

Marquand, Richard, dir. 1983. *The Return of the Jedi*. Twentieth Century–Fox.

Mascelli, Joseph V. 1965. *The Five C's of Cinematography: Motion Picture Filming Techniques Simplified*. Hollywood, Calif.: Cine/Grafic.

Minnelli, Vincente, dir. 1950. *Father of the Bride*. MGM.

Nichols, Mike, dir. 1966. *Who's Afraid of Virginia Woolf?* Based on the play by Edward Albee. Warner Bros.

Pakula, Alan J., dir. *Klute*. Warner Bros.

Polanski, Roman, dir. 1974. *Chinatown*. Paramount.

——, dir. 1979. *Tess*. Based on Thomas Hardy's novel *Tess of the D'Urbervilles*. Columbia.

Reisz, Karel, dir. 1981. *The French Lieutenant's Woman*. Based on the novel by John Fowles. United Artists.

Shakespeare, William. [1609] 1983. "My Mistress's Eyes Are Nothing Like the Sun." In *The Norton Anthology of Poetry*, 3d ed., 190. New York: Norton.

Sophocles. [c. 429–425 B.C.] 1939. *The Oedipus Cycle*. Trans. Dudley Fitts and Robert Fitzgerald. San Diego, Calif.: Harcourt Brace Jovanovich.

Spielberg, Steven, dir. 1982. *E.T.: The Extra-Terrestrial*. Universal.

——, dir. 1985. *The Color Purple*. Based on the novel by Alice Walker. Warner Bros.

Thorpe, Richard, dir. 1952. *Ivanhoe*. Based on the novel by Sir Walter Scott. MGM.

Vadim, Roger, dir. 1968. *Barbarella*. Paramount.

Walker, Alice. 1982. *The Color Purple*. San Diego, Calif.: Harcourt Brace Jovanovich.

Weston, Jessie. [1920] 1957. *From Ritual to Romance*. Reprint. New York: Doubleday Anchor.

Yeats. William Butler [1893] 1983. "When You Are Old." In *The Norton Anthology of Poetry*, 3d ed., 876–77. New York: Norton.

Zemeckis, Robert, dir. 1985. *Back to the Future*. Part 1. Universal.

Zinnemann, Fred, dir. 1977. *Julia*. Based on the autobiographical writing of Lillian Hellman. Twentieth Century–Fox.

12

Writing About Yourself

John A. Gould

Hidden on two pages in the middle of John Updike's *Pigeon Feathers and Other Stories* (1973) lies a tiny and mysterious monologue, "Archangel." I love to teach this piece to writing students. For one thing, Updike has chosen a fascinating ethereal persona, an archangel, who describes an Eden filled with exotic food and shelter. This voice startles the students, who until now have not thought about choosing a persona when writing an essay. They respond immediately to the archangel's rhythms and images, but they are baffled by what it is saying.

"My pleasures are as specific as they are everlasting," says the mysterious voice (170). As it elucidates, the first pleasure turns out to be a book: "The sliced edges of a fresh ream of laid paper cream stiff, rag-rich" (170). Indeed, some of the archangel's further pleasures recall Updike's own work:

> ... the candy sun slatting against the bleachers. The fair at the vanished poorhouse. ... The microscopic glitter in the ink of the letters of words that are your own. (170)

The archangel mentions other artists, other art, and concludes, "Your praise of me is praise of yourself" (171). What the students can see at last is that in this monologue, Updike is giving us a peek at aesthetic theory. In "Archangel," the artist talks through a mask of divinity, singing us simultaneously a celebration and a definition of art, particularly of literature. It asserts that art touches us at the most elemental junctures of human existence, right down there at the levels of satisfying hunger, of providing shelter. It is a hymn of praise to the way we praise ourselves.

At this moment, for the purposes of this essay, I am drawn to "Archangel" by its praise of specificity:

> Such glimmers I shall widen to rivers; nothing will be lost, not the least grain of remembered dust, and the multiplication shall be a thousand thousand fold: love me. (171)

Good writing rises from specificity as springwater from earth.

In teaching writing, we constantly extol the specific, the concrete. In *The Elements of Style* (Strunk and White 1979) a call for writing to the bones is echoed again and again: "Omit needless words" (23), "Prefer the standard to the off-beat" (81), "Use definite specific, concrete language" (21). William Strunk and E. B. White offer the plainsong to Updike's liturgy. The specific, the concrete, the definite object, the particular event—these constitute the bricks and mortar out of which all writers build their best sky-castles.

So, writing about oneself would seem at first consideration to be the easiest, most natural act of writing there is. Every child has owned objects dear to her, has visited places beautiful in his memory. As e.e. cummings noted "in Just-/spring," every eddie has a bill, every betty an isbel (1954, 23). The specific and concrete—people, places, things— are everywhere in all our lives, waiting to be tapped.

Why, then, do students of any age have such difficulty writing about themselves? "Write about something significant, something important to you," we ask them; and they so often give us dreck—sincere dreck, God knows, but dreck nonetheless: explanations of hopes gone astray, of loves gone awry, of plans gone agley. They *explain*, sometimes with wonderful clarity and precision, though more usually with verbal blushings and sweatings and avoidings of gaze. In consequence, my assignments get rather wearisome and repetitive in their efforts to eliminate explanation:

> 1. Write an account of a specific incident that happened to you recently. It should be tightly focused, without any more background than is necessary. You may use dialogue, but do so sparingly and effectively. The incident should have significance, *but do not explain what it is*. Rather, let the details *show* where the significance lies so that we as readers may discover it. 300–400 words.

Occasionally someone in the class will do as Rebecca did in the following piece, hit oil with the first drill. It doesn't happen often, though.

The Wake

My grandmother died on a Friday morning. The following Saturday evening I found myself sitting in her living room. Ever since my family had arrived that afternoon, a steady stream of neighbors and friends had come in bearing cookies, cards, cakes, and flowers.

I didn't understand why I was so tired after a seven-hour car trip, especially because I slept through most of it. But I wasn't the only one who was exhausted. Slumped in chairs, the family surrounding me wore bleak expressions as they went through the motions of thanking the latest well-wishers for their help.

I looked around at the meticulously neat and carefully decorated room. As long as I could remember, pink had been my grandmother's favorite color. I was surrounded by pink pillows, pink flowers, and pink curtains. On the coffee table was a pink candy dish, half-filled with leftover Easter candies my grandmother had put out.

My aunt showed me the obituary for Marjorie Glasow that had been printed in the local newspaper. "That's nice," I commented as I handed it back to her. She just nodded blankly and returned the clipping to the table.

Shirley Ann, a close friend of the family, arrived with a casserole. She joined us in the living room where the forced conversation faded into silence. Suddenly, Shirley Ann pointed to the beautiful pink sunset visible through the bay windows.

"Oh, look," she said, "Marjorie is up there decorating already!"

The first smiles of the day crept onto the faces of everyone in the living room.

I rejoiced when I saw this piece, although I had a feeling that Rebecca had been lucky as well as good. This narrative virtually told itself, and all the teller had to do was set up the punch line — which she did exquisitely well by showing the event and completely avoiding explanation. As with a joke — and this piece shares jokelike elements — to explain is to fail.

But most of the students don't believe me at first, and they embrace explanation as moths do open candles. They begin with the old thesis statement. "My feelings were torn by both expectation and sadness when I left my family for a school year in France." Clearly stated, and doubtless true — but all that follows will be explanation. Strong writing grows, not from the *why*, but from the *what*.

After a great deal of pressure to write with concrete details, students will quite reasonably start responding more precisely and concretely; but still most of them hang on with a death grip to their desire to explain.

> 2. Write a sketch of someone who has influenced you. Include a bit of narrative (i.e., have something happen — but not much). *Show, don't tell*. 300–400 words.

At this stage of the course, the light bulb inside Cameron's head clicked on.

The Player

I hear the music as I sit on my porch, reading by the last of the sunlight. I put down the book and push through the overgrown path between our houses. When I emerge from the brush I see him sitting on his porch, holding the guitar. He hears me climbing the wooden stairs; he turns his head and throws a casual "What's up?" at me.

"Not much," I reply as I sit down in one of the lawnchairs that cover the porch. He sits and strums on the guitar, I sit listening, watching the sun beginning to set. The porch perches atop a steep inclined lawn, splashed at the start of the summer with the brilliance of Indian Paintbrush, but now covered only with thick, dark green grass. The incline runs right down to the edge of the lake. On the left a dock, rickety and weather-beaten, extends out into the water, on the right is a tiny beach. Over the beach hangs a rope from which we used to swing out into the water when we were younger. Pulled up on the lawn next to the dock is his windsurfer. The board gleams a smooth white. On either side of the lawn are the woods, already beginning to grow dim.

He wears untied Nike high-tops, blue jeans, and a large red T-shirt. The shirt is loose, yet he is obviously strong, with the look of a wrestler about him. Muscular chest and strong arms seem incongruous with quick hands as he smoothly and confidently plays. He sits in a fold-up lawn chair, slightly hunched over the guitar, resting it loosely but carefully on his left knee. His hair is straight and brown. His lower lip looks swollen from the wad of chewing tobacco he has crammed between his lip and gum, and every so often he stops playing, leans over and spits into a tall, green, plastic cup at his side. The fingers of his left hand dance across the frets. Sometimes he watches the hand, sometimes stares out at the lake, not really seeing it but concentrating instead on the notes. He reaches a particularly tough passage and he cocks his head, turning it and leaning forward, intent on picking every note, every vibration from the polished hollow shell of the guitar. Now he stops—he gently shakes his head and starts again, his attention focused on his fingers and the steel strings. It sounds the same to me but this time he likes what he hears; he nods to himself and keeps on going, keeping time with his foot on the weathered wood of the porch.

He stops and sits back and we look out over the water. The lake is still and quiet. The setting sun sets fire to the tall birches that grow by the water's edge. They are the last trees to catch the sun's rays and they seem to glow in the special light you see only at day's end. Absentmindedly he rubs the callouses on the palms of his hands, the skin rough from hours of hanging onto the boom of his windsurfer. He strums a few more chords, watching the horizon, and turning to me he states, "Hope there's wind tomorrow."

"Yeah," I reply, "me too." He sits back and looks out at the gold-tinged water.

Cameron was pleased with and proud of that sketch, as he had every right to be. The picture of his friend is interesting and complex, and the class discussed the conflicting elements of windsurfing, chewing tobacco, and playing virtuoso acoustical guitar. His details about the setting, too, showed us a great deal about both boys, Cameron and his friend.

With most of the rest of the students, however, at this stage the thesis expands, but it's still a thesis. The student writing about going abroad tries again: "When I was getting ready to leave home for a school year in Rennes, France, I felt excited by the opportunity to live abroad, but the prospect of leaving my four-year-old brother made me feel sad." Clearer than that earlier version, and every bit as true. Most of us would applaud the improvement. Still, underneath the text the voice is crying, "Understand me; please, let me explain."

Somewhere in the use of the concrete and the specific must lie an act of faith. "Show, don't tell," I tell them over and over; and here is the glory of the concrete and the specific: *they have the power to show*. If a writer eschews explanation utterly and chooses concrete events and specific details carefully, "such glimmers . . . shall widen to rivers." So the most important direction to give young writers intent on writing about themselves is "don't explain anything."

At the start of every term students come to class certain that self-expression requires self-explanation. Every assignment I give presses them to abandon that belief, and invariably they resist, sometimes valiantly. Finally when their frustration begins to sputter over, I know they are ready, and I hand them the following essay, written by one of them, Adlai Hardin, during his senior year. Then they understand. Ad took the plunge. He decided not to explain anything—and wound up showing everything.

> 3. MAJOR PERSONAL ESSAY. Choose a topic you've already treated before or think of a new one. Develop it by using a number of the techniques and types we've already done. Write on a person, a place, or a thing, and expand on it with concrete description, dialogue, clear narrative. 800—1200 words.

Last View of Four

Standing in the narrow hallway outside his room, I reach for the doorknob and hesitate before turning it. The melodic rhymes of Hans Christian Andersen drift through the cracks in the moulding of the doorframe. The little hallway is dark, and the light from the overhead fixture in his room strikes my eyes like a direct blow from the beam of a flashlight. As I inch the door open, he looks up from his Lincoln Log creation and flashes a smile of delighted recognition.

"Hi," he says as he picks up an orange and white Matchbox Lamborghini that I gave him. "Come look at my thing." He motions toward a towering architectural marvel in the center of the room. He is four.

"Can you play with me?" His tone is beseeching, but he does not whine. I follow his gaze which jumps from me to the light fixture and then to the car in his hand.

"I don't really have time," I say with as much intonation as I can muster. "I've gotta go to the airport pretty soon." The smile drops and the glitter in the corners of his eyes disappears. He looks down at the row of cars lined up in front of him, his fingers lightly stroking the top of each one. The expression on his face reveals the intensity of the thoughts and questions which pass though his mind as he contemplates my departure. He sits perfectly still, Indian-style on the plush green carpet, mouth half-open, his lower lip protruding, exposing his bottom teeth. I sit down beside him.

"But ..." he starts to say, but stops with a frustrated sigh. "It seems like you're always GO-ing." His face crumbles into a full frown. He looks up at me, his eyes shining with tears now. "I mean ... do you really want to go to France?"

"I think so," I say flatly, wondering for the first time whether I really do.

"How long are you going to stay there? For twenty days?"

"Probably for about nine months."

"How many days is that?"

"A lot of days," I say, turning away from him.

"Why?" he asks. I realize that this is the first time he has said "why" in the conversation, because he is in the middle of that stage that children go through when they ask "why" to everything and everyone. I don't have any answers for a four-year-old brother.

"You look like you're sad," he continues. "Just stay here and play!" I stare in silence for a minute at the little round face which I will not see for such a long time, and which will be so different when I return.

"Why don't you make me something really neat with your Legos?" I suggest. He raises his head, chin thrust forward, and starts to utter a cry, and then stops. A little finger then darts into the corner of his mouth and all expression runs away from his face.

"'Kay," he says, taking the finger from his mouth and wiping it on the front of his overalls. He gets up a little awkwardly and walks toward the closet in the corner. The hole in the left elbow of his red turtleneck reveals yesterday's wound suffered in a Big-wheel race. He rattles the box of Lego out of the closet into the center of the room. The box is heavy, and he has to tug at each corner individually and keep switching off; his whole frame tightens and strains with each little tug, his straight blond hair flying about his head with each motion.

He plunks himself down in front of the box and digs in with both hands, eying the plastic pieces with a faint half-smile. He turns to me, his eyes shining and asks in his familiar chirp, "What d'ya want me to make?"

Before I can move my lips, he lets out a little gasp and covers his mouth with both hands, eyes wide open.

"What time is it?" he asks, without removing his hands from his face.

"Four," I say, wondering why he could possibly want to know.

"No way!" he exclaims, scrambling to his feet. "Adlai," he says emphatically, "Sesame's on!"

"I've gotta go now," I say as he runs toward the door. He stops, turns, and comes over to me.

"Can you turn off the record?" he asks. Our eyes are for once at the same level, me sitting on the floor, him standing beside me, belly sticking out hands in pockets. We remain silent for a minute or two, eying each other.

I put out my hand, palm open. Seeing it, he removes his right hand from the pocket of his overalls, raises it above his head, and brings it down as hard as he can on top of mine. Then with a giggle, he turns and races through the doorway and I hear the patter of his feet as he runs down the hall to the kitchen.

Works Cited

cummings, e.e. 1954. "in Just-spring." In *Poems 1923–1954*, 23. New York: Harcourt, Brace & World.

Strunk, William, Jr., and E. B. White. 1979. *The Elements of Style*. New York: Macmillan.

Updike, John. 1973. "Archangel." In *Pigeon Feathers and Other Stories*, 169–71. New York: Knopf.

13

Students, Writing, and Vietnam

Seth Bardo

I will never be you/But I am me trying to understand you

In January 1984 a ninth-grade student wrote a startling entry in her journal, which she ironically titled "What I Did over My Vacation." The piece was all about her father, who had served in Vietnam. He had never spoken to his daughter about his war experiences before, but one night over the winter break he

> had had a little too much to drink and it was late. He started telling my mother about waking up in the middle of the night the night before in a flashback. He had been back in 'Nam he said, and was remembering sliding a knife into somebody's ribs.
>
> "What do you mean," I said more than a little shocked.
>
> "It was him or me and I did what I had to do." He shrugged his shoulders and stared sightlessly at the floor.
>
> My mother smoothed over the moment by suggesting that I go to bed, which I did. Later, when she came to say good night, I asked her the question I couldn't ask my father: "Did Daddy really kill someone?"
>
> Mom looked at me with a tangible sadness in her eyes and said "I don't know."

The student concluded the piece:

> I've come out of this vacation with my eyes opened a little wider and a sort of void inside. I guess what it comes right down to is my attitude toward this country has changed. I love it because I believe in

159

what it stands for; I hate it because of what it has done to my father. And this is how I spent my vacation.

I know the above isn't very well written, it was something I had to express.

Honest and unguarded, the journals of ninth graders often make for compelling reading. This piece, however, haunted me for weeks.

When I was in ninth grade, President Kennedy was assassinated. Coming of age in the sixties had a profound effect upon me as well as those I grew up with in suburban Long Island. At our twentieth high-school reunion it was evident by career choices and political commitments how strongly our values were shaped by the movements we witnessed and participated in. In college many of us had been arrested. Now we were employed, with our own children, but many of us were deliberately making less than our parents. Our lives were changed due in part to a period in time which left a legacy that the student's journal tapped in me, especially as a teacher.

When questioned about Vietnam, about the sixties, it turned out that students were familiar with the music from that time period but knew virtually nothing related to the war or the social and political struggles that occurred then. Thus, they recognized Woodstock, the Grateful Dead, and Jim Morrison, but had not even heard of Ho Chi Minh, Spiro Agnew, or General Westmoreland. There is nothing new about this lack of information. We know from polls that some staggering percentage of teenagers have no idea who their political leaders are and are clueless about the location of India. But there was a crucial difference between other subjects and the Vietnam era; kids desperately wanted to know all about it.

"Were you at Woodstock?" "Did you ever get arrested?" "What about the draft?" A litany of questions always surfaced whenever a reference to the sixties came up in class. What the journal entry cited above crystallized for me was that these questions were generated not only from music still popular and a proliferation of films but also from a time period's impact upon their parents. For the student writing in her journal, Vietnam's influence disturbingly resonated in her life. For others, adult conversations at the table or discovering a military uniform or tie-dye shirt in the attic sparked inquiry.

The quest for self is rooted in the knowledge of where we come from. Absorbed in this search, kids wanted to learn what shaped their parents because consciously or unconsciously they understood these forces helped determine crucial relationships in their lives.

To offer a course on the Vietnam era was different from offering one on English poets or the Transcendentalists. Or at least when I began the project, it seemed to be because I felt so personally connected to the material, as did some of my students. The academic challenge was to design a course that would tap into a viscerally loaded subject and to explore that emotional connection. The personal challenge was to make sure this class was offered as a course, not as a crusade.

Curriculum choices came quickly for a senior English elective dedicated largely to the films, literature, and music that were engendered by Vietnam. Bob Dylan's early music, (notably the album *The Times They Are A-Changin'*, 1963), the poetry of *Carrying the Darkness* (Ehrhart 1985), David Rabe's dramatic trilogy (1973, 1977), Philip Caputo's *A Rumor of War* (1977), Stephen Wright's *Meditations in Green* (1983), and the films *The Deer Hunter* (1978) and *Coming Home* (1978) — all these and others turned out to be provocative and immediate. Appearances by parents, veterans, and activists powerfully added to the course's intensity in a way I had never before witnessed in a classroom. But what to do with this intensity, what vehicles should be chosen to express the unleashed feelings and thoughts, the "I know the above isn't well written, it was something I had to express"? What kind of writing would best help students express what they needed to say?

Essay questions such as analyzing Cimino's use of the Russian roulette metaphor in *The Deer Hunter* (1978) or Rabe's naming his characters Ozzie, Harriet, David, and Rick in *Sticks and Bones* (1973) seemed flat. They were important questions but did not resonate. Students would be grappling with intellectual issues as they did in all their classes; yet it seemed incumbent upon me to provide a more accessible mode for the emotional response to the materials, to personal conflicts that inevitably would ensue over the issues of patriotism, moral imperatives, and many others. I had witnessed devastated students leaving a screening of *The Killing Fields* (1984). Writing had to offer an avenue for them to focus on the source of their turmoil instead of the teacher trying to divert or redefine that upheaval.

A colleague in the English department suggested using the course's genesis, a journal. Intuitively, this made sense. Equally important, it made sense to establish from the outset that the journal entries had no prescribed length, no defined subject, and would be ungraded. (The only grade given in the course during the term was the final one for the report card. This grade was determined during a teacher-student conference by mutual consent. Participation in class as well as engagement in writing assignments became the valued criteria for both parties. Due to the nature of the course, the materials, and the assignments, most students felt, even after doing some of their very best work, that only a pass/fail grade be given because grades had become irrelevant in their minds to their learning process.)

When I announced on the first day of class that a major facet of work would be a journal and that the first entry would be due in a week, students immediately wanted more structure. Their guiding principle, their modus operandi, was that each teacher possessed a magic formula; once the code was broken, a student could consistently score. Students justifiably felt abandoned, as though they now had to run a 100-meter dash without any starting blocks.

Pressed by their anxiety I reluctantly offered broad suggestions for the initial assignment such as choosing a central image from a reading or a film and exploring the reasons for this choice. This provided the starting block most students sought. After the first assignment was returned, few students requested additional guidelines. Their entries had no grades and were filled with my comments, sometimes several pages in length. This response assured each writer on at least two important levels. First, that the reader took each individual's writing seriously by reacting personally and extensively; second, it was understood immediately that whatever was turned in would be acceptable. Thus, instead of a grade there was a dialogue. Instead of formulaic responses, there were many voices.

What liberation this was for students! It freed them from the belief in a mythical construct. It permitted them to write for themselves, to meditate on what they found vital. Once students discovered the importance of their own subject, of their thoughts and feelings, then their prose reflected this intensity in the effort to express what they felt compelled to describe.

And what a liberation for the teacher! Each student came to the material with unique choices. Each name became associated with a separate and distinct voice. Disturbed by images, troubled from the knowledge of an Asian genocide with American participation, moved by a poem or lyric, excited by political activism, these entries frequently achieved what writing should be — a tool for self-expression and through it self-discovery.

At the beginning, as the following two writers illustrate, this process often started with the articulation of an overwhelming despair that an individual could not affect events or just of the confusion of bombardment from the materials.

Writer One

My roommate just went to sleep, but before doing so, she wished me goodnight, and after looking into my sullen face, she advised, "Don't get depressed about the war. It's over." But it's not. There is still fighting in the world, there is still suppression and aggression. And it seems to me that our country is more than just casually involved in such things. Is there anything casual about death? My dad tries to explain the importance of war tactics and the U.S. military involvement, and some of it really does make logical sense. But what could possibly be logical about murder? War has played a key role throughout history, shaping the destinies of men and their cultures. So why should I have hope that it could ever end? The pain, the destruction, the heartbreaks. Aggression has controlled people for what seems forever. But why?

Writer Two

I want to add, that although I'm gaining a sense of where we human beings have gone wrong and where we have gone right, I have become even more aware of the almost impossibility (is that a word?) of finding solutions, of making this world a better place and realizing the common goal of happiness and self-fulfillment for all people. Maybe I'm getting too bogged down in concentrating so much on the huge scope of the problems that we face, maybe I should be content in just adding my drop of water to the rushing, singing river. But sometimes, it's so hard to be content with little things when you see the larger sadness that cloaks our world.

As an adult reader, as the teacher responsible for setting up a course that would raise fundamental value clarification issues, I felt that it was essential in my written comments as well as during class discussions to balance *The Deer Hunter's* (1978) nihilistic Russian roulette with the Emersonian dictum that "if a single man plant himself indomitably on his instincts, and there abide, the huge world will come around to him" (1983, 70). However, equally important was not to intercede too much during debates and in personal struggles. The least successful moments in class were the ones when I expounded my views, because whenever I spoke I stifled a potentially dramatic and lively dynamic between students. The same held true for journals.

Most students guided themselves through their own journeys, often with the aid of course materials that each found singularly appropriate. *Shallow Graves*, a book of poetry by Wendy Wilder Larsen and Tran Thi Nga (1986), offers just one example. In the following journal entries, two students illustrate how their approach to the book, their use of this vehicle — one by association of experience, the other through direct imitation of form — enabled them to cope with daunting questions.

Student One

Although Larsen did not fight in the war or see the dead and the dying, the subtle irony she saw in the more trivial aspects of her own daily life becomes a biting commentary on the larger picture — the United States in Vietnam, ignorantly trying to help it, to Americanize it, attempting to teach the Vietnamese morals and values which were not their own and were completely alien to them. This is an issue that I have struggled with in my experience overseas, and I could easily relate to her uneasiness and embarrassment sticking her foot into a culture which she didn't fully understand but which needed some kind of assistance and support. ... I've seen it and lived it so many times.

Of course it bothers me that as I live with my parents in our large white air-conditioned house complete with swimming pool in Sudan, starving children are struggling to stay alive in the refugee areas outside of Khartoum. I'll never forget the time when I went with the Ambassador's wife and another Embassy woman to Mother Teresa's clinic. Although they acted sincere as they smiled and shook hands with the sick and disabled Africans, when they had finished their rounds, they took a bar of Ivory in plain view of the patients, and washed any reminder of those sick, calloused hands from their own delicate white ones. I was thoroughly ashamed of how these Americans acted. But I did not know how to show that I really cared, that I wasn't like them. I think Wendy Larsen often felt ashamed to be an American in Vietnam, just as I have many times felt ashamed to be an American in Africa.

Student Two

The "real American"
felt empty and inexperienced with life.
"You cannot imagine, a real American
like you."
I can't imagine, Phuoc, and I will never fully understand.
I will never understand the way life looks to one
who has accepted death.
I will never know what it is to leave the shoreline behind you,
never knowing if I will return.
I will never be you
But I am me trying to understand you.

The journal turned out to be an ideal medium for examining images and issues because by its sanctioned subjectivity, by its lack of definition, entries allowed students the independence to isolate content and determine format. Finally, journals also invited them to risk what we as teachers could not responsibly assign students to attempt.

The first movie that really "moved" me was *Streamers*. I elected not to include it in my last journal because it is very difficult for me to write about. The movie brought to the surface my own great prejudices. I found myself thinking thoughts that I know must be wrong, but I have them anyway. I realized that I hold a prejudice towards homosexuals. I can understand why a man might want to be gay, but I don't know why he must "flaunt" it. Now, I realize that this must sound totally ignorant, but it is the conformist in me. ... These people must just be showing their pride in who they are, and simply living true to their culture. Maybe I lack these things. I don't know. I applied early and I am waiting to hear from Wesleyan University. They have a strong gay population. I am scared that they might reveal me for what I am. I think that I am hoping that they will.

In addition to three journal entries, students were required to hand in a documented paper the eighth week of a ten-week term. Due to the Vietnam War's recent place in American history, students were encouraged to incorporate a primary source. Each course section has produced a remarkable representative range of parents, relatives, neighbors, refugees, veterans, journalists, nurses, and activists.

Much to the students' delight and relief, they found that almost everyone they contacted immediately assented to being interviewed; people wanted to tell their stories to members of the next generation. Only one wife of a veteran expressed reservations to her husband's interview because she feared his recounting of his time in Vietnam would stir the nightmares that periodically haunted him, a symptom of posttraumatic stress syndrome, a condition familiar to all students in the course.

For those who chose this route, the paper quickly was transformed from an assignment to a mission as soon as they made favorable contact. Their excitement became palpable because they connected sometimes intimately with others' lives. In listening to stories, in knowing that someone was sharing an often painful experience, students took on a new responsibility as writers who must convey each interviewee's story. This was not only a challenge, it became an imperative. The process also led to numerous special relationships between students and their contacts, which again fed into the sense of mission and, for a few, had a profound personal impact.

One student interviewed her father, a veteran. He gave her the letters he had written to her mother while he was in Vietnam. These led the student to read *Dear America: Letters Home from Vietnam*, edited by Bernard Edelman (1985). Father and daughter shared a past that had not been discussed before, a past that led to opening a new dimension in their relationship. Months after the course concluded, I saw them together at the Lawrence Veterans Outreach Center where they were viewing a photography exhibit.

Another student, who had to overcome understandable trepidation because she did not know these neighbors, contacted a couple in her town whose son had been killed in Vietnam. President of his senior class, a varsity athlete, he had left an Ivy League college because he believed it was his duty to serve in the armed forces. A room in the local high school had been dedicated to his memory.

On the phone this couple urged the student to visit with them. When she arrived they showed her all of his mementos from school as well as his commendations from the army and letters he had written them from boot camp and while in country. Other meetings followed. The result was not only a superb paper but a special bond between three people — or four. As the student explained to me and said directly to the parents, she felt when she completed the paper as if she knew their son. As for the couple, they felt the meetings and resulting paper kept their son's memory alive. It pained them to think that other sons and daughters would die like their son. They believed that if his story was told and retold, similar deaths could be prevented.

After reading Wallace Terry's *Bloods* (1984) and "What Did You Do in the Class War, Daddy?" by James Fallows (1975), a student decided to do his documented report on blacks serving in Vietnam. In Roxbury, Massachusetts, he found an outreach center exclusively devoted to black veterans. When the white student returned to Andover, he was excited because he had two hours of taped material and, more importantly, he had experienced something that he felt altered his life. Never before had he gone to a place where he was the minority, "the only one." His sojourn presented a new perspective. Deep into what he had been conditioned to believe was enemy territory, he had found folks not only helpful but willing to share their lives with him.

What to do with these stories became the next critical step and a formidable one. Impassioned by the power, vitality, and uniqueness of their material, students were unsure as to how to translate this information to an audience. These stories were now theirs in a way other material gathered could never be; they believed they had a sacred trust. Many students in their need to honor this trust, to express the resonance that inspired them, decided to shape the documented report in ways they had not initially conceived. As a result of their experimentation, they shattered the notion of a conventional research paper while forging original works.

Example One

December 20, 1968
Dear Murph,

Hey, buddy. I got your letter yesterday, and was really thrown. I mean you've never mentioned it before. All your letters were about class and shit. I didn't know you were involved in the protest movement. I can't believe you were arrested. Your mom must have fainted when you told her. I don't know what to say. I'm sure you understand the politics of this whole mess a hell of a lot better than I do, but I'll tell you this much, "if we're fulfilling any useful purpose over here they sure are keeping it a secret."* And God knows what the next four years have in store for us now that Nixon's in. Still though, I feel kind of strange that you're dedicating yourself to opposing what I live everyday. Are you anti-government or anti-soldier?

Love,
Nick

(* quotation from personal letter of veteran interviewed.)

Example Two

I was never so vulnerable, knowing Charlie was there but not where. I'd sit there listening, afraid to move for fear of upsetting any types of balance keeping me alive. The possibilities crawled over from the back of my brain, went out through my eyes and immersed themselves in the darkness down the tunnel. Paranoia outraced reason, bumped it off the road. Sent it flying into some ditch laughing and screaming all the way. So how was he going to get me, a grenade that wallpapered the tunnel with my insides or the roar of an AK-47 opening up across? Maybe Charlie had the tunnel rigged to collapse. Please not fucking that. My older brothers used to smother me when I was asleep.

Journals opened a forum for probing personal reactions in the first person. What students shifted to in their documented reports was a different persona, written in first or third person. Committed to their subject matter and their interviewees, students wanted to get as close as possible in their writing to what they had heard and read about but not experienced. It was almost as if through writing about their subjects directly they could make the unknown known for them and their readers. When Sam, the teenage protagonist of *In Country* by Bobbie Ann Mason (1985), is cautioned about asking questions concerning Vietnam, where her father was killed, she replies: "All I can see is a picture postcard. I see palm trees and rice fields. And that's it" (135). As teachers, no matter what innovative techniques we employ, we cannot make a subject real. Yet students have the capacity to make it real for themselves.

It was after one week on the boat that Ling's days and heart started to turn sour, and her childhood started to drift off the boat, only later to drown in the water below her. Eating their rice, as they had every day, Ling and her mother sat talking about how lovely it would be when Ling could be in school again. Suddenly a noise so painful and so familiar lodged itself in the ears of every person on board. It was the sound of machine gun fire. Ling looked to the open sea and saw a Vietnamese security patrol boat. "That, that is what's trying to kill us," Ling discovered. Her boat was raked with machine gun fire for an hour.* The end result: 19 people were killed. These were the first casualties of this new war, albeit an extension of a very old war and Ling knew, as the children in Vietnam knew, war and its consequences.** But as the blood hardened and gave the floor a new glaze, and as Ling watched as the bodies were dumped overboard, she became reacquainted with something she had hoped was left behind in Vietnam: the emptiness of death. Neither Ling nor her mother had spoken more than a couple of words to any of the victims but some part of them was thrown to the bottom with the bodies. "What will be left of me when all of this, this suffering, this injustice, this war is over?" Ling wondered.

* David Butler, "Agony of the Boat People," *Newsweek* (July 2, 1979), p. 42.
** Robert Rosenblatt, "We Go Together in One Boat," *Time* (January 11, 1982), p. 55.

American Civil War veterans wrote Stephen Crane praising his battle accuracy in *The Red Badge of Courage* (1951). Some even believed Crane had soldiered with them though he was born in 1871. We know that authors have realistically created numerous settings outside of their personal experience. What this course brought home to me and to others who read the work produced in the elective (through the publication of its own magazine, as well as two prize-winning papers in the nationally sponsored "Walk a Mile in My Shoes — Interview a Vet" contest) was that high-school students, when given the freedom to determine their own paths of learning and responding, can achieve notable results. As a teacher I had little to do with the success of my students. I offered reference sources about subjects, but basically I was a coach consulted on the sidelines as students converted their own learning from passive to active.

As indicated in the opening of this paper, Vietnam as a subject offers an immediacy created by numerous factors in our culture, such as a virtual explosion of music, films, plays, and novels. However, clearly Vietnam is not unique. Our culture produces a fabulous array of topics. At the moment I am completing this essay, the headmaster of Phillips Academy is offering a special symposium for seniors on gender. A profusion of films, speakers, books, and articles is available. And once immersed in this issue, once set free to question teachers, lecturers, parents, peers, and people in their communities, students begin to look differently at advertising, at their culture, and at themselves.

Topics abound. Think of all the resources available for a course on the environment or diversity. These topics also immediately invite teachers from other disciplines to join with you and the students as they continue their work. Many teachers at Phillips can identify students who have taken the Vietnam course because these students use what they have learned as a touchstone in every other course. The Vietnam course's value is not that it teaches a student about Vietnam, but that it allows students to discover the interconnectedness between event and culture. It could be any event or theme. In *Absalom, Absalom!*, William Faulkner (1964) devotes a long passage to the effect of a single pebble thrown into a lake. After the Vietnam course, this concept no longer is an abstract one for students. Implicitly, they not only under-stand this concept, but they are empowered to seek out as many ramifications of an idea or event as possible. As active learners, they become in effect students who refuse easy answers to issues and problems that they know are complex.

Let me leave you with this observation: the resources and desires of students to journey for themselves and to set this experience down in their own way is what is special and limitless. I am convinced that students do not like passively sitting while listening to our wisdom; they want their passports stamped so that they can begin. And once they set off, the classroom becomes converted from a dry dock to a port.

Works Cited

Caputo, Philip. 1977. *A Rumor of War.* New York: Holt, Rinehart, and Winston.

Coming Home. 1978. Dir. Hal Ashby. With Jane Fonda and Jon Voight. United Artists.

Crane, Stephen. 1951. *The Red Badge of Courage.* New York: The Modern Library.

The Deer Hunter. 1978. Dir. Michael Cimino. With Robert DeNiro, John Cazale, John Savage, Christopher Walken, and Meryl Streep. Universal/Emi.

Dylan, Bob. 1963. *The Times They Are A-Changin'.*

Edelman, Barnard. 1985. *Dear America: Letters Home From Vietnam.* New York: Norton.

Ehrhart, W. D., ed. 1985. *Carrying the Darkness: American Indochina, The Poetry of the Vietnam War.* New York: Avon.

Emerson, Ralph Waldo. 1983. "The American Scholar." In *Emerson: Essays and Lectures*, comp. Joel Porte. New York: Library of America Series.

Fallows, James. 1975. "What Did You Do in the Class War, Daddy?" *The Washington Monthly* (October).

Faulkner. William. 1964. *Absalom! Absalom!*, 261–62. New York: Vintage.

The Killing Fields. 1984. Dir. Roland Joffe.

Larsen, Wendy Wilder and Tran Thi Nga. 1986. *Shallow Graves: Two Women and Vietnam.* New York: Random House.

Mason, Bobbie Ann. 1985. *In Country.* New York: Harper and Row.

Rabe, David. 1973. *The Basic Training of Pavel Hummel, and Sticks and Bones: Two Plays.* New York: Viking.

———. 1977. *Streamers.* New York: Random House.

Terry, Wallace. 1984. *Bloods: An Oral History of the Vietnam War by Black Veterans.* New York: Random House.

Wright, Stephen. 1983. *Meditations in Green.* New York: Scribners.

14

Acting and Writing

Sheila McGrory Klyza

You drink the water, and then you sweat it out. And the water is other, and the sweat is your own. You need to do the same thing with your characters. You need to drink them and sweat them out, and then they'll be yours.

Is this a director speaking to an actor? A writing teacher speaking to a student? Or how about an actor speaking to a writer? None of the above? The third choice is the correct answer. But why would an actor give directions to a writer? Isn't it usually the other way around? Can writers, or students learning to write in a composition class, learn anything from working with an actor or from having others read their writing from the perspective of an actor—that is, from the perspective of someone trying to bring the words to life?

The answer is a resounding yes based on my experiences in the classroom and a study I conducted during the summer of 1989 while I was a student at the Bread Loaf School of English in Middlebury, Vermont. The opening words above came from Annie Scurria, who was an actor in residence at Bread Loaf during the summer. The person Annie was speaking to is Nancy Boutilier, an M. A. candidate at Bread Loaf enrolled in David Huddle's fiction writing class; Nancy teaches English at Phillips Academy during the regular school year. Over the course of the summer, Annie helped Nancy create characters and develop a consistent voice in her stories; they worked together, striving for specifics in writing that build strong, vivid images and "real" characters. Through my observations and interviews with them, I discovered a way for writing students to share a language about writing that is intuitive, natural, mutually rewarding, and free from the language of grammar and style.

Throughout the summer, Nancy and Annie met frequently to discuss first drafts and revisions. A mutual trust and respect for the other's work gradually developed and was evident in their uninhibited, friendly discourse. Creating an environment in the classroom in which such relationships are encouraged is essential to the teaching of writing. A workshop atmosphere certainly promotes trust and collaborative learning; students can even be assigned as partners for the duration of the course to provide a greater chance for a close working relationship to develop. As long as the two students work well together, such consistent feedback and steady development of trust can be of great advantage in a writing class. Having the students work on one piece for an extended period of time is also effective in making them feel confident and comfortable with their writing. In the following interview, Annie talks about her role in Nancy's work as a writer.

Annie: As I understand, we ... help students by telling them how we go about developing a point of view when we're working on a character, how we can't judge characters when we act them; it's just not possible, if you're going to do it well. So you have to get beyond the question of "is he a good person or a bad person?" or "is he morally right or morally wrong?" because none of us think of ourselves that way. ... So essentially it's what we do, it's really at the core of what we do, getting inside someone's skin; it's pulling up those parts of ourselves that we're going to use, and so it's helpful to the writers, I guess. We don't comment on the writing; we're not equipped to do that.

Sheila: What *do* you do when you look at a script? What is the process that you go through? You mentioned that you draw upon parts of yourself to become a character.

Annie: Yes, because my feeling is that I'm always myself. I don't become someone else. I don't think that's possible, unless you're a schizophrenic. And I certainly don't think that it's healthy. But what I try to do is find those parts of myself — it's like couscous. You know, when you put it in water and some stay at the bottom and some float to the top. For each different role it's different water so different kernels float to the top, and that's what you try to find. And maybe you might shake the pan and a couple of kernels sink down and a couple float to the top. That's really the process, what you're trying to do — find different parts of yourself that you can draw upon. ... As an actor, what you're trying to do all the time is create channels linking the instinctual impulses with your conscious mind so that you can travel back and forth from one to the other at will, or at least relax and let it happen, let it surprise you.

During rehearsals, much of an actor's work is expressive, exploratory. Just as writers will write for hours trying to get down ideas and tap feelings and intuitions that lie beneath the surface, so too will actors try to discover parts of themselves that are deep within them, within what Annie refers to as their "pool of tacit knowledge."[1] According to Annie, while the explicit knowledge, or conscious thought, may differ in the two creative processes because the actor and writer are engaged in two different activities, the reliance on tacit knowledge, or the instinctual and intuitive awareness, is the same in both cases. Whatever the creative endeavor — sculpture, poetry, musical composition — we draw upon our individual pool of tacit knowledge.

Everybody possesses this pool of tacit knowledge, children and adults alike. Thus, when students complain that they haven't experienced enough to write anything interesting, they are victims of an unproductive misconception that unfortunately is often furthered by their adult authority figures. Every student, having lived on this earth for fourteen or so years, has a pool of knowledge upon which to draw — a pool that expands exponentially when the imagination is included. So gaining access to this pool becomes merely a matter of losing inhibitions and feeling confident enough to tap into that intuitive source. And one of the most important jobs of the teacher is creating an environment that promotes this self-discovery.

An activity that serves to demonstrate to students the power and diversity of their tacit knowledge involves having the whole class write a description of a dramatic natural scene, such as a canyon at sunset or a tumultuous river. The students should have different stories in mind that are not mentioned explicitly in the descriptions but that will definitely inform their perspectives.

Another useful activity involves bringing in a single photograph or print, preferably one that captures a scene, such as Renoir's *Luncheon of the Boating Party* or a Doisneau photo. Students are then asked to write a story in the third person based on what they perceive to be going on in the scene. Having the students read both sets of stories aloud demonstrates powerfully the endless possibilities that dwell within their realms of experience and their imaginations.

So, what exactly does Annie do when she reads one of Nancy's stories, and what might a teacher or student do when reading another student's work?

Sheila: When you read one of Nancy's papers, do you go through the same process as when you read a script?

Annie: No, because it's not a play, but I mostly think about questions that would be good to ask, and maybe questions that she hasn't thought of already. Things that I would need to know if I were going to play that part, but that I the reader don't need to know.

Sheila: But that the writer needs to know even if she isn't going to put it into the story?

Annie: Right. Because I think it helps get away from the general and make it more specific, and that's when you get surprised by yourself. I know that's what I work for as an actor — to get to the point where I'm controlling what I'm doing. Because if I'm thinking of things all the time, I'm limited by my own conscious imagination. What I try to work for is getting to the point in rehearsal, and certainly for performance, where I can surprise myself and not do anything that I have thought up, but only that which comes from my reaction to the person I'm working with, and I just let something happen. . . . I think that wanting to surprise yourself is important, and then you will surprise the reader, and then it will be real, and then it will be yours.

In discussing with Nancy one of Nancy's stories, Annie emphasizes again the importance of being specific in writing. This search for the specific is what she undergoes in her creation of a character, and through this heuristic process she elevates her work to an art form.

Annie: Just go into detail for yourself. Not a lot of that will be included. But if you have it concrete in your mind, it will come through somehow and inform it. You really have to know all about your characters, about their families. It may seem like a lot of unnecessary work, but it isn't. Something about it is just so informing. It also just helps you to get into the world of that person. . . . For me, when I'm working on getting more specific on my character in one area, I'll come up with something that will key me off to something else — it will surprise me. So it really isn't unnecessary, because what you're doing, what we're all trying to do, is create a world, a universe. And then you have to bring the camera into your people in your story, but they still have to be in this universe, so you have to do a lot more that's not ever in the story. . . . Some of the relationships between your characters are a little general, and you need to keep taking it from the general to the specific. . . . Then you will come up with things that are surprising and interesting. It will seem natural to you, but if it seems surprising to the reader, in a good way, then you know a lot about it.

Nancy nods in agreement, and Annie proceeds to ask a series of questions about one of the characters. "For me," she says, "I have to do this for one person every time I do a play, but a writer, my God, you have to do it for every character." She puts her hand to her forehead to emphasize her awe for the writing process and continues by reiterating that, as people, we define ourselves by the way we react to other people; characters on stage and in print must do the same.

Nancy laughs and says, "We define by how we react; I like that. I can hear myself telling that to my students."

Annie: And that's how other people define us, how we fit into our universe. It would seem to me that a writer would know how each character would react if three of his characters were in a room and then a thunderclap struck. . . . It's so hard because when you think you need more information about a character, we think, "Oh, the reader or audience wants to know how old the character is or whatever," but they really don't need to know those specifics. It's usually *you*, the writer or the actor, who needs to know.

Annie is asked if she could use her acting skills in reading a piece without characters, such as a purely descriptive piece.

Annie: I think so because it's always got to be from somebody's point of view. Once you write something down, somebody is writing it. I mean, we could describe simply this table. You could describe it first of all from points of view from positions around the table, and then from one position but from different perspectives, like a two-year-old and an alien. You can find out something about the character through what is important enough for them to notice. Really only a camera is completely objective, but even then, it's being operated by a human who wants to control your point of view.

Sheila: How could a teacher somehow use this process to help students with their writing?

Annie: I guess you could go about it in a couple of different ways. One would be, if there are any actors around where you are, you could get them to come in. Another way, if that's not possible, would be for the teacher to make the students aware of the basic acting questions: Who am I? What do I want? And just to ask students to try to really see someone else's point of view without judging it. And by asking as many questions as you can think of — what makes the person laugh, what is the person's favorite color — even if the students don't use that information directly. The more a writer can flesh out a character, the better. I think it's very important because it creates a feeling that everyone has equal validity and there are more ways of seeing something than just one, and that there is more than one interpretation, and that everyone's interpretation is valid.

Clearly the average high school does not have access to the resources of a professional acting company. Drama instructors can be helpful collaborators, but teachers should not feel limited if no full-time drama instructors are available. As long as the teacher is aware of the basic acting questions and can probe the students for details and explain what an actor or writer looks for in a piece of writing, then it makes no difference if the teacher has never appeared in a professional play. Instead of focusing on structural problems, which tends to discourage students, the teacher reads the paper for content, for meaning — interpretively not evaluatively — thereby elevating the student's writing to the level of a text. Students in turn usually respond in an overwhelmingly positive manner and begin to feel like true writers. They gain confidence in their abilities and feel assured that they have something valuable to say. And the mundane grammatical editing gains a new purpose when they begin to take pride in the content of their writing.

In a workshop situation, however, students are usually the teacher's best resource. Student actors can be called upon to explain to other students what process they go through when they approach a part in a play. And students with no previous acting experience whatsoever can work with partners and take turns reading each other's writing with the intention of bringing the words to life.

An exercise that illustrates this process involves having students write a character sketch — a two- to three-page essay in which they describe thoroughly, from appearance to mannerisms to personality characteristics, a person they know. When one partner reads an essay, the other writes down a series of questions and answers based on what might be deduced from the description. For example, what kind of car does the character drive? A small economy car. What is his favorite flavor of ice cream? Plain vanilla. Where would he choose to go on a vacation? Camping in Yellowstone. From the accuracy of the guessed responses (allowing some room for inconsistencies in personalities), the writer is able to ascertain just how accurate a portrayal she or he presented.

In a similar assignment, students are asked to write a description of an imaginary person. The partner, in this case, poses a variety of questions to help the writer create a more vivid portrayal. If the writer does not know how to respond to a question or, more specifically, how the imaginary character would respond to a situation, she or he will then be aware of a need for further thought about the character. When creating a character, a writer, as well as an actor, must know as much as possible about the person, even if the information is not found within the story or description, because that knowledge will be communicated to the reader through an informed, convincing portrayal.

When students begin to read each other's writing for meaning and not for grammatical errors, they become excited about their own and others' writing. Classes move from dull editing sessions to interpretive brainstorming workshops. Since no right or wrong answer exists, the oppressive weight of judgment is lifted from the classroom, and the teacher is free to become a collaborator instead of an evaluator. And when students begin to think of themselves as writers and believe that what they say has significance and is not merely grist for the teacher's red pen, then they will begin to write from within and not merely crank out a paper because an assignment is due.

Another way in which students can work collaboratively and use acting techniques in the writing process is through improvisation. Viola Spolin, in her text, *Improvisation for the Theater* (1983), defines this elusive term:

> Playing the game; setting out to solve a problem with no preconception as to how you will do it; permitting everything in the environment (animate or inanimate) to work for you in solving the problem; it is not the scene, it is the way to the scene; a predominate function of the intuitive; playing the game brings opportunity to learn theater to a cross-section of people; "playing it by ear"; process as opposed to result; not ad-lib or "originality" or "making it up by yourself"; a form, if understood, possible to any age group; setting object in motion between players as in a game; solving of problems together; the ability to allow the acting problem to evolve the scene; a moment in the lives of people without needing a plot or story line for the communication; an art form; transformation; brings forth details and relationships as organic whole; living process. (383–84)

This process works best again with descriptive pieces, such as an assignment in which the students are asked to write a description of a family member. A student's partner then reads the piece interpretively and tries to act out the character based on the writer's description. The writer can direct the actor to make the character seem more real, closer to the idea that the writer had in mind. By seeing the description acted out, the writer can more easily discern gaps and weaknesses in the piece, which can be eliminated in the revision process. If the actor, for instance, interprets the description in a way that is entirely different from the writer's intent, then the writer can take a second look at what was actually said, in contrast to what was intended. For example, a student writes a description of a much older or younger relative but is unable to state explicitly the age of the person in the piece. Instead, he or she must rely on description to communicate the age. If, upon reading the piece, the actor is led to believe that the character is twenty when he is actually forty-five, the writer must then determine the reason for this discrepancy. Not only does such as exercise make the writer more aware of how the piece is interpreted, but it demonstrates the creative process that the reader undergoes as well. Students then begin to recognize the two-way creative street shared by writer and reader and to learn that they can control, to a certain extent, the effect of their writing on their audience. Through this exercise, the writer also can be made aware of, and consequently rectify, problematic characters that are not fully developed or are confusing because of their inconsistencies.

Assignments similar to the one described above can focus on occupations or emotions. Spolin outlines numerous exercises designed to teach theater and acting techniques in the classroom. Many of her ideas, however, can be applied to the teaching of writing since the primary goals are essentially the same:

> ... making the theater techniques so intuitive that they become the students' own ... [helping] both teacher and student find personal freedom ... [establishing] an environment in which the intuitive can emerge and experiencing take place ... [so] teacher and student can embark together upon an inspiring, creative experience. (1983, 4)

In Spolin's exercise "How old am I?" (1983, 168) students take turns acting out characters of specific ages in a previously determined situation (such as a person waiting at a corner bus stop). The other students try to guess the character's age and discuss whether the actor showed or told the information, whether age qualities are always physical or are part of an attitude toward life. In the same way, this exercise can focus on occupations, with the students trying to guess what occupation is being presented by the student actor.

Spolin's exercise "Jump Emotion" (1983, 243) can be helpful to student writers learning to write about various emotions. After the who, what, and where are agreed upon, the student actor chooses some radical change of inner action to fit into the scene, such as a mother's feelings ranging from fear to courage. Instead of merely trying to act out the scene, the actor should concentrate on what the character is feeling and try to communicate those emotions as believably as possible. Through exercises such as this, students begin to realize that writers must inhabit their writing, like actors; otherwise it will be contrived and unconvincing.

Reading students' papers interpretively seems to work most effectively when students are writing what James Britton defines as "poetic writing" (1970, 170). This form of writing represents a move away from "expressive writing" (the putting into writing of whatever comes to mind, such as free-writing) toward more formal writing in which the writer concentrates on giving the piece a more satisfying shape, more of a construction, so that the piece becomes a story. Indeed this type of writing lends itself well to interpretive readings by both teacher and students. But what about all the other writing that students do, writing that is more informative, less narrative? Can this too be read interpretively?

"Transactional writing," as defined by Britton (1970, 236), represents a move in the other direction, away from expressive writing toward informational, opinionated, or factual writing. Cause-and-effect essays, comparison essays, and all the other expository exercises that teachers generally assign in high-school composition classes usually fall into this category. While acting these essays out demands a creative effort, it can be done; however, acting the essays out is not necessary in order for the students and teacher to read the essays interpretively, which is the primary goal in this pedagogical approach. By the time the students are writing transactional essays, they most likely will have had experience reading their poetic pieces interpretively; therefore the transition, although not a painless one, will be smoother than if they have never read their essays interpretively before. An effective way to bridge this gap is to have students write an expository piece and a short story or a poem on the same subject, thus enabling them to see both the differences and the striking similarities in the two forms of writing.

One way in which teachers can incorporate a more interpretive approach to the teaching of transactional writing is by staging an oral debate in which two students argue two sides of an issue. The students work together to prepare two airtight arguments and then present those arguments in debate form to the rest of the class. Creativity should be encouraged, as students may wish to debate from the perspective of a certain personage, such as the president; costumes, too, can add to the fun. While the first half of the debate should be fully prepared, the second half can be devoted to open discussion in which the "audience" poses questions to both debaters, who must respond impromptu. This exercise is very helpful in demonstrating to students the importance of presenting information in a reasonable, logical format. When the arguments are brought to life in front of the class, students are much more conscious of what they are saying and are extra careful to avoid fallacious reasoning (prior to the debates, students will have become familiar with the various logical fallacies and argument pitfalls they should avoid). Moreover, the entire class becomes involved, as both listeners and arguers, as performers and audience.

Not only the argument essay can be brought to life in the classroom. By establishing a mock news station in which students are assigned various roles — such as movie critic, restaurant critic, world news reporter, local news reporter, weather person, sportscaster — teachers can further transform their classrooms. Evaluative essays, cause/effect essays, and many other standard assignments can be brought to life "on the air." And if a videocamera is available, the broadcast could even be taped.

In exercises such as those described above, student writing is given validity and importance through a caring, supportive "audience." The content, again, is focused upon, while the editorial work becomes the necessary, expected polish.

During my observation sessions in the Bread Loaf Barn, a lively interchange went on between Nancy and Annie. Annie questioned, and Nancy reconsidered; Nancy questioned, and Annie explained; both were teachers, both were learners. In an interview, Nancy comments on the ways in which Annie has been particularly helpful and actively makes connections to her own work as a teacher.

Nancy: Annie is good at pinpointing where I should sharpen, where characters seem not to be distinct; I can't really see that when I write it. She's really into the content. She is taking it from the perspective of "would this be enough for me to go on to create a character?" She is not looking to critique; instead she really focuses on the content, on the characters, which takes the pressure off. I'm thinking that, as a teacher, that's one more way to set up a collaborative, nonthreatening workshop environment. ... She is convincing me of the need to have the character set in my own mind. I'm changing my approach; I'm making sure I know my characters better. Instead of just putting down words that they said, I have a better sense of why they said it, where they're coming from. Reacting is very important. What makes them laugh, what makes them cry, all those questions she asks, I wouldn't have thought of before. I'm watching myself going into a story with a much better sense of background information I felt I had to know about the character before I wrote it.

When asked about the connection between acting and writing, Nancy pauses.

Nancy: In both of these forms you're creating characters or trying to somehow convey to an audience something that the character is thinking or feeling. So whether you're using words to do that on stage or on paper, I think it's similar. ... In a production or in a story, the important thing is that the characters all act consistently. As long as it's believable, it doesn't have to be definitive, as long as it's consistent, not judgmental, as long as human nature would allow that particular situation to occur. ... Any kind of writing is trying to capture the specific that will somehow express the universal.

Nancy has never taken an acting class, but her dynamism and expressive, vibrant face suggest that she would be well-suited. Similarly, Annie has never taken a writing class, but she says that she would like to one day.

Annie: One thing that I've been amazed by this summer is that the process is very similar. Except for some vocabulary, the way she talks about writing is really the way we talk about acting, and what we're trying to do, and what we're trying to derive, and where the editing comes in. Sometimes you want to edit here, and sometimes you don't want to worry about it and just let it come. It really is a very similar process. . . . I'm aware of words and the sounds of words and the feel of how certain words go together. Because of what I do, I think I have an instinctual feeling for that.

Sounds like the words of a writer to me. Interestingly, the interchange between Nancy and Annie has made each one more of what the other wants to be; they have developed within themselves multiple capacities as creators. Younger students, too, will find that trying to read their work through the eyes of someone else will make them simultaneously much more broad-minded and focused readers and writers.

The common vocabulary that Annie refers to can be very helpful to writing teachers because certain acting terms that can be translated directly into the writing process carry no evaluative associations; therefore, teachers can make suggestions that are free from the inhibiting effect of judgment statements. Terms such as *characterization*, *conflict*, *detail*, *dialogue*, *energy*, *heightening*, *objective reality*, and numerous others that can be found in a theater glossary are applicable to writing as well and can be used by teachers when discussing both creative processes.

Of course, differences do exist between writing and acting, particularly, it would seem, in the degree to which they are collaborative processes. Writing is seemingly more solitary, in both creation and reception, although this doesn't have to be the case. While only the individual actor or writer can tap into his or her pool of tacit knowledge, the involvement of other people can aid that process. As for the reception, one of the fundamental differences between acting and writing has to do with audience.

Annie: As an actor, I try to think very simply about what I'm doing, and then the director will give me feedback. Sometimes it's very explicit, like "it needs to be faster or slower." And sometimes it's "let it work on you a bit more." Now I take that in and what it means to me is what it means to me, and then I let it come out. It might not be what he wanted, so then he has to tell me something else to try to get me to do what he wants. What he sees or what comes out of me as angry might not be what I'm thinking of as angry. I might be trying to do something else, but it might be eliciting from his point of view what he wants so I don't have to be thinking of what the product or outcome is. I can be thinking just about what I'm doing. So for a writer you have to be thinking of what you're doing, but how can you be aware of how people are perceiving you? As a writer, you leave your work on the page and that's it. As actors, we're constantly working off the audience, so the performance will be very different every night because we're feeling how we're doing. ... At least in the theater we have some control over our audience. They come and they sit in the dark. I guess it was John Irving who said that it drove him crazy that he had no control over his audience, that people could read his book on the toilet. It's different with acting.

Clearly, acting is by nature a more collaborative process than writing. An actor constantly is working with other actors, with the director, with the audience. This difference is minimized, however, in the classroom when students can receive immediate feedback from the teacher and from other students, when writers have an interactive audience that responds to their work. That audience can consist of one person (teacher or student) or a room full of attentive student writers.

Based on what the actors and writers and teachers in this study have said, acting and writing *are* similar and when integrated, can provide a highly creative teaching/learning experience. As Annie points out, through practice actors cultivate the explicit knowledge, but to act truly, they need to be able to tap their core of tacit experience and thereby personalize that facet of the character they are trying to create; the more in-depth the personalizing, the clearer and more specific, the more real the character will be. And to write truly, writers need to do the same thing. This approach dramatizes an idea that most beginning writers have a hard time conceptualizing: the more specific and concrete the writing, the richer and more complex it will be. To use an apt metaphor, specifics lend flesh and bones to the writing.

Actors have directors; writers have teachers, and those teachers can very easily be other students in the class. If students are taught at an early age to be sensitive, intelligent readers, to read interpretively instead of evaluatively, then the collaborative process really can work. Students, in turn, also will read their own work in the same way, thereby elevating by several notches the quality of their writing. So, even though the pool of tacit creative knowledge belongs to only one person, and the sweat is her or his own, no one else's, other people can assist — can offer the water and wipe the brow as they sweat alongside.

Note

1. Annie derived this phrase and the ideas behind it from the work of Michael Polanyi (1962).

Works Cited

Britton, James. 1970. *Language and Learning*. London: Penguin Books.

Polanyi, Michael. 1962. *Personal Knowledge: Towards a Post-Critical Philosophy*. Chicago: University of Chicago Press.

Spolin, Viola. 1983. *Improvisations for the Theater*. 1963. Rev. ed. Evanston, Ill.: Northwestern University.

15

A Literate Culture
Courses for an Active Education
Craig Thorn

E. D. Hirsch's book, *Cultural Literacy* (1988), was right to express concern about the average American's literacy, particularly his or her awareness of a Western culture. Summarizing Ernest Gellner's *Nations and Nationalism*, Hirsch argues that teaching a common culture through a national system of education is at the heart of modern nationhood (73). Without cultural literacy young people are disenfranchised and consequently ineffective citizens. I would add, and I think he would agree, that without cultural literacy, young people cannot truly know who they are.

I tried an experiment in journal writing with my seniors in a course our department calls "Literature of Two Faces." Using N. Scott Momaday's imagistic autobiography, *The Way to Rainy Mountain* (1969), I asked students to imitate his approach to his personal history in their own journals when writing about themselves. Momaday divides each brief section into three vignettes exploring some part of his Kiowa mythic/folkloric past, his cultural history, and his childhood. The next day I met a group of very frustrated seniors. It seems they all could relate some childhood experience with great difficulty, but they found the first and second parts impossible to recreate in any way that was relevant to their own lives. Either what they imagined to be their mythic/folkloric past and cultural history had nothing to do with them, or they felt they had no myth, folklore, or culture from which to "re-create" personal experience.

My little experiment and Hirsch's point of view differ in two fundamental ways. He would argue that first we have to make the classic themes of Western Civilization relevant to the average high school—aged student in the form of pure information—not just titles, but names, dates, phrases, places and events—representing the shared experience of what he defines as our American identity. While I wholeheartedly agree with his concerns, I question the means by which he would have educators achieve cultural literacy in the classroom and what these means imply about our American identity. I prefer to teach students how to think about facts rather than facts themselves, though you certainly cannot think without them. Furthermore, I find that themes in American culture, however we define it, are much more compelling than facts about it. In fact, facts are more compelling when presented in the context of compelling themes. The themes Hirsch mentions—such as our belief in self-help, equality, freedom, altruism, free-thinking, and the frontier spirit—are compelling and inclusive of many American voices, as is his idea about an American civil religion (1988, passim). These *ideas* represent the emphasis in our ideal curriculum, for such emphasis is closer to our complex American identity. Hirsch writes of a school's responsibility to its students:

> The acculturative responsibility of the schools is primary and funda-mental. To teach the ways of one's own community has always been and still remains the essence of the education of our children, who enter neither a narrow tribal culture nor a transcendent world culture but a national literate culture. (18)

However, as a relatively young nation with a multiplicity of cultures in our brief history and increasingly intimate and intricate relations with new nations and cultures in our immediate future, we need to recognize that tribal and world cultures have been and will be significant aspects of our national literate culture.

These differences, then, are ones of process and emphasis. To these I add a pedagogical reluctance to embrace Hirsch's methodology. I respectfully argue that his approach implies a return to education as the application of distant authority, distant in time and experience from contemporary adolescent life. Not surprisingly, his book renewed the debate between the classic and contemporary approaches to education and specifically the teaching of literature.

I suggest that there is an approach to literature and cultural literacy that unites classic and contemporary literatures. Furthermore, this approach addresses the challenges of teaching students in the electronic age. It incorporates the literature of our multicultural community in ways that are provocative and pedagogically sound. I argue, in short, that the various experiments our department has allowed its teachers to try in literature courses would satisfy both Hirsch and his critics. The key advantage to our varied approaches is that they emphasize the student and his or her ability to find a voice in a cultural continuum that includes T. S. Eliot and the rock band The Clash, Joseph Conrad and Joan Didion, Sophocles and Francis Ford Coppola, Thomas Hardy and *The Thornbirds* by Colleen McCullough.

Whether in a public or private school, the average student today is alienated from culture, specifically cultural history. This is the age of the short-term memory, the electronic age. Expecting teachers and students to read *Oedipus Rex* without acknowledging the way we live today is wonderfully idealistic at best, unfair to the teacher at worst. Studying the courses some of my colleagues teach, I suggest that the first rule in designing a literature course goes something like this: *Try to include contemporary and classic works that can be compared thematically and perhaps even stylistically.*

The argument I make elsewhere about grammar applies here to classic literature in a course that includes contemporary literature. Grammar is most appreciated when it is seen as a means to an end: improving and/or understanding the sense of a student's piece of writing. Showing the similarities between the classics and contemporary experience does not demean the former; on the contrary, students experience precisely why classics are classics. They are timeless. They discover, therefore, that the classics can be relevant to experiences closer to their own. As for contemporary literature, the best of it is as good as any good literature from any period in our cultural history. It invents and challenges, and it often does so in a language that is smart about today's language. Much of this literature, furthermore, shrewdly dissects the very forces that have led to what Hirsch perceives as our cultural illiteracy: the nearly immoral, formulaic simplification of human experience by the electronic media and the entertainment industry. Consequently, many of us try to organize our literature courses around some general theme that is relevant to American culture (Seth Bardo's course described in Chapter 13 is an example). A few examples of such courses demonstrate the point:

America After the Wars

A study of the way America has dealt with the horrors of its involvement in wars. The course addresses issues of national conscience, religious and moral beliefs, personal and cultural identities as they are challenged by the chaos of major conflict. The course can be broken up into two parts: America's wars against itself and America's wars against other superpowers. A course like this allows teachers to teach literature from the Civil War (Stephen Crane) to literature about our relationship to South and Central America (Joan Didion). A course could literally begin with a few poems by Hart Crane and end with Don DeLillo's *White Noise*. The teacher could include films, music, even television documentaries. The poetry of Robert Hayden, the drama of Amiri

Baraka, and the stories of Leslie Marmon Silko all respond in one way or another to our nation's internal wars.

Of Men and Women in America

A study of our changing views of men and women. This course could start with Edgar Allan Poe's "The Fall of the House of Usher" and end with Anne Tyler's *Breathing Lessons* or Margaret Atwood's *The Handmaid's Tale*. It could study the music of Joni Mitchell and the poetry of Emily Dickinson (Mitchell alludes to Dickinson in several of her songs). It could compare the show "Rosanne" to Evan S. Connell's *Mrs. Bridge*, Hemingway's short stories to Frederick Busch's short stories. Henry James's *Daisy Miller* and Rachell Ingalls's *Mrs. Caliban* make for an interesting combination as do Grace Paley and Anne Sexton. The movies of Sigourney Weaver raise interesting questions about America's view of the contemporary woman as do the striking contrasts between singers like Rickie Lee Jones and Paula Abdul.

America's Poor

A study of what American writers have to say about our poor. The course might include John Steinbeck's *The Grapes of Wrath* and Mary Morris's *Vanished*. The teacher could introduce the student to Walt Whitman and James Welch, Carolyn Chute's *The Beans of Egypt, Maine* and the Compson family in William Faulkner's *The Sound and the Fury*. The students could "re-listen" to Bruce Springsteen's and John Cougar Mellencamp's music. They could read *Ironweed* and see the movie. John Dos Passos, James T. Farrell, Theodore Dreiser all write about the poor. The students could read the poetry of Phillip Levine and Louise Erdrich.

The American Family

This course could use many of the same texts as the above course. *The Grapes of Wrath*, *Machine Dreams*, *The Beans of Egypt, Maine*, and anything by Faulkner seem appropriate. John Updike's *Rabbit Run* and John Cheever's *Bullet Park* offer challenging visions of American families. The television drama "Roots" would offer a dramatic view of family as would *Kramer vs. Kramer*. Susan Minot's *Monkeys* and John Irving's *Hotel New Hampshire* are provocative as well. What is happening to the American family is of great interest to young people. Contemporary fiction in which mother and father both work or the parents are absent would be very relevant. Along these lines, Bobbie Ann Mason's *In Country* and the movie based on it would reach many students. Comparing works by May Sarton and Maya Angelou or Paula Fox and William Saroyan would demonstrate strikingly similar experiences in radically different settings. Asking students to consider why most situation comedies focus on changing family configurations might yield a lot of rethinking about popular television and the values it reflects.

Outcasts

A study of people in America who don't seem to belong anywhere. The teacher might start with Nathaniel Hawthorne's *The Scarlet Letter* and end with *Sula* by Toni Morrison. *Invisible Man* by Ralph Ellison and Saul Bellow's *The Adventures of Augie March* strike me as a particularly rewarding combination. *Catcher in the Rye* and *The Outsiders* are specifically about alienation among young people. Writers Herman Melville and Flannery O'Connor, and directors Woody Allen and Michael Cimino, all study people who don't fit into the fabric of American culture.

There are countless ways to organize such courses. Robert Penn Warren's *All the King's Men* and Garry Wills's *Nixon Agonistes* could be the focus of a course on perceptions of power in American life as could Joan Didion's *Slouching Towards Bethlehem* and Don DeLillo's *Libra*. A teacher could ask students to research the Jim and Tammy Bakker debacle and then give them Sinclair Lewis's *Elmer Gantry* to read. I think that Coppola's *The Godfather, Part II* and Oliver Stone's *Wall Street* would fit nicely into such a course.

Courses can be simple — a course on nature writers featuring pairings like Robert Frost and Galway Kinnell, Emily Dickinson and Annie Dillard, N. Scott Momaday and Ernest Hemingway, Jean Stafford and Amy Clampitt. Or courses can be more complex — a course on America's terror of and obsession with junk featuring writers as diverse as T. S. Eliot and David Byrne of the Talking Heads, Frederick Barthelme and e. e. cummings, Updike and Twain, or Whitman and Howard Nemerov.

Courses like these render the literature a means to an end that is relevant to students: what it means to live in this country. More importantly, such courses invite student experience as relevant to discussion about the course material: everyone has a family, feelings about the opposite sex and their own, some awareness of war either through the experiences of a family member or exposure to movies and music on the subject. I have found that the best way to pull off these courses is to rely in part on a mode of thinking familiar to all young students: comparison and contrast. This mode exploits a natural tendency young people exercise daily. Using the comparison-and-contrast approach as a modus operandi yields gratifying results in the second type of course some of us teach, which stems from our second tacit rule: *Introduce works that expose students to cultural diversity in a way that is relevant to their own experiences.*

Literature of other cultures challenges students to reconsider the formulaic ways (usually evoked by the electronic media) they view human experience by reaffirming, in new and exciting ways, basic experiences all people share. The course entitled Literature of Two Faces focuses on the relationship between ethnic and mainstream culture. Thylias Moss and I try to introduce students to the myth, magic, and hard realities of ethnic experience in this country. What students discover, of course, is that America's complex cultural identity challenges *all* Americans to adopt two faces, public and private. Furthermore, the course has direct application to the student's understanding of his or her own culture. Native Americans, Japanese-Americans, African-Americans, Italian-Americans, Jewish-Americans, Mexican-Americans—all these peoples struggle with this difficult responsibility: to be a part of and apart from the larger community, to succeed as responsible citizens in America without compromising the integrity of their cultural heritage. At its best, this literature touches on a deep-seated experience all students share: being your own person and a positive contributor to the group. Furthermore, this literature shows students that all behavior and experience is potentially ritualistic, even mythic. Over and over again, the protagonists of these works (frequently young) find the will to live productively by sifting through their recent and deep pasts for clues to their cultural/familial/tribal identity as it relates to their national identity. Learning about the importance of this process would seem to be what Hirsch's book is ultimately about. All people, whether they are white or of color, have such a history that is important. That is the point of this course. In fact, Thylias and I have included works by Faulkner, O'Connor, Emerson, Thoreau, Adams, Cather, and others in our possible reading lists. Watching students comparing their experiences with the experiences of young Native Americans, for instance, is enormously satisfying.

Courses that address other cultures in light of American culture need not be confined to various cultures within our own borders. What we define as classic literature surely includes works by Italians, Germans, Spaniards, South Americans, the French, and Japanese. While all cultures pose challenging new ways of looking at life to the American teenager, great literature celebrates the human spirit. Two courses that come to mind are (1) a course that introduces students to German works by writers like Friedrich Dürrenmatt and Heinrich Böll and Japanese writers like Yukio Mishima and Yasunari Kawabata; and (2) a course that introduces students to Czech writers like Vaclav Havel and Jaroslav Seifert, Hungarian writers like George Konrad and Ivān Mandy, and Polish writers like Czelaw Milosz and Bruno Schulz. These courses need not be intimidating. The quantity of what students read is never as important as the quality. In light of world events, courses like this help to make more responsible Americans out of our young students. Havel's speech before the House and Senate (1990) moved his audience precisely because it reflected a personal vision inextricably connected to a world vision, and it spoke in the language of Czechoslovakian *and* American cultures. Havel punctuated his speech with specific references to Lincoln and Jefferson. In those allusions he spoke directly to deep-seated values we cherish as Americans. Isn't Havel's the kind of cultural literacy to which we should aspire as educators? How many of us could embrace a personal and world vision in language that would speak directly to a Czechoslovakian congress? Awareness of other cultures is not just a nice idea; it is a pragmatic necessity. There is no reason why history and geography instructors alone should bear the responsibility of reminding students that Japan is not just south of Africa.

How do these courses address student writing? Won't such texts be as "foreign" to students as *Silas Marner* or *A Tale of Two Cities* can be when isolated from contemporary adolescent experience?[2] The teacher can empower students to feel at home with this literature when it is presented as a means toward understanding what they see on the news every night. Students know something about German cars and Japanese tape decks. They see what has happened and is happening in Poland. What they hear is part of the white noise of our electronic culture and therefore part of their experience. But what about courses that focus on the classics? Is there no place for them without relying on "thematic tricks" with which to make them relevant to the student who hangs on Axel Rose's or Bon Jovi's every word? The best way to beat the competition — and that is what Bon Jovi is, like it or not — is to absorb it. Many of us tacitly follow a third rule: *Introduce the classics in ways that inform our understanding of contemporary experience.*

Though Ada Fan's course (described in Chapter 11) is not specifically concerned with the issues raised in this essay, her course nicely addresses them. Inviting students to find similarities between *Oedipus Rex* and *Chinatown* does not belittle *Oedipus Rex*. On the contrary, it makes *Oedipus Rex* immediately interesting to the student, and it also suggests to students that if they are discerning and thoughtful viewers and listeners, they will find that the electronic media is not always concerned with pure entertainment. Entertainment can be educational. Education can be very entertaining. Again, there are numerous ways to develop courses that focus on the classics successfully. Ada's is one excellent way. Another is to study Shakespeare's history plays or tragedies in the context of contemporary problems in society. So, for instance, the teacher can teach *Macbeth* and Coppola's *Godfather* films. Or study Richard Nixon and *Richard II*. Doesn't *Gulliver's Travels* speak today about the world's religious wars, England and Ireland's continuing struggles? The great irony about teaching the classics in opposition to contemporary culture is that this approach denies the classics much of their wonder: namely, their continued relevance. Worse, this approach implies that what the student knows is not only irrelevant, but also antithetical to meaningful experience. John Gould's piece on getting students to show what they mean rather than say what they mean implicitly urges students to trust the inherent value of their own, highly personal experience. The same effect can be achieved in any of the above courses. In a course that studies *A Tale of Two Cities* in the context of today's complex revolutions, the student can *contribute his or her own information* to an understanding of Dickens's surprising work after reading newspaper or magazine articles about the countless revolutions around the world that promise an end to the oppression and instead perpetuate it.

Students can make new discoveries about *Antigone* based on their own experience or the experiences of adults close to them. Some of our students could learn about *Antigone* by talking to their parents. Weren't many of them struggling with tough choices about America's role in Vietnam? Was it easy to fight for your country in a war that was not easy to understand? Was it easy to stay home because of your conscientious objections when people you knew and loved were going? Sheila McGrory Klyza's suggestion that student writers and actors collaborate on written work has the same effect because her exercises implicitly remind the students that all great literature must address real experience.

Introductory and advanced literature courses must not hide from the challenges of a contemporary culture that seems counter-literary and alienates young people from their own deep experience. In *Ceremony*, a novel by Laguna Indian Leslie Marmon Silko, Abel has an important revelation while retrieving some stolen cattle:

> The ride into the mountain had branched into all directions of time. He knew then why the oldtimers could only speak of yesterday and tomorrow in terms of the present moment: the only certainty; and this present sense of being was qualified with bare hints of yesterday and tomorrow. (1986, 192)

Courses that try to bring literature to the students' experience as well as insist students identify with the author's immediate culture are courses that empower students with their own voices.

Concerns about courses such as those mentioned above might include the following:

1. These courses lead students to believe that what they have to say off the cuff is as important as what great writers like Hardy have to say.

2. These courses may become more polemical than pedagogical in their intentions, allowing teachers to espouse political/social/moral beliefs under the guise of instruction about literature.

3. These courses assume that teachers have the time and/or energy to read everything from Yukio Mishima's works to The Clash's lyrics.

With respect to the first concern, I would argue that we as teachers must first attract students to Hardy. Worrying that Hardy will not stand up to the voices of our students and contemporary experience, that he will not interest students in his own right, implies that we don't have much faith in Hardy or ourselves. All that these proposals attempt to suggest is that there are ways to make the challenge of teaching literature more rewarding and relevant. The fact that Hardy wrote some of his stories as serials for magazines can make his work less daunting to students who have watched a television miniseries. The teacher can remind students that judging a work solely by your own lights does not make for good writing. With some exceptions, of course, most students will find that Hardy has given considerable thought to issues of native wisdom and learned wisdom in, say, *Return of the Native*.

As for the second concern, I agree that these kinds of courses may encourage proselytizing as opposed to teaching. However, I would argue that teachers who are prone to do this will do it in any course. Ultimately, the quality of any course has little to do with its broad outlines: the quality of a course comes down to the relationship between the student and teacher. Teachers who use their position to insist on a political or social viewpoint need to reconsider their intentions, maybe not their teaching, which might be superb. In fact, the course this teacher teaches might be an excellent course.

The third concern may be the most telling for all of us. Limited funds, time, and energy might seem to preclude such courses. I disagree. One needn't teach half a dozen books to make the basic points argued here. A course that includes *Heart of Darkness* by Conrad, "The Hollow Men" by Eliot, *Song of Solomon* by Toni Morrison, and *Apocalypse Now* by Coppola accomplishes everything this essay hopes for in a literature course. It introduces students to great works. It implicitly invites them to compare classic work with contemporary experience. It employs one of the very mediums with which we compete for their attention. It suggests that there is a cultural continuum of which they are an important part. It consequently gives students an active voice in the discussion of literature initially foreign to them. If those four works seem like too much, *Heart of Darkness* and *Apocalypse Now* achieve the same effect on their own. *The Diary of Anne Frank* and Paul Auster's *In The Country of Lost Things* constitute a legitimate course in literature. Students could "imagine" their own letter from a war-torn land. You could read the two books and "send" them off to Saudi Arabia as an American or Arab soldier. They could write letters to their spouses from the desert. They could assume the role of journalists covering the struggle in Nicaragua or El Salvador. They could keep a journal from the urban ghetto or from the front during World War I. Or they could just talk about why Auster chose to pattern his very modern book after the style of Anne Frank's diary. It's all up to the teacher.

Notes

1. The Talking Heads and many other bands like Love and Rockets, R. E. M., PiL, and the B-52s have written songs on the subject of language and meaning in contemporary culture. Dozens of writers, from F. Scott Fitzgerald and Ernest Hemingway to Nathanael West and Kurt Vonnegut, are concerned with the same issue. Again, exciting combinations abound. Take, for example, Steve Martin's wild adaptation of *Cyrano de Bergerac* in his movie *Roxanne*.

2. The argument that courses concentrating on the classics perpetuate an education that deemphasizes multicultural diversity is as simplistic as that point of view that finds multicultural literature a threat to Western traditions. Most literature before 1945 may as well be thought of by educators as foreign to the contemporary student. Few Anglo-European students are any more acquainted with the Bible than they are with Chinua Achebe. Doesn't Momaday's *The Way to Rainy Mountain* tacitly challenge *all* readers to learn their own histories? Anglo-European students might want to read the Bible or *Paradise Lost* after reading this story of a Kiowa Indian. Dickens's *David Copperfield* can and should be read by every young student because it speaks to all people at what Ralph Ellison's invisible narrator called the lower frequencies (1972, 568).

Works Cited

Ellison, Ralph. 1972. *Invisible Man*. New York: Vintage Books.

Havel, Vaclav. 1990. Address Before a Joint Meeting of Congress on February 21. "The Revolution Has Just Begun." *Time*, March 5, pp. 14–15.

Hirsch, E. D., Jr. 1988. *Cultural Literacy*. New York: Vintage Books.

Momaday, N. Scott. 1969. *The Way to Rainy Mountain*. Albuquerque: University of New Mexico Press.

Silko, Leslie Marmon. 1986. *Ceremony*. New York: Viking Penguin Books.

Afterword

Very early in putting this book together, we realized that the process of gathering our ideas and putting them into essays we could share had become the desired end. Making a book out of them was incidental to the real benefits for us as a diverse group of teachers who rarely have time to sit around and talk about what is flying or flailing in our classrooms. We found the experience of making this book rewarding in ways we could not have anticipated when we started. For one thing, the act of encouraging each other to write about what we do in the classroom forced us to consider our approaches critically. In some cases, perhaps we had not considered what the motives were behind what we were doing. In others, the motives were clear, but we had never taken time to consider how or why our methods had evolved the way they had.

What we discovered when we examined our approaches to teaching composition were wonderful parallels and coalescences in our class-rooms. They crop up here and there throughout our curriculum. Peter Gilbert and I find Vaclav Havel's words, written and spoken, extremely useful in encouraging good writing. Several of us invite students to write poetry and fiction as a way of breaking down barriers between the text and the reader. Seth Bardo's and Thylias Moss's pieces study different ways of introducing students' personal voices into the living text of a literature class. John Gould's essay relies on a similar premise, insisting on the primacy of personal experience when crafting an essay or story that speaks with a true voice. Together Sheila McGrory Klyza's and Ada Fan's pieces argue persuasively for provocative ways students can "visualize" literature. Lynne Kelly's work puts into practice some of the theories and assignments discussed in Kevin O'Connor's article. Paul Kalkstein's "grading system" seems a nice way of com-plementing Carole Braverman's peer-editing ideas. Knowing that we shared common ideas about writing — the need for it to be tied closely to the writer's experience, the importance of experimenting with many kinds of writing, the emphasis on the writer's involvement in her or his development as a writer — legitimized our diversity as a department and our autonomy in the classroom. The simple rewards of sharing our ideas may be the most immediate reward of an endeavor like this book.

I use Kevin's piece whenever I need help dreaming up writing topics for a course. I use Ada's ideas about film when I muddle through Peter Sellers's films in my course on satire in literature. Someday when I get up enough nerve, I'm going to try Tom McGraw's great ideas about having young writers experiment with in-depth studies of authors. If I'm really brave, I'll try Ed Germain's ambitious and highly successful projects. If I get stuck, I know that the experts are just outside my classroom door. Teachers should be able to turn to their colleagues when they want to improve the writing that goes on in their classes.

In these times when education is an embattled art, when all kinds of people outside the classroom insist on programs for what should go on between teacher and student, teachers must recognize the potential they have to make their own courses. In the same way that these approaches to teaching composition empower the student writer, valuing our own efforts enough to share and improve on them empowers us as teachers. Appropriately, we learned that our collective effort is greater than our individual contributions precisely because we are free to experiment with our own ideas.

C. T.